Praise for *Gaysia*

'Benjamin Law has put together a book that at first glance starts as a sexy romp through Asia, bringing him to the gay hotspots coming into consciousness, in what he calls the gayest continent on earth. It's the truth, of course, based on census figures in this most populous area of the world. Law digs deeper though, bringing us far under the surface, giving us keen observations on emerging gay rights issues in these regions, along with the poignant contrasts and issues that tourism of all kinds brings, destroying paradise even while lifting countries and destinations out of poverty. Of Asian extraction, Law also straddles two worlds—he is a part of the cultures he is seeing, and yet not, as a native-born Australian. Law has achieved what seems the impossible in *Gaysia*: a sensual, enjoyable read, full of titillation, at once part of the gay travel circuit, yet deep with sociological observations along with a clear understanding of Asian history. Whether you're planning a trip to Asia, an armchair tourist, or merely curious, *Gaysia* is a book you should add to your collection.'

—Michael Luongo, editor of *Gay Travels in the Muslim World*

'*Gaysia* is Brisbane-based Law's first attempt at book-length journalism and it consolidates him as one of the most surprising and entertaining voices in Australian non-fiction writing.'

—*Weekend Australian*

'Law is a very funny writer.'

—Andy Quan, I

NOV 2014

'Law comes across as not just fun to be with, but sensitive, quick to empathise, sharp-eyed and, well, extremely nice.... *Gaysia* is focused, observant (within its own limits) and often thought-provoking in a refreshingly upbeat way.'

—Robert Dessaix, *Monthly*

'Benjamin Law is a really good writer and *Gaysia,* a book exploring homosexuality and its reception in Asia, is a fantastic book.'

—Readings.com.au

'This is investigative journalism carried out with style, empathy and unflinching honesty.'

—Emma Perry, artsHub

'*Gaysia* is one of the most entertaining and truly wonderful non-fiction books I've ever read.'

—Georgia Dixon, Under the Stilts

'Law has an incredible talent for storytelling, and the anecdotes told to him by his diverse cast of interviewees are as riveting and illuminating as his own first-person accounts.'

—Ramona Ketsuban, blogger

GAYSIA

GAYSIA

ADVENTURES IN THE QUEER EAST

BENJAMIN LAW

FOREWORD BY AARON ALLBRIGHT

CLEiS
PRESS

Published in the United States by Cleis Press, Inc., 2246 Sixth St., Berkeley, CA 94710.

Printed in the United States.
Cover design: Peter Long
Cover photo: Tammy Law
Text design and illustrations: Peter Long

First Edition.
10 9 8 7 6 5 4 3 2 1

Trade paper ISBN: 978-1-62778-036-0
E-book ISBN: 978-1-62778-053-7

First published in 2012 by Black Inc., an imprint of Schwartz Media Pty Ltd, in Australia.

CONTENTS

For Scott Spark

FOREWORD

AN OLD TIBETAN PROVERB says that on every journey, you must die once. The person who returns should not be the same person who left. I invite you to travel to Indonesia, Thailand and China, to Japan, Malaysia, Myanmar and India with an observant and sensitive explorer as your guide. It will be an adventurous trip in which you meet the moneyboys of Bali, the ladyboys of Thailand, the hidden gay Internet of China, the Chinese gay ghosts and their homowives and the grand gay celebrities of Japanese television in a country that pretends to have no other kind of LGBT person. You will be befriended and taken around with Christian and Muslim fundamentalists who claim to cure homosexuality. And yes, they have been named after and trained by American fundamentalists and the folk at the Christian ex-Gay organization called NARTH. The extreme poverty and rampant AIDS in Myanmar will open your heart in sadness. And you will get to know the inspiring activists of India, gay and straight, along with a gay swamiji who thinks that being gay is sick and must be cured. There is a theme of fear and self-hatred here—that runs throughout the world—but it is balanced out by the Queer Azaadi Mumbai Pride Parade, the biggest queer event in the world's most populous democracy.

There are a lot of ingredients here, but they are blended together with a rare skill: over-the-top beauty pageants, sacred in their depth of feeling for lives lived truthfully, no matter how difficult it can be; religious institutions and persons, profane in their betrayal of that which is best in us; dangers and gay celebrations; an exotic itinerary through seven of Asia's (and the world's) most interesting countries; a fast, fabulous, funny, sad read of life, love and the great gay happening world of Asia. Cheers to the future! And to your guide and friend through *Gaysia*, Benjamin Law.

Aaron Allbright

Author of *The Land Near Oz: Two Gay Yankees Move to New Zealand*

AUTHOR'S NOTE

THIS IS A WORK OF non-fiction. For brevity or clarity, the chronologies of some incidents have been condensed or altered. Some names have been changed to protect the identities of people or organisations.

The meaning and usage of the terms 'transgender' and 'transsexual' vary between countries, communities and individuals. In this book, 'transgender' generally refers to people who express their *gender* in non-conforming ways through behaviour, dress and appearance. 'Transsexual' refers to people who have undertaken hormonal and/or surgical procedures to physically affirm the *sex* with which they identify.

The choice between the names Myanmar and Burma – and the names of the country's former capital (Yangon and Rangoon, respectively) – is subject to debate and often contested. Usage varies among countries, and even among news organisations within the same country. (In the United States, the *New York Times* and Reuters use 'Myanmar'; the *Washington Post* and *Time* magazine use 'Burma'.) I have used Myanmar for several reasons, including the burgeoning democratic reforms that took place shortly after I left the country, and the fact that every local person I spoke to called their country 'Myanmar'.

INTRODUCTION

OF ALL THE CONTINENTS, Asia is the gayest. Deep down, you've probably had your suspicions all along, and I'm here to tell you those suspicions are correct.

Let's do the maths. Of the world's ten most populous countries, six of them (seven if you count Russia) are in Asia: China, India, Indonesia, Pakistan, Bangladesh and Japan. Across the continent are close to four billion people, making Asia home to the majority of the world's people. So doesn't it stand to reason that most of the world's *queer* people – lesbians, gays, bisexuals, transgender and transsexual folk – live in Asia too, sharing one hot, sweaty landmass and filling it with breathtaking examples of exotic faggotry? I would think so.

Perhaps I'm biased. You tend to reach for massive generalisations after spending nearly a year skipping between seven Asian countries, sitting backstage with Bangkok ladyboys prepping themselves for beauty pageants, chatting to Tokyo's celebrity drag queens, marching in the heat with Mumbai's fierce queer rights activists, listening to the testimonies of Melaka preachers who claim they can heal homosexuality, and hanging out with Bali's moneyboys and the old foreigners who hire them.

But in 2009, *Time* magazine ran a major story, 'Why Asia's Gays Are Starting to Win Acceptance'. It was an interesting piece about globalisation and a region in flux, one exploding economically but still wedded to strict religious and cultural traditions when it came to sex and marriage. The story started in Nepal and moved through developments in China, Japan and India, and argued that when it came to gay rights, momentum was building.

'If nothing else, people aren't denying the existence of homosexuality anymore,' said one commentator. 'The Asian social institutions and beliefs that often stood in the way of tolerance – religious conservatism, intense emphasis on marriage and having children, cultural taboos against openly discussing sexuality – are weakening.'

Was that true? Eventually, I would discover nothing is ever so straightforward, especially in Asia. Some countries embraced their transsexual people, but didn't care for lesbians. Other countries didn't *hate* homosexuals as such; they just didn't really *get* them. Some celebrated transsexuals but denied them basic rights; others didn't mind if you were a gay man, just as long as you married a woman.

I might have been Australian, but I was ethnically Asian too. For me, it was time to go back to my homelands, to reach out to my fellow Gaysians: the Homolaysians, Bi-Mese, Laosbians and Shangdykes. I would journey through their cities by foot, plane, cross-country train, bus, rickshaw, trishaw, tuk-tuk, taxi, motorcycle, scooter and a utility truck that was originally designed to carry livestock. I would experience the deathly cold of Haridwar, get drenched in Bangkok's downpours and feel my face melting off in a Beijing heatwave. I would contract heat rash, whooping cough and dehydration from Indian food poisoning so intense that, by the end of it, I saw the eye of God. (From what I remember, it was brown.)

Asia is a big place, a sprawling and intoxicating mix of landscapes and languages. Where to start? I decided to begin where most Australians did: taking it easy on the Indonesian island of Bali, leisure-filled paradise and island of the gods. But first, for reasons you will soon understand, I would have to get naked. Very, very naked.

INDONESIA

*In which we travel to Bali and stay in establishments
catering to foreign homosexual nudists, and encounter
various local moneyboys and the men who love them.
Things we learn: (1) how to roster several international
boyfriends at a time; (2) sometimes sex work ain't so bad
(you get a motorcycle!); (3) every man in Bali – at least
according to one local – is a slut.*

WE COME TO BALI after reading *Eat, Pray, Love*, but most of
us just come here to eat, drink and fuck. We come for the nasi
goreng and Bintang, the towering Kuta waves and luxury
resorts, the ten-dollar spa treatments and surf lessons. We
come to scuba-dive, bird-watch, elephant-ride and monkey-
gawk. We come to trek through sun-drenched rice paddies and
find our inner selves at yoga retreats, or have foreign strangers
drunkenly fondle our inner selves after too many drinks.

Holiday budgets don't matter in Bali. If you've ever felt
poor, come to Bali just for the feeling of going to an ATM and
withdrawing a million of something at one time. One million
rupiah will get you around 100 US dollars, which will yield a

week's worth of food and drinks on this island if you're smart. Here is a currency so devalued and littered with zeroes that shops give breath mints when change gets impossibly small.

Bali itself is also small – on the right roads, it takes just over three hours to drive across the island – but it manages to cater to every imaginable urge and need. For gay visitors, those needs might include clothing-optional, male-only resorts, gay night clubs, drag performances, go-go boys, 24-hour house staff, nude sunbathing spots and a cute Indonesian moneyboy you can fuck until you're utterly spent and walking like a duck. It's rumoured that there is a place near Denpasar airport where you can go for a special eight-hand massage, where two men massage you while another two masturbate each other for your visual pleasure, and all for a cheap, cheap price.

It wasn't always like this. In a single decade, Bali's gay scene went from almost nothing to being *the* premier hotspot for fabulous homosexuals the world over. If you were a foreigner, especially a *bulé* – a Caucasian Westerner with pockets presumedly lined with cash – you could buy anything you wanted. Or anyone.

A lot of the gay *bulés* in Bali ended up where I'd been invited to stay: Spartacvs Hotel, a men's-only nude resort in the beachside tourist area of Seminyak. What started in 2007 as 'the only Hotel in Bali dedicate [sic] to those who enjoy an alternative lifestyle' had become the region's only exclusively gay resort that provided a 100 per cent clothing-optional environment. Women and children weren't allowed and neither were ladyboys. It said so on the sign as you walked in.

Everything about the place made me nervous, not just the clothing-optional thing but also the purposeful misspelling of Spartacvs with a V instead of a U (apparently the V made it more edgy). There was also the email I'd gotten from the owner who had invited me to stay. When I assured him I didn't have a problem with public nudity – looking back, maybe I was trying to convince myself – he responded by simply saying: *So I might get to see you naked around the pool, hmmm nice.*

The driver who picked me up from Denpasar airport was Ketut, a big-toothed, goofy-faced guy in his early thirties. Ketut had worked at Spartacvs since it opened and he'd been pro-moted over the years from simple housekeeping duties to admin and management. Working at Spartacvs was a good job, Ketut said, but getting there every day was a killer: a two-hour drive and another two back, sometimes in traffic that refused to budge.

Like most of the male staff at Spartacvs, Ketut was straight. He was also local, while most of the other workers had moved from Java, Jogjakarta or Sumatra to find better jobs in Bali. Some of Ketut's friends knew he worked at a nudist hotel for gay men, but his parents didn't. Guests were usually naked, he said, but staff remained uniformed the whole time. I asked Ketut whether the male guests ever hit on him, and he giggled and squirmed, knowing it was unprofessional to answer.

'Noooooo,' he said. Then, after some encouragement, he said it actually happened pretty regularly. Ketut's approach was to turn them down gently with a boyish laugh and give his standard response: 'Yeah, but me straight!'

We laughed. 'Is it weird to work at a place like Spartacvs?' I asked. 'I mean, every day you're surrounded by naked men ...'

'No! Because I enjoy! Is no problem!' He paused. 'Maybe at first, was little bit ...'

He trailed off.

'Strange?'

'Yeah!' he said, grinning. 'But now, is fine!'

Ketut's funniest memory of working at Spartacvs took place within the first few months of the resort's opening, when three naked foreign men had hooked up poolside in broad daylight, completely going for broke, fucking each other in front of the staff and all the other guests, doing – as Ketut put it – 'jiggy-jiggy'.

It was the first time Ketut had ever seen anyone have sex in public, much less a gay threesome of foreigners. Spartacvs's Indonesian staff had quietly watched the live sex spectacular from discreet vantage points with their hands over their mouths, curious and happily scandalised by the ways of Western men. Stuff like that didn't happen too often at Spartacvs, Ketut said, to my relief and – if I was completely honest with myself – slight disappointment. It was as if I'd been told about a terrifying natural phenomenon – a volcano exploding, a blood-coloured lunar eclipse – that happened once every few decades, then discovered I was probably going to miss out on seeing it.

When we arrived at Spartacvs, a doorman rolled my suitcase through miniature Jurassic Park gates, and across a stone walkway hovering over a pond filled with koi. Past a small concrete modesty wall, a lush poolside landscape of baby palms and frangipani trees opened up, framed by clusters of two-storey bungalows. Naked middle-aged men lazed around the pool, their bodies spread out on deckchairs. They looked up at me sleepily. I was wearing a t-shirt and shorts, but I had never felt so clothed in my life. A couple of men wore one-inch-on-the-hip speedos, but everyone else went nude. Penises were everywhere. And these penises weren't just attached to humans, but also appeared as sculptures and decorations: penis-shaped ashtrays and cement water features in the shape of erect phalluses. Timidly, I smiled and politely waved.

The atmosphere was a cross between a relaxing island getaway and a marine zoo, with everyone lounging around like so many seals – or walruses, depending on the body. Most were over fifty and nearly all were *bulés*, except for a lone sixty-something Japanese guy who was skinny and completely hairless from the neck down, roasting his skin in the sun to a rich shade of gravy brown. From his deckchair, he smiled at me though John Lennon sunglasses (the only thing he was wearing) as he continued to oil himself with the loving intensity of someone polishing their favourite boot.

Gary, Spartacvs's owner – the one who had encouraged me to get comfortable and naked, *hmmm nice* – was a super-friendly bald Australian who was fifty-nine years old and had a generous barrel-shaped body. Gary's accent was thick, the kind that comes with spending most of your life driving giant, 25-metre-long trucks between Australian towns. When Gary first started holidaying in Bali in the mid 1970s, he wasn't openly gay. He had originally come here with a straight travel buddy who liked to surf. When he was by himself, Gary would try looking for something gay in town, but all he encountered were droves of female prostitutes.

Then in the late '90s, Gary came back to Bali and fell in love with a local guy he had met on the internet. Around this time, he also met a British entrepreneur who pitched the Spartacvs idea to him: a proper hotel that could fit between twelve and twenty-four men at a time, exclusively gay, targeted at foreign homosexuals. The British guy would take care of the logistics – there was already a failed family resort on the market that would be perfect to renovate – so all Gary needed to do was supply the money.

Around opening time, Gary discovered the Brit was embezzling his funds. Receipts for one million rupiah would equate to two million missing rupiah. After getting rid of the guy, Gary did the sums and found he had lost between 40,000 and 50,000 Australian dollars. On top of that, he now found himself having to start and run an all-gay resort – the first of its kind in Indonesia – completely on his own. Gary sat down and thought, *Well, what the fuck do I know about running a hotel?*

'What *did* you know about running a hotel?' I asked.

'Nothing!' Gary said. 'I'm a truck driver! I didn't have a fucking clue!'

People had tried to capitalise on Bali's fledgling gay-tourism market in the past by starting hotels similar to Spartacvs, but they had all flopped. Another gay hotel manager, who'd tried what Spartacvs was doing but on a smaller scale, warned Gary off.

'You're wasting your time,' he said. 'There's no market for it. Oh, and don't call it Spartacvs; it's too gay.'

'Excuse me!' Gary said. 'What's so gay about "Spartacvs"? He was a Greek warrior.'

After it opened, Spartacvs started turning a profit within months. Gary opened the hotel in September. The books were tipping in his favour by January. While other hotels in Bali went through peak and non-peak seasons, Spartacvs was different. In his office, Gary showed me a computer monitor displaying the resort's colour-coded bookings. Vacancies were represented by white space, and for months ahead, there was barely any white space at all. The spreadsheet was a wince-inducing rainbow. Visitors streamed in from Australia, Germany, France, the United Kingdom, the United States and Canada. Increasingly, with the global recession, visitors had started to pour in from across Asia, Africa and the Middle East, too. Bookings now came from Saudi Arabia, Qatar, Egypt and South Africa. International homosexuals had become a non-stop market.

It helped that the place was clothing-optional. That wasn't originally in the business plan, but now it was one of Spartacvs's strongest drawcards.

When it first opened, guests had asked whether they could just walk around naked. Everyone kept doing it, Gary reasoned, so why not just make it 100 per cent clothing-optional?

'You weren't a clothing-optional guy yourself?'

'No,' Gary said, guffawing. 'You'll never see me walking around nude with my body.'

A grinning Spartacvs staff member led me up to my room. An online review had harshly described Spartacvs's rooms as 'horrendously camp' and 'if Liberace had designed a hotel, this would be it'. That was unfair. The rooms felt more like Jean Paul Gaultier and David LaChapelle had been jointly commissioned to design a wonderful sex dungeon. The walls were painted asphalt, with fuchsia highlights and satin black privacy curtains, and the open-roofed bathroom was fitted with wall-to-wall mirrors, which meant that finally – *finally* – I could see what it looked like to have my butt reflected into infinity whenever I took a shower. (Overall effect: hypnotic.)

On my shared balcony, I met an extremely toned Chinese guy from Macau who wore a designer muscle top, shorts and sunglasses. He had magnificent calves. When he said hello to me, he was busily punching things into his phone, and explained he was holidaying in Bali with his Western boyfriend. They were only at Spartacvs to meet up with friends who were staying there. He wasn't staying at Spartacvs himself, he wanted to emphasise. He would *never* stay there; he wasn't that kind of guy.

'What kind of guy?' I said.

He laughed conspiratorially. 'Well so many DOM stay here, you know.'

'Dom?' I said blankly.

'DOM!' he said, taking off his sunglasses, appalled. 'You've never heard of DOM? Dee, oh, emm. DOM. It means' – he whispered – '*dirty old men*. Hahahaha. Me? I'm a DYM: dirty young man.' He cackled again.

I headed down to the pool to order a late lunch, still feeling too covered up. I nervously took off my shirt, leaving my shorts on as a salute to decency.

At this time of day, Spartacvs became an ecosystem worthy of an Attenborough documentary. Back when it first opened, Spartacvs had a problem with local moneyboys loitering outside its doors for business, but they'd solved that by allowing a few in at a time to hang around the pool, order drinks and use the wi-fi. Policy was strict: moneyboys weren't allowed to approach guests, but guests could approach the moneyboys if they wanted to chat and take them into their rooms without fuss.

On this day, there were only a couple of men trading themselves. One moneyboy was less 'boy' and more 'tank'. He was rugged, with tightly coiled muscles covered in barbed tattoos. Another moneyboy was clean-cut in preppy white shorts, looking like a Tommy Hilfiger advertisement, with his hair cut short back and sides. They were the only clothed men around the pool besides me. Because they weren't allowed to talk, they ogled and seduced with their eyes, zoning in on the naked *bulé* Spartacvs guests with silent intense stares.

As I ate my sandwich, I watched one of the *bulés* approach the moneyboys. He was an Australian man in his fifties with a kind face and a soft belly who wore black speedos with an opal pattern on the hip. The tattooed guy grinned and made staggered small-talk with the *bulé*, before the pair silently headed back to a private room, drawing the black satin curtains shut. Everyone else around the pool casually pretended that nothing was happening. I stared and chewed on my lunch, cow-like, unable to turn away.

This place is amazing, I thought.

Another Australian man – white and in his late thirties – now approached the pool completely naked. He was one of the younger *bulés* here, tall and toned. It was hard not to notice his penis: an enormous, semi-erect thing that hovered in mid-air like a fairground ride threatening to go higher. Behind him, his short, cute Indonesian boyfriend – or maybe he was a money-boy too, it was hard to tell – approached the pool in high-cut running shorts that made him appear practically naked from the side. Giggling, they dived in the pool together. As they surfaced for air, the naked Australian guy swam over to his boyfriend and wrapped his legs around him, making out with him hungrily, like a large animal trying to eat some smaller creature's face.

It felt as if I'd stumbled across some wonderful sex matinée. It was riveting. This was the closest I'd ever come to watching another couple have sex right in front of me, and the realisation was both exciting and depressing.

Though he was in the water, it was clear the Australian guy had a full erection now and was enthusiastically humping his Indonesian boyfriend through his wet shorts. After making sloppy kissing noises that sounded like a draining sink, the Indonesian guy climbed onto his boyfriend's back, and they swam across the pool like the scene in *Whale Rider* where Keisha Castle-Hughes rides a humpback.

'You two are so cute!' I wanted to call out to them, but real-ised this might send the wrong message.

When they got out of the pool and towelled each other off, the height difference between them was stark. From behind, the tall *bulé* reminded me of a parent drying off his young son after swimming lessons. The two of them then disappeared into their room, drew the curtains and shut the door.

The entire pool was now silent, except for the PA system that was playing the Joe Dolce 1980 hit novelty song 'Shaddap You Face'. I had finished my lunch. I felt both full of food and moderately aroused, which wasn't a great combination. I stared at the empty water, wondering whether I could bring myself to swim in it, considering what I'd just seen.

*

People said Bali's gay scene had only taken off in the past decade, but the island had actually been quietly hosting foreign homosexuals for close to a century. In 1925, the German artist and writer Walter Spies landed in Bali after travelling through Java and Jogjakarta, and was instantly smitten by the island's glassy blue water, lush rainforest and chirpy, handsome locals. He started an artists' colony first, then built a house in Karangasem that became his famous mountain hut boasting unending views of lakes, rice paddies and mountains. It was here that Spies hosted guests such as Charlie Chaplin, Noël Coward and the anthropologist Margaret Mead during the day, before making love to his handsome Balinese lovers at night. Spies romanticised Bali in his dreamy art and writing, casting the island in heady myth with a homoerotic undercurrent. The artists came, the gays came, then everyone else followed.

From the late 1960s onwards, large groups of gay and lesbian travellers would fly to Bali on cheap flights bound for Denpasar

14

airport, making it their holiday hide-out. At the time, the airport was little more than landing strips cut into thickets of coconut trees. Even then, it wasn't hard for gay visitors to find masseurs who were willing to be extra-accommodating with their massages, or poolside boys who said they would be your special friend for your entire stay.

By the '90s, Bali had Hulu Café, its first proper gay bar. It was a basic set-up over two wooden floors, where muscled men would perform scantily clad dances with giant pythons suggestively wrapped around shoulders and between legs as homoerotic homages to the Balinese snake gods. Hulu had since fittingly gone down in flames, but the island's appetite for the pink dollar had only grown and grown. Now there was Club Cosmo for the rich kids, Mixwell's for the tourists, Face Bar for the ladyboys, Bali Joe for the moneyboys and the seedy Bottoms Up for those who were either lost or too drunk to know where they were. Gay villas were everywhere. Tourist guides told me they couldn't keep up with the new ones being built.

Local attitudes towards gay travellers ranged from happily oblivious to outright welcoming. Everyone now knew there was a buck to be earned, especially from commission.

'You travel in Bali one person?' local taxi drivers would ask me.

'I'm by myself, yeah,' I'd say.

'No wife? No girlfriend?' they'd say.

'No,' I'd say. Sometimes I'd add, 'But I have a boyfriend.'

After a moment's realisation they'd say, 'Ah, boyfriend! Maybe you look for Balinese boyfriend too? I can take you!' They'd whisper, 'You know, beautiful, beautiful boys in Bali …'

If you were an entrepreneur, it made sense to start your venture in Bali. Before long, tourism would account for 10 per cent of Indonesia's GDP and nearly half of all foreign visitors to the country would make their way through Bali's international airport. Occupying only 5632 square kilometres, Bali had become a crucial economic hub, and the island's standard of living far outstripped the rest of the archipelago's. If you had a vision and a dream, you came to Bali to build your empire. And if you were building a gay empire, you were almost guaranteed a good return.

Josh was one businessman who knew this well. Ethnically Chinese, he had grown up in Bali and did most of his business there. He was in his late forties, but looked alarmingly young in his white t-shirt with its fashionably small pocket, and pants cut in a fabric you could tell was expensive just by looking. At all hours, he was hooked to his Samsung Galaxy Tab, checking emails and taking calls.

Josh was the owner of Bali's Antique brand, which encompassed a luxury spa, villa and restaurant. Although he had studied business in Australia, most of his projects – including the hotel he was currently building – were based in Bali. No regulations, lower costs: it was just far easier to build here. Even when Josh was growing up in Bali as a kid, the local tourism industry had been robust.

'In some ways, it was much better,' he said. 'It wasn't commercial, really more cultural. Before the development, it was more about family holidays. It was more …'

He looked up, searching for the right word.

'Wholesome?' I said.

He laughed and pointed at me. 'Right. Everyone used to come to Bali for the culture. Now, having a good time is more important. It's more about singles. And all those gay bars there are actually quite new. Nothing was basically a gay place until I opened the Antique restaurant, then that whole area started to become very specific. Gay bars, gay restaurants, gay villas.'

Not that Josh minded. If anything, it was working to his benefit. On Dhyana Pura Street, between Mixwell's and Bali Joe, Josh was building a new upmarket gay club called the Birdcage that was scheduled to open in a few months. There was also his upcoming hotel – the nearly completed Grey Hotel – that was perched between Legian and Seminyak and would aggressively target the gay market. It wouldn't be a gay-exclusive place like Spartacvs (Josh didn't think it was nice to discriminate against straight people), but zoning in on the gay market was crucial to its success. For instance, at Josh's Antique day spa, over 70 per cent of the spa clients were gay, so Josh ensured most of his massage therapists were handsome men.

'I'm *always* thinking about that,' he said. 'If you want to make something, you have to ask the gay people. They *know.* They're always setting the trend. Where the gays go, the straight people go. They spend money and they have no kids, nothing. They know how to live in style. They spend and they want to have a good time. So Bali is like Bangkok now, except we don't have go-go boys to pick up at the bar.'

'Really?' I said. 'But I've noticed heaps.'

'There are moneyboys, but they're more discreet,' Josh said. 'We have a border – a social, cultural border – because we're a mix of Hindus and Muslims here.'

Josh thought about how to phrase it properly, how to best draw the distinction between his island home and a seedy city like Bangkok. 'There is a line,' he finally said. 'There is a line.'

*

On my first night at Spartacvs, a Dutch couple checked into the room next to me. I only found this out when one of them started spying on me through my blinds. I was working on my laptop wearing nothing but Y-fronts (it was hot), before looking up to see a white-haired Gianni Versace lookalike in his fifties locking eyes with me. I nearly screamed.

To defuse the situation, I leaped up to open the door with the giddy, sexless enthusiasm of an American housewife welcoming a new neighbour to town. 'Hello!' I said, opening the door to shake his hand enthusiastically. 'My name is Benjamin! I am from *Australia*! And where are you from?! Did you just arrive?!'

Perhaps he thought I was brain-damaged. But with all the lights on and the volume of my voice turned up high, every potential trace of sexual tension between us quickly evaporated. Unimpressed, the Dutchman cleared his throat and introduced himself and his boyfriend, who was unpacking in the room next door. His boyfriend was a few years younger – balding, with a handsome, equine face – and merrily said hello. After standing at the doorway awkwardly for a while, we made our excuses and the older Dutch guy grumpily crept back into his room with his partner.

Some time later, a twenty-something Indonesian swaggered past my room. I didn't see his face, but heard murmurs between him and the Dutch guys at their door. The Indonesian guy went inside and everything went quiet. Outside on our shared balcony, they had left half their curtains open, almost like an invitation. All the lights were still on, which meant that anyone could easily make out something weird was happening on the bed: a single organism made of three torsos and twelve limbs; a six-armed beast thrusting into itself; a tanned butt nestled into a mound of

pale Dutch flesh. Seeing them made me feel simultaneously perverted and curious, like a kid who'd caught his parents screwing
on top of the washing machine and couldn't stop watching.

Quietly, I went back inside my room, closed the door, show-
ered and prepared to head out. At Spartacvs's reception, the
guys at the front desk told me to go to Dhyana Pura Street. Not
only was it the gayest street in Bali – full of drag queens and
bulés and moneyboys and muscly-butted go-go dancers – but it
also had decent places to eat.

Just as I was about to walk down the road for a taxi, the
Indonesian guy who had just visited the Dutch couple appeared
next to me. He had mischievous eyes, big puffer-fish cheeks
and wore his hair in a heavy-fringed boy-band cut. His cotton
shirt was unbuttoned right down to his navel. Big wooden
beads framed his torso suggestively, giving him the look of
someone who'd been cast as a seaside monk in a gay porno.

'You need a taxi?' I said. 'I'm about to catch one if you want
to share.'

'No, I have one of these,' he said, mounting one of the scooters parked outside. 'Where are you going?'

'Dhyana Pura Street,' I said.

He gave me a look. 'I *live* at Dhyana Pura,' he said.

'Shut *up*.'

He backed his scooter onto the dirt road and cocked his head
at me in a way that told me to get on. As I straddled the bike
behind him, he grabbed my thigh and pulled me close into him.

'Closer,' he said. 'Like this.'

My groin was right up against his butt.

'Comfortable?' he said.

'Uh –'

Before I could answer, we were speeding off down the road.

The dirt road leading out of Spartacvs took us past a narrow creek that snaked its way between other newly built villas and luxury homes. It was perfumed with a hundred smells, none of them good. When I later walked past it in the daytime, I discovered that it looked exactly like it smelled: choked and strangled with hastily disposed-of chemicals and garbage. It was a place where things came to die. Every street around here was a construction site, with the foundations of homes emerging from mounds of stone, rubble and crap, and the detritus of the sites seeping right back into nature.

On the ride, I learned my new friend's name was Bumi. Bumi was twenty-two years old and worked at Club Cosmo, one of the more expensive and exclusive gay clubs. He usually served drinks but sometimes worked as the guy who stood at the front of the club, flirting with male tourists, kissing them on the cheek and dragging them in by the hand.

Like most guys who worked Seminyak's gay circuit, Bumi wasn't Balinese himself. He came from Jakarta and a rich Muslim family. He was one of ten children, each of whom had grown up with their own room in a giant house in the country's most expensive city.

As Bumi and I settled in at a pasta restaurant, he bemoaned conditions in Jakarta.

'So boring!' he said. 'Jakarta is much better for work, but so *expensive* for life. If you have skills, if you have good speak-English, it's easy for find job in Bali. And Bali is much better for gay life.'

Bumi didn't believe in true love, which suited him fine. In Bali, he explained, it was all about sex, and sex came with a price tag he was happy to charge.

'If you come to Bali for sex, if you want to fuck us, you must pay!' he said.

'Does that mean the ultimate goal is to find a rich sugar daddy?' I asked.

Bumi looked angry and offended. 'Not true!' he said. 'I don't want to find!'

Horrified, I started to apologise.

Bumi laughed. 'I don't want to *find* sugar daddy,' he explained. 'I want him to come to *me*, because I'm younger. Hahahaha!'

Bumi was only interested in white Western guys: Italian or Swiss especially. Roughly half the sex Bumi had ever had in his life – and there had been a lot – had involved a monetary transaction. He didn't consider himself a moneyboy or a prostitute and definitely wasn't desperate for cash. Bumi already had a job that paid the bills. He just didn't see the point in giving away his assets for free. A couple of months ago, for instance, Bumi had had sex with a Japanese guy he wasn't particularly attracted to, so he had charged him 10,000 yen – about 120 US dollars – and all parties came away happy. On his Gay Romeo and Scruff internet profiles, Bumi had even set up a Western Union account, so that if a horny *bulé* wanted to see naked photos of him, they could easily transfer 100 euro to Bumi for quick access. In a way, I admired Bumi's entrepreneurial spirit.

'And what do you get to see for 100 euro?' I asked.

'Cock-cock, naked-naked,' he said.

Bumi hadn't actually gotten any money from the Western Union set-up yet – too many guys were showing off their naked bodies for free, he said with contempt – but he was still proud of coming up with the idea himself. And because of his online profiles, there was one American *bulé* who wanted to fly Bumi to Texas for the sole purpose of having Bumi fuck him really hard in the arse, which I said sounded like a lovely trip. Bumi hadn't yet set a price for that particular arrangement, so the emails had stopped for now. I joked to Bumi that if he ever became a proper moneyboy, he wouldn't be a very efficient one. He fluttered his eyelashes at me and shrugged innocently.

Later, over drinks at Club Cosmo, Bumi got out his Samsung phone and showed me the photos he charged foreigners 100 euro to see. There was one spectacular shot of Bumi getting out of a pool naked, perfectly capturing the arse I had seen only hours ago at Spartacvs, thrusting at the Dutch men. I thanked Bumi for not charging me 100 euro to see the photo and he laughed so loudly that everyone around us could hear, then locked his phone. As I paid for our drinks, Bumi kept on tapping his phone, checking his Facebook and Scruff accounts and showing me all the men who were interested in him.

'So is this the kind of thing you were doing at Spartacvs tonight?' I asked.

Bumi covered his mouth and let out a scandalised shriek, followed by a jackhammer laugh. How did I know about that?

'Um,' I said.

Bumi explained that he had met the younger Dutch guy via Scruff, and when Bumi found out he was staying at Spartacvs, they had arranged to meet. But tonight, Bumi had been surprised – no, shocked; *shocked* was the word – to discover the Dutch guy had a boyfriend there with him already! And an *old* boyfriend, no less. Gross, yuck, ugh. Bumi didn't know they were looking for a threesome.

'He wants to get fucked from me, but I cannot!' Bumi said, looking as though about to gag. 'I'm not interested in his boyfriend; no, no, no! *Because he lie.* He tells me before he came to Bali he was coming alone. I love Dutch guys – and he is from Dutch – but I don't like threesomes! Oh my *god.*' Bumi shook his head, almost morally affronted. 'You want a threesome with me, you must pay me!'

'And because he wouldn't pay –'

'I don't want to sex!'

'How much would someone have to pay?' I asked.

Bumi shrieked, scandalised.

'Why is that so scandalous?' I said. 'How much did you ask?'

Bumi bit his lip. 'Um, 100 euro!' he said, breathlessly.

'That seems reasonable,' I said. 'And they still didn't want to pay?'

Bumi shook his head. 'He wants to get fucked by me? He must pay me! I'm attracted to the younger guy, but I would not *touch* with the boyfriend. And I'm not interested! Because he *lie*.'

'So,' I said delicately, 'exactly how far *did* it go?'

Bumi sighed. 'He wanted to see my cock ... so I just showed him. I mean, as you already know: Balinese. There are many sluts in here.'

'Oh, sluts!' I said enthusiastically.

'Oh yeah, many.'

'You mean the local guys?'

'Local guys, but not just local guys. Western guys also.'

I sipped on my drink, thinking about it. 'So what you're saying,' I said, 'is that everyone here is a slut, then.'

Bumi put his hands together and nodded sagely.

*

Dhyana Pura Street was a human stew of sunburn, alcohol and breathtaking crimes against music. At night, diners were serenaded with weird cover hybrids, funk-reggae versions of Kings of Leon's 'Sex on Fire' and Spanish guitar chillax versions of

Beyoncé's 'Crazy in Love'. In this street, there seemed to be more Australians per square foot than in Australia itself, all of them red-faced, flushed and thrilled at their good fortune in having found themselves in a country where they could dine in the best restaurants wearing nothing more than Bintang singlets, rugby shorts and sand-crusted thongs. Snot-nosed kids ran around with newly braided hair as their mothers cooed to each other, comparing cheap pedicures and sipping on giant cocktails.

Across from Dhyana Pura's string of gay clubs was a kerbside where Bali's moneyboys gathered seven nights a week to steal your heart, take your breath away and, sometimes, pinch your wallet. Rows of them waited patiently, standing on one leg with a crooked knee planted on the wall behind them, the international pose for male hustling. No one ever said they were a moneyboy outright. Partly this was out of modesty, partly because prostitution was technically illegal in Indonesia. But many of them just didn't see themselves as hustlers. They weren't moneyboys; they were opportunity-seekers. Their attitude was the same as Bumi's: *We've got something you want and we're not giving it away for free.* In a sense, ensuring that you got paid every time you had sex – irrespective of whether you liked the guy or not – was a way of respecting your worth.

The diversity was astounding. Some looked barely out of high school and wore the kind of screen-printed, block-coloured t-shirt you find in the boys section of a suburban department store. Others weren't young at all: one guy was in his forties and slouched with a paunch that hung off him like a pregnancy. He nonchalantly smoked cigarettes as he waited for trade. Some looked poor and didn't speak English when I said hello, while others spoke English as a first language and preppily texted their friends on BlackBerries as they waited for men. One man styled his hair in a greasy mullet and wore a shredded singlet with the words 'PUNK'S NOT DEAD' scrawled on it; another looked vaguely homeless and was missing a couple of teeth. There was someone here for every taste and budget.

One thing unified them: they all looked crushingly bored. They were also evasive when I asked them what they were up to that night. One guy told me he actually sold mobile phones in Denpasar full-time – a well-paying job, he added – but hung outside the clubs on Friday and Saturday nights because he 'just liked to'. Generally, none of them talked to each other. When they figured out that I wasn't in the market, they didn't talk to me either. Instead, they stared at me, baffled that I wanted to chat. Later, someone told me that because I was in my twenties and also Asian, they probably saw me as competition. Feeling a little rejected, I shuffled across the road to Dhyana Pura's bars for a drink, when a hand reached out and grabbed me.

'Who are *you?*' a voice purred excitedly, clutching my forearm with one hand and stroking it with the other. 'Where do you *come from?* You are *gorrrr-geous.*'

Eelga was twenty-three years old and was all mouth and coiffed hair. Along with his giant quiff, he proudly displayed teeth covered in expensive braces. His jeans were so tight that they looked painted on and he had a feather tattooed on the left side of his smooth-skinned neck. Eelga's friend Leo was an older ethnic Chinese guy with a pugdog face and a weird haircut that looked like Justin Bieber's fringe turned ninety degrees to the side. Leo strutted up to us with a supermodel's walk, sandwiching me between him and Eelga.

'What is your name?' Leo demanded, in barking English.

'Uh, I'm Benjamin,' I said, casually trying to release myself from Eelga's weirdly strong grip. 'What are you guys up to tonight?'

'Oh, I want to hang at the gay bar,' Eelga said, 'because I want to relax! Maybe meet someone there, becaussssse ...'

'Because?' I asked.

'Because maybe someone *sexy* is on holiday! Maybe I'll meet someone there.'

'You want to meet a tourist? A foreigner? A *bulé*?'

'Exactly!' Eelga said, snapping his fingers. 'I'm not interested in local people; I'm interested in *Western* people. I don't know why. I'm just not interested in Indonesian people! I like Westerners because they're *hot*. HOT. Especially white people.'

He turned his palm down then flicked his hand upwards, as if scalded. *Hot.* I laughed while still trying to worm my way out of his vice-like grip.

'And what do you like about them?' I asked. 'Their looks?'

'I want to have *sex* with them!' Eelga said.

Eelga demanded I take photos with him on his smartphone, using our posing as an excuse to kiss me all over the face like a persistent and hyperactive dog.

'EELGA,' I said.

'You are *gorrrr*-geous!' he said.

'You say that to everyone.'

Eelga pretended to look hurt.

Eelga could come out clubbing only once a week because he worked full-time as a waiter in Legian. He mainly chased after older European guys aged between thirty and forty ('Because hot!' he helpfully explained), and unlike other Indonesian guys, he insisted the whole money thing didn't matter.

'I don't expect the money or the rich man,' he said. 'No, I don't expect about that. I just expect the HOT SEX. Of course I like old men, especially when he is *gorrrrrr-geous*. Especially when I was with good-looking men' – he lowered his voice and touched my arm – 'like you.'

I stared at him, baffled.

'I'm not white,' I said. Remembering that he preferred older men, I had a horrible thought: *But am I old?*

'You *white!*' Eelga said, as if I was stupid.

'Eelga, I'm not white!' I said, pointing to my face. 'I'm Chinese?'

Eelga looked confused. 'But you said you live in the Brisbane?'

Eelga was familiar with my Australian hometown because he had a boyfriend there right now. Actually, Eelga had a couple of boyfriends, neither of whom knew about the other's existence. He had one boyfriend in France and another in Australia, whose photo he showed me on his phone before saying, 'He is not good-looking,' which I thought was sad. Eelga's Australian boyfriend sent him about 200 dollars every month and had invited him to Australia for Christmas. Eelga's French boyfriend was even more generous, sending him 300 euro every month, and was already proposing that they marry each other in Quebec. Eelga's boyfriends flew to Bali in successive months to visit him and he made sure their paths never crossed.

'That's a nice system you have,' I said.

'*Exactly,*' he said, snapping his fingers.

'And are you looking for Boyfriend #3 tonight?'

Eelga giggled, scandalised. Then he got really close to my face and looked into my eyes. 'Maybe,' he said.

I rocked my head back and swallowed.

Eelga, Leo and I headed to Mixwell's together. As I bought us all beers, two German men in their late fifties latched onto Eelga and asked, without any introduction, whether he would come home with them for sex right now. Eelga wasn't afraid to be rude and bluntly told them both that they were too old for him. It didn't matter: within minutes, the German men were surrounded by swarms of other young Indonesian guys who had sniffed old blood and good money.

At Mixwell's, hard-bodied go-go dancers climbed on top of the bar wearing nothing but white briefs, the outlines of their crotches and butts not so much suggestive as anatomical. Middle-aged women from Australia and England on holidays stared at the men's bulges as they thrust to the club's beat. The women were hypnotised, almost dewy-eyed at the beauty of it all. Watching them was like seeing someone's sexual awakening occurring before my eyes. Middle-aged gay men stuffed money into the go-go dancers' briefs. Emboldened, the women followed suit, sliding in 20,000 and 50,000 rupiah notes, almost visibly shuddering as they made skin-to-skin contact. The go-go dancers winked at the women, making them blush.

Leo had lost his drink but was already, somehow, weirdly drunk. Or maybe he was on something. He was incomprehensibly slurring, but he had been sort of like that when we had met outside. Boisterously, he shoved his way past the crowd of dancers and drinkers, leaving angry looks in his wake, before storming up to me. With his mouth in a pout, he locked eyes with me, swiped my beer right out of my hand –

'Leo!' I said.

– and sculled the drink without breaking eye contact. He handed the bottle back to me dramatically, nearly empty. When I rolled my eyes and reached out for it, Leo leaned in to kiss me like a giant, slobbering Saint Bernard. I turned quickly so all he got was my neck.

'Leo, I have a boyfriend!' I said, pushing him off.

Leo made a face. 'Your boyfriend is ugly!' he barked.

He rolled his eyes at me then sashayed back into the crowd, leaving me holding a beer bottle that was now nearly empty. With the back of my hand, I wiped Leo's spit off my neck.

'I think he likes you,' Eelga said into my ear bitchily as we watched him walk away.

We kept drinking hard. The rest of the night was a blur of alcohol and go-go dancers and terrible drag queens dancing to Lady Gaga in wigs that looked inspired by both Elvira and Susan Sontag.

Outside on the road, an elderly, wrinkled *bulé* aggressively shoved his hand down the pants of a young Indonesian guy and pretended he was a puppetmaster. Another Indonesian guy, barely out of his teens, swung flirtatiously off the back of a wizened, goblin-like white man. Both of them looked thrilled with the other as they poured themselves into a cab. Judging by the older man's clothes, he was loaded. Both parties had clearly done well out of this transaction. All the *bulés* were well over fifty.

Seeing this, I was reminded of what an elderly Australian expatriate man had told me. He had lived in Bali for years and enjoyed the clubs and attention when he was younger. Nowadays, he avoided them. The older you were, he said, the more aggressive the attention from the young boys.

'You see this?' he said to me, pointing to the deep lines in his forehead. 'ATM,' he said, tapping out the wrinkles with his finger. 'ATM.'

*

I woke up at Spartacvs feeling as though my vital organs had been rearranged. My mouth tasted as if it belonged to a dead man. Morning sun crept through a tiny slit in the curtains, carving a blinding and exact path across my face, like a laser bisecting my skull. Groaning, I brushed my teeth, grabbed my towel and sluggishly hauled myself downstairs towards the pool, dipping my feet in. I looked around at the surrounding bungalows. No one else was awake. Everyone was sleeping in, recovering from the night before. *Fuck it*, I thought. I took off my clothes and dived in naked.

When I broke through the water, there was movement nearby. Panicked, I quickly swam to the side of the pool and watched as a sleepy-looking moneyboy crept out of a ground-floor room. Earlier, I had met the Belgian guy who was staying in that room, an affable man in his late fifties who seemed to have a different Indonesian guy on his arm every night. This moneyboy had bed hair and smiled at me as he put on his shoes. He couldn't have been much older than eighteen. He looked like a kid sneaking out of someone else's dorm at a school camp following a late-night junkfood binge, all guilt-ridden but helplessly pleased with himself. We waved to each other sheepishly.

I'd been told the best place in Bali for a gay visitor to nurse a hangover was Callego Beach, a twenty-minute walk from Spartacvs. Callego was a gay hotspot where you could get snacks and legitimate massages, or disappear into the bushes for blow jobs with local men who didn't ask for much money. If you were lucky – or unlucky, depending on your tastes – you might also encounter the Balinese guy who was said to actually *live* in these bushes, animal-like: a puckish man with long curls who made a living entirely out of selling hand jobs and blow jobs for 20,000 rupiah (two dollars) a pop. Someone told me he slept under Callego Café's ramshackle roof whenever it rained.

Only a year ago, Callego Beach was still beautiful. It'd had voluminous duvet-like lawns and carefully landscaped plants that grew in explosive floral clusters. Until recently, it had been public property and the locals had taken pride in maintaining the grounds. But a few months before I arrived, the site had been bought out by a new 300-room hotel development that was in the process of bulldozing the entire site. The master plan was to erect an enormous resort as direct competition to the brashly luxurious designer beachside hotels here that charged up to 1000 US dollars a night.

By the time I got there, Callego looked sad and derelict. Past the little archway entrance, the stone paths leading to the beach had become rubble, smashed by bulldozers to make way for the new hotel's foundations. The grass was brown and flammable-looking, crunching as I walked on it. Local boys had used to have regular volleyball competitions and visitors would gather here for sunrises and sunsets, or to celebrate birthdays. Now, as I set up a deckchair and sun umbrella, Indonesian and Chinese inspectors in business attire tiptoed between the sunbaking men, taking notes on clipboards and surveying the site for demolition. By the end of the year, this would all be torn down.

Around the site, there were some battered remains of small statues depicting Hindu gods, some embodying the concept of *trimurti*: the creator Brahma, the preserver Vishnu and the destroyer Shiva. In Hinduism, at all times, there was supposed to be a balance among the three, a cycle of creation, preservation and destruction in order for things to regenerate. Whatever: it wasn't long before the statues would be bulldozed too.

Next to the *bulés* sunning themselves at Callego, I was shamefully skinny and pale. One sixty-something Caucasian guy was so alarmingly tanned that he seemed to belong to a new race entirely. He lay flat on his stomach wearing what was technically a G-string, although the way his giant butt consumed the fabric he may as well have been naked. Every so often, he blinked and looked around confusedly, before getting up and shuffling off, smacking his lips and gently flossing his anus as he walked to the bathroom.

At the nearby Callego Café, an old man sat by himself smoking cigarettes while wearing the tiniest white rugby shorts. He had an interesting face that changed depending on the angle. When he took a drag on his cigarette, he looked craggy and villainous – like someone being tried at a war crimes tribunal – but then he exhaled the smoke and looked utterly charming and dapper. The old man smoked languidly alongside a younger, compactly muscled Indonesian guy, and they both caught my eye. Their names were respectively – no joke – Steve and Irwin.

Steve and Irwin were just friends. Australian Steve had an Indonesian boyfriend, while Irwin's *bulé* boyfriend had recently passed away. As Steve smoked, he told me about the first time he came to Bali in 2000, having just broken up with his long-term Australian boyfriend back home.

'You came here looking for a rebound?' I asked.

'I wanted to come and fuck everybody I could, actually.'

'Oh,' I said.

'I'd never had sex with an Asian until then,' he said, 'so I thought, I'll go and have a look. And since then, I've never been with another *bulé*.' Steve laughed to himself.

When he first arrived in Bali, Steve found himself at an Australian bar called Peanuts. It was a standard mixed club, because that's all he could find. Despite what he'd heard, there were no obvious gay bars and he hadn't seen any advertisements for them. Steve started talking to the Indonesian barman and asked him if there were any close by.

'Oh, there are no gays in Bali,' the barman had said. 'No gay scene.'

The barman was friendly, but also looked nervous talking about this stuff. Steve was convinced he was covering up, so bought him a few drinks to loosen him up.

'Okay,' the barman eventually said. 'I'll call somebody. Just wait.'

Soon after, a guy on a motorcycle came to pick Steve up and usher him to the newly opened Hulu Café – the one that would eventually burn down – where a ladyboy greeted him at the bar.

'No,' Steve said to the motorcyclist. 'I want a man who looks like a man.'

Overhearing what Steve was saying, two young Indonesian men immediately approached him.

When I asked whether the men were good-looking, Steve shrugged.

'Actually, looking back,' he said, 'they weren't so handsome.' He laughed croakily at me. 'I looked at some photos yesterday.'

Nonetheless, the next morning, Steve sauntered into the hotel breakfast area, a young Indonesian man on each arm, completely without shame. Only twenty-four hours earlier, he was heartbroken and bereft; now he was in a foreign country having fucked two perfectly lovely young men in one evening. He felt radiant. His fellow hotel guests were appalled. Children at the breakfast tables giggled quietly, silently appealing to their parents for answers while mums and dads shook their heads at each other, absolutely disgusted. As Steve took a seat with his straight friends, the owner of the hotel came to tell him that he was very sorry, but they'd unfortunately made a double booking for his room and he would now have to vacate the premises.

One of Steve's friends leaned over and said, 'You dirty old bastard. Bringing *two* of them over? If you had only *one* of them, you might've gotten away with it.'

Steve wasn't concerned. He had heard about a gay-friendly hotel in Legian that had just opened up, so the threesome stayed there for a week, fucking each other senseless at every opportunity. Steve was generous with the boys, paying for their taxi rides and shouting them meals at the expensive Jimboran seafood restaurant where they both demanded to be taken every night. He was still getting used to the currency, but everything seemed cheap enough. Just before Steve left, he gave them each an extra 300 dollars before happily waving them goodbye, leaving them to revel in their modest new fortunes.

The way Steve told the story made it seem happy and idyllic, but I still had my reservations, and the image of this old man with two young boys on each arm burned in my mind. *Was this okay?* I wondered.

'Everyone's got to make money somehow,' Steve said, as if reading my mind. 'No one here judges the moneyboys.'

Plus, he added, they made for the most beautiful, loyal boyfriends. And despite anyone's preconceptions or judgements about sleaze or sordidness, once the locals hooked up with you, Steve said, they were fiercely loyal. Steve's boyfriend Imam had been a moneyboy when they met, he said. Steve had been walking along the shoreline at dusk when he heard someone call out, 'Hello, hello.' In the half-light, Steve couldn't see anyone, but could discern Imam's smile: Cheshire-cat teeth glowing white. The young man was deeply tanned from walking up and down the beach all day in the full sun, looking for customers. Steve liked the look of him.

'He stayed with me that night,' Steve said. 'I woke up in the

34

morning and he was still there, and I thought, Wow, okay: he didn't steal my money.'

'Your organs hadn't been removed,' I joked.

'No!' Steve raised his eyebrows and chuckled. 'Well, *almost* ...'

I nearly spat out my drink. Steve roared with laughter.

Steve and Imam had been together ever since, in a devoted and happily non-monogamous relationship. It was a recurring story with *bulé*–Indonesian gay couples: many started out with a frisky money-fuelled session of jiggy-jiggy, but often these relationships developed into something far deeper and unexpectedly solid: romances, friendships, partnerships and even business arrangements between equals. Gary, who had started Spartacvs, was another example. The young Indonesian man he had met online years ago was now a business partner in Spartacvs. While they were no longer lovers, Gary's relationship with him had laid the basis for his future. Often the dynamics of male sex work in Bali were more complicated than basic exploitation. For some moneyboys, it was a quick and creative way out of poverty, if you played your cards right.

*

By the end of my time in Bali, I caved. I embraced who I was and became a shameless, bona fide tourist. For years, I had avoided travelling to Bali because of the clichés of what it meant to be a foreigner there: the drunk Australians with braided mullets; the Europeans buying shitty souvenirs and pirated Viagra; the sunstroked Brits sporting second-degree sunburn; the vomiting; the hooting.

But it was only when you embraced Bali that the island embraced you back. I had surfing lessons at Kuta that were almost spiritual, experiencing the natural high of standing on a wave, and the agony of fibreglass chafing that nearly eroded the nipples from my chest. I rode my bike to organic restaurants in the middle of nowhere and experienced the specific yet name-less guilt that comes from cycling past Kerobokan Prison to get a luxuriously long twenty-dollar massage at a nearby spa. There were dinners on timber decks overlooking the ocean by night, and afternoon bike rides where I'd get stupidly lost before find-ing myself watching the sunset in the middle of endless rice paddies, built like the tiered green seating of some natural amphitheatre. If this island wasn't paradise, it was getting close.

From Spartacvs, I roamed from nudist gay villa to nudist gay villa. One was a giant old Dutch house that had been turned into a gay clothing-optional homestay. It was secluded and homely, and often played host to married businessmen who liked to fuck men on the side. These guests would check into five-star hotels so their wife and kids had a place to leave phone messages, but in reality they were staying here, having affairs with the foreign and local men who stayed at this place. With everyone under a single roof, it had the feel of a hostel crossed with a colonial-era homosexual harem.

It was sort of gross.

'I think you'll have a lot of fun here,' the manager told me when I arrived. The communal living environment was designed to be conducive to sex, and it wasn't long before I opened my dorm room one night to find two portly Malaysian men making out and taking off each other's shirts enthusiastically.

'Oh shit, sorry!' I said.

Neither of them paid attention to me and they kept making out, grabbing each other's bulky chests and licking each other's nipples. It was a long time before I went back to the room to sleep that night. Because the one communal shower was almost constantly in use, I'd just take my showers in the open by the pool.

At another four-bedroom villa, I had the place to myself while it was being done up. Yandi, the houseboy who lived on-site – a tall, lean and muscled guy with teeth as white as bleached paper – walked around wearing nothing but brash designer underwear in colourful patterns. He was quite forward when introducing himself.

'I'm Yandi!' he said. 'I like Asians! Japanese, Chinese, Singapore. *Like you.*'

'Okay!' We stared at each other. 'And do you live here, Yandi?'

'Yeah, I live here, live here all alone,' he said, lowering his eyes seductively. 'But tonight, I sleep with you.'

'Uh …'

'You like?' he said.

'Yandi, I have a boyfriend.'

He barked with laughter. 'Ah, you have boyfriend!' he shrieked. 'I'm naughty!'

Then he lowered his eyes again and looked me up and down. 'But you can still *call me*,' he said, rhyming, 'if you're *horny.*'

'You are bad, Yandi,' I said.

Yandi laughed really loudly, then looked me up and down again.

At night, when Yandi had gone to bed and I had the house to myself, I'd strip off and float in the pool, making the most of the dark and washing off the day's sweat and weird conversations. As I floated in the warm water, staring past the silhouettes of palms and into the starry night, I felt like a really small kid float-ing in a giant bath.

I was a little conflicted. Bali's tourism had lifted the island out of poverty, but there were other costs. The island's entire tourism model was a Catch-22: the pace of tourism steadily eroded Bali's native culture, environment, language and religion, but economically Bali couldn't live without foreigners. Tourism was the island's lifeblood. After the bombs in 2002 and 2005, visitor numbers contracted by a third and employment figures sank. People got poor quickly and non-Balinese workers returned to their home islands and awful jobs. People still spoke about that period like a recent horror they had only barely scraped through.

Meanwhile, sex work had become such an ingrained part of Bali's gay scene that nearly all young gay men in Bali – and a lot of straight ones – had scored money from sex with *bulés* at some stage. They tried it for fun, out of boredom or because they wanted an instant hit of money. It had almost become a rite of passage.

Made was thirty-two, a skinny guy who seemed to be formed entirely out of sharp-angled, crane-like limbs. He was native Balinese. For young gay Indonesians from other islands, Bali represented an amnesty zone where they could be openly queer for the first time, away from the prying eyes of their family in Sumatra or Jakarta. It was different if you were Balinese like Made. Bali was a small island, and it didn't take long for word to spread from family to family. You had to be more discreet. While other gay boys openly cruised each other and *bulés* at Dhyana Pura, Balinese boys either went online or did old-school cruising along the riverbanks or in old derelict buildings: *uma hatu*, or ghost houses.

Despite this, Made told me he still went to the bars on Dhyana Pura Street occasionally. When he was in his twenties –

when he was more foolhardy and less aware of the consequences – he'd go there nearly every night looking for action. Usually he looked for other Indonesian men, but occasionally he went out sniffing for *bulés* or they'd come and approach him. Locals were fun, Made said, but the *bulés* were potentially lucrative. Made even once scored a *motorcycle* out of one old Australian.

'A motorcycle!' I said. 'How did that happen?'

'It was difficult. I didn't speak English,' Made said, grinning, 'so I had to use the language of my body instead.'

I nodded. 'Right.'

Made said the Australian *bulé* had been more than twice his age – in his sixties or older. Made had been only in his mid twenties. The age difference was so big that it made him a little embarrassed to think about it now.

'Was he good-looking, though?' I asked. 'Some older guys can still be handsome.'

Made grimaced and clarified for me: this particular dude was super-old *and* super-ugly. Made didn't say it in a callous or deliberately mean way. He was describing the *bulé* objectively, the way you'd describe someone's hair colour or the shape of their ears. This guy just happened to be ancient and had a seriously unfortunate face. But the old, ugly *bulé* also had money, so Made went through with it.

The only catch, Made said, was doing exactly what the *bulé* told him. But Made was usually passive in sex anyway, so he just lay there while the *bulé* did his thing. To Made's surprise, he managed to put on a convincing performance, and even got a boner.

'I don't think I need someone to be handsome,' Made said. 'I think I need someone to comfort me. I mean, at first I didn't exactly love this guy, but then slowly, slowly, I learned to like him.'

After a few months though, Made decided the *bulé* wasn't really his thing. He was young, and this guy was so old he may as well have been his grandfather, or a wizard. And there wasn't really a spark to speak of, so Made casually called the arrangement off. Furious, the Australian *bulé* took back the motorcycle he'd given Made, which made Made upset. But he knew better than to argue back. Made's problem was that he wasn't open about being gay to his family, and he didn't want the *bulé* to expose him.

Made was the sixth of seven siblings and none of his brothers or sisters knew he was gay. Neither did his parents. He *suspected* his family had their *suspicions*, but no one ever asked questions and Made never said anything. In his Hindu family, questions about his sexuality were framed by talking about how Made wasn't yet married, which was embarrassing for everyone involved.

'The difficult is with the community and the *banjar*,' he said. *Banjars* were the traditional councils upon which Balinese society was based, discrete micro authorities on the island. Even now, male heads of most Balinese families met every fortnight to discuss matters affecting the community, including marriage. 'I'm getting old,' Made said, 'so everyone in my family is asking me: "When are you going to get married?" In Bali culture, a man *has* to be married, but I'm not ready to be open to the family yet.'

Adding to his shame, every one of Made's siblings – four brothers and two sisters – was already married. One of his nieces and another nephew were now married off too, and *their* kids were old enough to talk and refer to him jokingly as 'grandfather'. Made laughed as he said this, but the laughter came out uncomfortably.

At thirty-two, Made felt too old – and was definitely too gay – for marriage now. But he was also beyond chasing *bulés*. There was way too much competition in Seminyak, with each new batch of gays moving to the island more handsome, muscled, charming and willing than the last. Nowadays, one Westerner would have between five and ten Indonesians close to him, trying to catch him.

'Locals have to be more aggressive,' Made said. 'And Westerners, they are the king here. They have money, so they get to choose which boy they want.'

Made's gay friends told me that none of this stuff – the gay villas, the gay clubs, the unceasing packs of rich gay *bulés* – existed when they were teenagers. Part of them still wished it didn't. Now it was crowded in Seminyak and tourists came and went, treating boys like trash. Boys became superficial, and it was all about comparing the gifts that *bulés* left behind. It was common for Balinese guys to pick up *bulés* and be given widescreen televisions they'd install in comically tiny bedrooms, despite not even having a flushable toilet.

'All this is good for the economy,' one of Made's friends told me, 'but maybe not good for our culture. Maybe more Balinese will forget the culture also. We're really afraid Bali will become a sex destination for tourists, like Bangkok, you know.'

He looked at his lap.

'Nowadays,' he said, 'tourists like drag queens more than they like Balinese dancers.'

He laughed a little at his own joke.

You heard this a lot: locals mournfully speculating that Bali was about to become the next Bangkok, that the island was on the tipping point from being famous for its culture to being synonymous with sex. There were other emerging problems too: in Bali, only around 26 per cent of sex workers reportedly used condoms. The rise of gay tourism, the blurring of occupational and incidental sex work, combined with a lack of sex education, meant HIV rates on the island amongst men who had sex with men had increased by 10 per cent in the past year alone.

I swam naked in the villa's pool at night, my junk floating about, stars shooting across the night sky. The luxury here was almost obscene: the frangipani flowers that dropped into the water would be removed by morning. I mulled over the stories and arguments: ethics versus economics; selling sex to know your worth. It was hard to think about, but it didn't take long to figure out what was distracting me. In the back of my mind, I was planning my next holiday here. Next time, I decided, I would bring my boyfriend too. It was both wonderful and awful, the way this island made everything – and everyone – so easy.

THAILAND

In which we attend the world's biggest beauty pageant for transsexual women. Key question: 'So why are there more transsexual women in Thailand anyway?' Key quote: 'You are a man who wants to live as a woman? But you're not a woman!' Average temperature for this story: forty degrees Celsius.

*

IT WAS THE KIND of weather where it felt dangerous to be wearing pants. By early morning, Bangkok's air was already thick and warm like bathwater; by midday, it was scorching. On my walk over to the Si-Yak Bang-Na intersection, I worried about how the heat would affect the busload of twenty-eight glamorous young beauty contestants I was scheduled to meet. I was particularly worried about what it would do to their meticulously applied make-up and hair extensions. I hoped they'd brought tissues.

This wasn't a regular beauty pageant. In a country synonymous with sex-change, Miss Tiffany's Universe was Thailand's most famous pageant for transsexual women, and reputedly the world's biggest such event. All that you needed to enter was documentation proving you were born male and were between the ages of eighteen and twenty-five. The contestants had been culled from a larger national pool of sixty and I'd been told they were supernaturally beautiful. Today marked the beginning of a gruelling week of sponsorship commitments between Bangkok and Pattaya, leading up to a live TV broadcast finale that attracted 15 million viewers nationwide – roughly a third of the number of Americans who tuned in to the Oscars every year. The stakes were high. The winner received 100,000 baht (3000 US dollars), lucrative advertising deals, performance contracts, a new car and an automatic spot in Miss International Queen, which saw transsexual women from countries including Brazil, Australia, the United Kingdom, the United States, Sri Lanka, China, Russia, Columbia, India, Lebanon, Japan, South Korea, Nigeria, the Philippines and Argentina compete head-on.

By the time I got to the intersection, I was sweating freely and had soaked right through my shirt. Si-Yak Bang-Na intersection wasn't really an intersection at all, but a flat island of sticky dirt and gravel, an ugly patch of rubble in the middle of one of Bangkok's busiest traffic zones. Above and around us, cars, motorcycles, scooters and buses wove their way through a multi-level concrete braid of bypasses and turnpikes. Everything was loud and smelled of mould and exhaust fumes. It didn't exactly scream 'glamour'.

In the middle was a large chartered coach, parked with the engine still running. Outside, a small crew of TV camera operators from Thai broadcaster VTR milled about alongside publicists and photographers, gossiping and smoking cigarettes. Everyone was waiting for something to happen. Not knowing anyone, I popped my head inside the coach to introduce myself. I climbed up the stairs and let the coach's air-conditioning caress me.

'Hello?'

A motherly-looking Thai woman with a bob haircut spun around, blocking my view of the girls sitting behind her. This was Kuan Lek, one of the organisers. I smiled as I introduced myself, trying to look over her shoulder.

'Benjamin!' Kuan Lek said, waving her hands. 'Please wait outside! Girls are still doing make-up and hair.'

'Oh!' I said.

I hadn't seen a thing, but her reaction made me feel as though I'd caught the women naked. Apologising, I stepped back onto the dirt as the coach doors closed behind me. It had rained the night before. Mud steamed up and stank beneath my shoes as if I'd stepped on a hot turd. Embarrassed, I smiled at the TV crew and staffers. Some jutted their chins in cool acknowledgement, then turned their backs on me to talk in Thai and smoke cigarettes.

I tried spying on the contestants through the coach's tinted windows like a sweaty, dreadful pervert. All of the girls had hand mirrors and were grooming themselves. One girl had a mirror in the shape of a gerbera. There was one in the shape of Hello Kitty's face; another, a teddy bear. Through the tinted windows, I could make out one girl touching every single strand of hair in her fringe, arranging it meticulously with the back of her comb. Her neighbour had curlers in her bangs and was applying mascara. I grew up in a household of women but had never met any girls who paid this much attention to their appearance. Then again, I had never hung around many women like these.

'This year's ladyboys are so beautiful,' someone said. 'You'll see soon.'

Behind me was a petite, lithe and effortlessly pretty woman. Pear ('like the fruit') smiled at me, shielding her eyes with a pair of oversized designer glasses. At first I thought she might have been a ladyboy herself, but Pear was actually a rarity on this tour – what people called a 'genetic girl', a woman who had been born in a female body.

'You actually call them "ladyboys"?' I asked Pear. 'I thought maybe that was offensive.'

Before she could answer, the coach's doors opened. The crew lifted video cameras to their shoulders and photographers sprung into action. Kuan Lek stepped out first, beaming proudly as she made way for the girls.

'Sawadee-*kah*,' the first girl said, putting her hands together and bowing at the TVR video camera.

Finalist #1 – Chanya Denfanapapol; nickname: 'Bank' – looked like a Thai version of Scarlett Johansson, all cheekbones and pillowy lips. With her hair held back in a simple ponytail, she was naturally and alarmingly attractive. Bank had a blue-and-white #1 tied to her wrist – all finalists were required to wear their number for the duration of the competition – and was already the odds-on favourite to win.

Other girls strutted out of the bus and introduced themselves for the cameras, each one a vision in white. They wore white jeans so tight it was as if they had been born wearing them, and low-plunging white V-neck shirts that clung to their breasts like plastic wrap, emblazoned with the neon-pink Miss Tiffany logo. Their skinny waists led to curvy hips that shimmied and swayed, their white clothes catching the midday sun like sails in a brightly lit sea. The effect was blinding.

'Sawadee-*kah*,' they said, one after the other, pouting-smiling-flirting at the cameras.

After posing for the cameras, the girls walked off-screen and stumbled badly, giggling. They all wore sharp, long stilettos that looked capable of breaking their ankles with a wrong step. I felt a rush of sympathy for them.

Poor things, I thought. *They must still be getting used to heels.*

Then I remembered they were walking in mud.

We all gathered at the other end of the intersection as an assistant handed the girls a neat stack of flyers for G-Net, a Thai mobile phone company. The girls were instructed to wait until the lights turned red, then weave their way between cars to hand out flyers to passengers and drivers, before racing back to the kerbside when the lights turned green.

'Isn't this dangerous?' I whispered to Pear. I'd had enough experience to know that Bangkok drivers ignored road signs and drove straight over lane markings. 'It's not like traffic here is exactly … polite.'

'Oh, it's definitely safe,' Pear said. 'Don't worry.'

When the lights turned red, the girls shot out, twenty-eight white-clad gazelle-like women wading among grimy traffic in heels. Pear was right. Bangkok traffic might have been unwieldy, but it was also so congested that the girls had plenty of time to hand out flyers even when the lights were green. A man dressed as G-Net's mascot – a blue bumblebee–robot hybrid – walked among them while G-Net reps waved advertising placards around the group. Onlookers smiled. Kids waved.

Pear saw me smiling at the scene. Ladyboys hadn't always been embraced in Thailand, she said, but over the last thirteen years or so, more and more people in Thai society had begun to accept transsexual women. In Pear's mind, it wasn't a coincidence that Miss Tiffany's had been running for exactly that length of time.

'Before then,' Pear said, 'people saw them as a joke, only for funny or comedy, something like that. Ladyboys weren't as public.'

'So they were there, but hidden.'

Pear nodded. 'You'll find out, a lot of these girls have been through a lot with their families. You see what they're like now, but it's been hard to get to this point. Especially with their fathers: they expect their son to be a boy. They have to work very hard for their family to accept them. That's why they have really good manners. These girls are very polite. They go to university, go to school, study hard to get a good job.'

'So they won't disappoint their families further,' I said.

Pear looked solemn and nodded.

Keang, the pageant's young, smartly dressed choreographer, came over to hand the girls tissues, Wet Ones, disposable cotton towelettes and bottles of ice water. I was surprised the girls' make-up wasn't dripping off their faces. The G-Net mascot removed his costume's head, revealing a young man's pink face drenched with sweat, his hair stuck to his temples like seaweed. When I smiled at him, he smiled deliriously back and gave me the thumbs-up.

The Miss Tiffany's girls dabbed themselves with tissues, swabbing their foreheads and pulling down their shirts to collect the sweat around their boobs. I couldn't help but stare. Some of the girls caught my eye and smiled. I felt myself blush. It didn't matter whether you were attracted to men or women. Sometimes there were people in the world so gorgeous, so remarkably beautiful, that they made you feel as though you didn't belong in the same dimension as them.

At first I thought I wouldn't be able to tell any of them apart. When they had disembarked from the bus, they had been a blur of long legs and pretty faces, but now I was able to make distinctions. There was the Disney Cartoon Princess, the Bright-Eyed Kids TV Host, the James Bond Glamour-Puss, the Hot High School Slut and the softly spoken Nervous Wreck Who Constantly Looked Like She Was About to Spew, who had clearly surprised even herself by getting this far in the competition.

For me, Contestant #8 – Numpath Prasopchok; nickname: Nadia – was the prettiest. Her doe eyes, cut-glass cheekbones and lioness mouth belonged on billboards. When she caught me staring at her, she smiled and waved in my direction. I bashfully looked to the ground like a pigeon-toed, twelve-year-old doofus.

In among all the white t-shirts and jeans was the Vixen. Instead of the generic white outfit of the finalists, the Vixen wore an intricate gown of turquoise and purple sequins, with a bright yellow sash across her torso. The crown on her head was a series of spikes so long that they could have impaled a small animal. Her multi-level earrings dangled like tiny anvils.

'Who,' I asked Pear, pointing at the woman discreetly, 'is that?'

'Sorrawee,' Pear said. 'She was the winner of Miss Tiffany's last year.'

Apart from a smallpox vaccination scar on her left shoulder, Sorrawee Natee's skin was flawless. Statuesque and poised, she was not the most feminine-looking of the group but was definitely the most striking. Unlike this year's finalists, she didn't smile for the cameras. She smouldered. She looked at you like she was going to eat you and you would be completely grateful if she did. It was as if she were emitting raw heat through her eyes.

When I spoke to Sorrawee later, she beamed about the competition and spoke Thai in a slightly nasal, honking voice. She looked like Tyra Banks and sounded like Fran Drescher.

'I've had such great opportunities,' she said. 'Life's changed a lot. Winning Miss Tiffany's was already a big award, but after I won, it meant I could also get a better job. Now I have new opportunities to work and education.' She had been studying fashion design at a college, but she was now in her senior year and had national attention. 'This year's winner's life can be expected to change, the same way my life has changed. What I have experienced here, she'll get it too.'

I watched as Sorrawee knocked on the passenger side of a cab to hand the driver a G-Net flyer. When the cab driver refused to wind down his window, Sorrawee turned to us and raised her eyebrows – as if to say, *watch this* – and opened the door to climb right in. Everyone hooted and laughed. All of this traffic-stalling activity felt very dangerous and illegal. At one point, the girls simply stood in the middle of the road, posing for photos with onlookers and leaning on the braked cars as props. They had literally stopped traffic. Traffic police officers approached us in severe, tailored black uniforms and I flinched. Instead of arresting us, the officers directed traffic around the girls. When it was all under control, they asked for photos too.

On the taxi ride from Bangkok's airport, my cab driver – an enthusiastic guy in his late fifties called Mr T – had asked me what I was doing in Thailand. When I told him I was writing a story on the Miss Tiffany's pageant, he chuckled to himself.

'Oh, so you like *this* sort of thing,' he said, lowering his voice.

I wasn't sure what he was getting at, but I could guess. 'You know of Miss Tiffany's, then?' I asked.

'Yes, yes. Many people in Thailand know and see this.'

'Do you think there are more ladyboys here than in other countries?'

'In Thailand? Yes, I think so.'

'Any idea why?'

He laughed again, then shrugged his shoulders. 'Why?' he said. 'I don't know!'

Thailand has a long history of transsexualism. Before the 1960s, it had three gender categories: *chai* (masculine); *ying* (feminine); and *kathoey*, a sort of umbrella term that referred to in-betweeners – effeminate men, masculine women and people with intersex conditions. Afterwards, those categories splintered further into super-specific identities like *gay, tom* (masculine lesbian) and *dee* (feminine lesbian). Now, many Thai children and teenagers had a basic understanding of how to pinpoint their gender or sexual orientation if it deviated from the norm. Schools had an unusually high proportion of boys who identified as girls and openly declared themselves to be female from an early age. In 2008, a BBC journalist had gone to a secondary school in Thailand's north-east and found the school offered its pupils a transsexual bathroom option, signposted by a half-man, half-woman picture. Throughout Thailand's cities and villages, ladyboys were often the women who served drinks and meals at restaurants and worked in beauty parlours, grocery shops and 7-Elevens. No one knew why there seemed to be more transsexuals in Thailand. Maybe there was something in the water. Something fabulous.

The Miss Tiffany's entourage reconvened for lunch at a place called the Royal Dragon, a Chinese restaurant that had made the *Guinness Book of Records* in 1991 for having the world's largest seating capacity (5000) and the most staff (1200). It was spread over eight acres, as vast as it was absurd. We laughed as a man in a polyester Qing Dynasty outfit flew past our window strapped to a flying fox, sailing over an artificial lake with a tray of hot food in his free hand. We ate shredded chicken, seafood chow mein, deep-fried fish intestines with cashews, dim sum served with century egg, fungus and mushroom soup, crispy-skinned duck, Buddha's delight and tom yum fish soup. Going against my expectations of beauty contestants, the girls pigged out.

The lunch was a thank-you for sponsors and a recap of Miss Tiffany's pageants gone by. Now in its thirteenth year, the pageant had been running long enough to have created legends. One of the previous winners – 23-year-old Treechada Marnyaporn; nickname: Nong Poy – had been voted most beautiful ladyboy of all time. She was now one of G-Net's primary spokespeople. Poy was gorgeous and looked like the kid sister of Gong Li. Her voice was feminine – almost remarkably so, since a deep voice was something neither surgery nor hormones could really 'fix'. At age nineteen, Poy had won Miss Tiffany's before being crowned Miss International Queen in 2004. Since then, she had scored roles in two Thai soap operas – *Rak Ter Took Wan* ('Love You Every Day') and *Muay Inter* ('The Chinese Girl') – as genetically female characters, without any references made to her sex change. She was also the star of the hit Thai pop music video '*Mai Chai Poo Chai*' ('I Am Not a Guy') for an artist called Doo Ba Doo. She was living the dream.

Alongside G-Net, there were thirty major sponsors for Miss Tiffany's Universe, ranging from the big guns – the Tourism Authority of Thailand, Coca-Cola, the *Pattaya Mail* newspaper – to ones that had subliminally humiliating connotations, like Ripley's Believe It or Not! Museum ('Come see the freaks!')

and Louis Tussaud's Waxworks ('Feast your eyes on people who aren't real!').

Another sponsor was a computer chain called Banana IT. After lunch, we visited the computer store where the girls were made to pose sexily for the cameras with giant plush bananas, their lips brushing the toys sensuously. As far as marketing partnerships went, it was either a stroke of genius or hideously offensive, or possibly a hideously offensive stroke of genius. Another sponsor was something called the Asoke Skin Hospital. *That's nice*, I thought. *This thing isn't all about business. It's good to see the pageant supports burns victims too.* As it turned out, Asoke Skin Hospital was a cosmetic beauty centre that specialised in laser peels. For a facility that resembled the lobby of a Marriott Hotel, 'hospital' seemed an overly dramatic term.

By the end of the day, the girls were beaming but sleepy from all the public appearances. I still hadn't had a proper conversation with any of the finalists, just passing hellos and stupid giggles. I desperately wanted more. What were their stories? What did their parents think? What were their strategies for winning? Where could I buy a Hello Kitty hand mirror? As we waved goodbye to Asoke Skin Hospital, the girls boarded the Miss Tiffany's coach headed for Pattaya, while the staff and I boarded our own air-conditioned minibus.

After the brutal heat of that day, the two-hour bus ride was soothing and cool. Tech-heads fell asleep around me and the radio softly played old soft-rock classics. When we reached the highway, a power ballad from the '90s came on by a band I'd long forgotten. The song was called 'Wind of Change'.

When I woke up in Pattaya, it was night-time and my mouth was dry. Our minibus had parked outside a bar called the Bed, an ultra-chic, über-modern place that had avant-garde furniture in the lobby, the kind you can't actually sit on. We'd arrived before the Miss Tiffany's coach, so the staff and media got out and together we stretched our legs.

Pear introduced me to a fellow Australian called Kristian, a Eurasian guy in his thirties who was now based in LA as a freelance photographer. He'd shot Angelina and Justin, Zac and Miranda, and talked about them on a first-name basis. Affable and talkative, Kristian told me he'd been trailing the pageant for a few days already, but had decided to skip the Bangkok sponsorship trail.

'Did I miss any good photo opportunities?'

'You did miss their stint with a shop called Banana IT,' I said. 'There were plush bananas involved.'

I leaned over and showed him photos on my crappy point-and-shoot camera.

Kristian winced. He knew a missed photo opportunity when he saw one.

When the girls arrived, we were all ushered into the bar for rounds of alcohol-free cocktails. As Kristian, Pear and I stacked food from the buffet onto our plates, we talked about our lives back home. Kristian talked about his wife and daughter. I talked about my boyfriend. That piqued Kristian's interest.

'Can I ask you a question?' Kristian said.

'Sure,' I said.

'So, you're attracted to guys, right?'

I nodded.

Kristian glanced over our shoulders at the contestants, lowering his voice. 'So knowing these girls were – well, actually, *are* – guys. I mean, does that do anything for you?'

I looked at him blankly, then laughed. 'No, I'm attracted to *guys.* There's nothing remotely guy-like about these girls.'

He nodded, watching the girls, weighing things up in his mind. 'It's just, you wouldn't be able to tell with some of them, would you? Well, I mean, some of them you *can.*'

He gestured to one of the contestants whose cheekbones were stronger and had pretty broad shoulders.

'Well, what about you?' I asked. 'If you started having a relationship with one of these girls and everything about them was female – their brains, their mannerisms, their bodies – would you have a problem if you found out they were born male? Would that matter?'

'I don't know,' he said. He hesitated. 'There's just still *something* about it. I'm just being honest, you know. I think I would be shocked –'

'And then you'd end the relationship?'

He made the face of a seven-year-old kid who'd been asked a difficult ethical question. 'Probably,' he said, sighing. 'I don't know. I *think* so?'

Later, during evenings I spent in Pattaya's and Bangkok's tourist bars, drunken male tourists would have similar but far less subtle variations of these conversations with me. For them, ladyboys were nothing more than the punchline to every loud, obnoxious joke they told. 'Be careful which girl you take home!' they slurred. ''Cos she mightn't actually be a *real girl*, ya know!'

They laughed, but I also sensed a palpable fear. Or maybe it was arousal. Or both. These men invariably knew of someone – always 'a friend' – who had 'accidentally' ended up sleeping with a transsexual Thai woman. In most cases, the story was the same: the friend in question was drunk, before being fooled by a beautiful woman who – *quelle horreur* – had a penis. Or not! Maybe she had a surgically constructed vagina, but felt obliged to tell the man about her past anyway. And then – only because the guy was so helplessly drunk – they would have sex. Truly, they just weren't to know! Still, I suspected all these men had been willingly fooled. And it felt wrong to me that it was the woman who was always the butt of the joke.

I was guilty of it too, though. I hadn't encountered many transsexual women before. In high school, I remembered my friend Matt declaring his love and affection for 'chicks with dicks' at lunch one day to everyone's squealing horror. 'You get the best of both worlds,' he'd explained. 'They've got tits *and* dicks.' Then when everyone got dial-up modems, we'd run AltaVista searches for 'chicks with dicks', scream at the image results and forward the pornographic JPEGs to our friends' Hotmail accounts as pranks. At university, we'd buy each other she-male novelty playing cards for each other's birthdays, passing them around in lecture theatres and laughing so hard that we were nearly kicked out of class.

That was the thing about transsexual women: they were always either a joke or the extreme, off-limits sex object. And in a world where transsexual women were the outcasts, where access to hormone treatment was near-impossible and sex-change operations were either primitive and dangerous, surely there had to be one place – one country – that was their homeland, their safe house. Thailand was a country that seemed to give these women mainstream recognition and even a beauty pageant. Winners became famous and their faces sold products to housewives and young women! Surely, I thought, this was progress.

*

The next morning, I joined the Miss Tiffany's crew for breakfast. They were a bunch of sharply dressed young producers and tech experts. Because I am one of those irritating people who places bets on things like the Oscars and elections, I asked everyone to pick their favourites for the pageant. Eve, one of the tech girls, offered to translate our conversation. I told her to start the betting.

'But there are so many more pretty girls this year,' Eve complained. 'Way more than in the past. Normally, they have one or two standouts in the competition, but this time they've got a lot.'

'Come on, humour me,' I said.

'Okay,' Eve said, laughing. 'For me, I love #1. She looks natural.' Contestant #1 was Bank, Thailand's Scarlett Johansson. A sound guy sitting next to Eve picked Bank to win too. Keang, the competition choreographer, picked #8 – Nadia – the girl who had smiled at me yesterday and was already becoming my favourite. A producer named Ann picked Nadia too, as well as #29, who had the girl-next-door looks of a high school volleyball captain.

'It really is too difficult to pick, though,' Keang said in Thai. 'This year, a lot of the girls are already working as models.'

'Really?' I asked. 'Are they earning a lot?'

'No, not necessarily,' he said. 'Because they're not "real" girls, people don't really accept them. So usually, they can't be famous in Thailand.'

'Couldn't they just try to pass as ladies, though?'

'Well ...' Eve said quietly, 'there *is* their voice.'

'Oh.'

'I mean, you're right,' she said quickly. 'If they walked past you, you're really not going to know. But if they speak ...'

'You can tell with all of them?' I said.

'Almost all of them. Eighty per cent.'

Ann leaned over to Eve and whispered something in Thai. Both women laughed. 'Okay, okay, maybe *ninety* per cent,' Eve said. 'Plus, they're taller than normal ladies. Thai ladies are not that tall. Their shoulders are wider too.'

After breakfast, I joined the girls for rehearsal. Ann ran through her notes and Keang led them through their steps for the televised finale. Today they were dressed uniformly again, but this time they wore standard-issue Miss Tiffany's t-shirts coupled with micro miniskirts. Over the speakers, the opening disco beats of the gay anthem 'I Am What I Am' filled the room. The lyrics were empowering, but I would hear the song so often in the coming weeks of rehearsals that it would seep into my dreams. I'd spend my waking hours wishing I had a power drill to extract it from my brain.

After going through walks, poses and struts, Keang stopped the music. He told half of the girls to sit down so he could concentrate on one batch at a time. A brunette girl – adorably cute like a cartoon chipmunk – sat next to me. Contestant #10 – Parnrapee Tipjariyaudom; nickname: Noon – wore giant gold hoop earrings and arranged her long hair in a shiny, horse-like ponytail.

'Look,' Noon said, making a sad face and pointing to her feet. Her stiletto was damaged, its cork heel split right through the middle like an old carrot. It was irreparable.

'Oh man,' I said. 'That sucks.'

'Yes,' Noon said. 'It sucks a *lot.*'

Noon was twenty-three years old and tall. Her voice was powdery like talc. She had been living by herself in Thailand since she was a teenager, and was now studying for a business degree and thinking about a career in finance. When she was young, Noon's parents had migrated to the United States without her to start up a Thai restaurant in Massachusetts, while her sister lived in England. Each year since then, Noon had flown to the States for three months to earn enough US dollars at her parents' restaurant – around 200,000 baht (6500 US dollars) – to support her studies back home. It was a strange family situation, but Noon was purposefully vague about why it had come about. I suspected part of the reason was Noon herself.

'I told my mum I don't feel like a boy when I was seven or eight,' Noon said. 'They made me dress like a boy, but inside I was thinking, "This is not me." My mum gave me a hug. She cried. She felt pity for me, she felt sorry.' Noon's father was more hostile. Because Noon was their only son, he refused to believe she was a woman for years and years. 'So now my family don't have a son,' Noon said, a little sadly. 'My dad had hoped for a son so much.'

At sixteen, Noon started a course of female hormones. By eighteen, she had breast implants, paid for by her parents. At twenty, she underwent complete genital sex-reassignment, half-funded by her, half by her parents. That procedure alone cost roughly 300,000 baht (9700 US dollars). She estimated that over the years she'd spent around a million baht (32,300 US dollars) on her four surgical procedures: nose job, breast work, eye work and sex-change.

Noon was staring at me intensely. 'You want to see something?' she said.

'Uh,' I said.

She whipped out her smartphone and fanned through photos of her parents, before landing on a folder full of personal glamour shots: her modelling portfolio.

'Noon!' I said faggily. 'These are *gorgeous.*'

I meant it. Noon was attractive enough already, but these photos made her look like every straight teenage boy's pin-up dream. In studios and by the beach, she posed like a natural in tight shorts, skirts and bikinis. Some had her smiling innocently, others had her posing with come-hither, fuck-me looks. The shots were taken by a modelling agency called the Josie Model Society.

'I really love it,' Noon said, 'but it doesn't pay good money.' On a good day, Noon could earn up to 5000 baht (160 US dollars), but most days she only hit between 800 and 2000 (a miserable twenty-five to sixty-five US dollars). After paying for the petrol to get herself to the shoot, she was lucky if she broke even. It was her three months of American restaurant work that covered her university tuition and living expenses.

In so many ways, Noon was on her own. She didn't have a boyfriend, at least not right now. She'd had one boyfriend before, but he'd freaked out when Noon told him about being born a boy. 'In Thai society, they're not too open to this,' she said. 'If men know I'm a ladyboy, they say, "No way!" Some wouldn't even know I'm a ladyboy, but if they found out, they'd say, "*No, no, no.*"'

That made me sad to hear. Everything about Noon – her brain, her body – was so decisively and adamantly *female*. What was it that men feared exactly?

Keang started clapping his hands, signalling the girls to rejoin the main group. Noon got up and apologised, hopping away on a pair of replacement heels. Ann cued the music and Keang started clapping out the beats, running through the steps to 'I Am What I Am' again. I looked down momentarily at my notes. Before I knew what was happening, the girls were screaming.

When I glanced up, the girls were squatting down on their

haunches, stretching forward with their torsos at a horizontal angle, as though they were in the last few minutes of an intense tug of war. The position made their miniskirts hitch up around their waists and exposed their underwear. It was difficult not to notice some girls had a telltale bulge. Politely, I looked away. They continued to shriek with horror and embarrassment. Keang laughed and put out his palms, shaking them across each other as if to say: *Okay, okay. We won't be doing that.*

*

Later, I returned to Bangkok to track down two of Thailand's most prominent sex-change surgeons. First was Dr Pichet, a sharp-looking man who gave off the brusque, businesslike confidence of a finance broker. If you ran an internet search for 'Thailand sex-change', Pichet's website was the first that popped up. He ran the Bangkok Plastic Surgery Clinic in the city's shambolic Din Daeng district and had treated over 1000 people from all over the world. But even though Pichet was one of the country's most famous sex-change surgeons, he confided that barely any of his clients were Thai nowadays.

'They cannot afford my price!' he said.

Instead, most of Pichet's clients came from America, Europe and Australia. And even then, Pichet said, people seeking sex-change procedures didn't make up the bulk of his clients. At most, they accounted for a fifth.

'It's not *quite* common,' he said. Leaning in conspiratorially, he lowered his voice. 'You know how many people allow you to *cut off their penis* every day?'

'Uh,' I mumbled, caught off-guard. 'I guess it's a pretty extreme thing to do?'

Pichet nodded. 'Correct!'

Of course, it was more complicated than just slicing off part of the anatomy, he explained. Pichet listed all the motions of the surgery as though running through a grocery list. 'Build a new vaginal canal. Remove all of the testicles. Use the scrotal tissue to do the labia – a large labia. A small labia? We use your penis skin and some part of your glans penis to make a new clitoris there. That's it.'

I nodded, gulping.

'Say if *I* wanted to be a woman,' I said, 'what could you do about this?' I pointed to my Adam's apple, which had been weirdly prominent since puberty. You could hang a coat off the thing. 'Could you make this go down?'

Pichet studied my throat. 'Hmm. After you take the hormones,' he said carefully, 'I think maybe your "Adam's" will go down. Then we could open it up, remove some part of cartilage. But I do not perform the voice; only the shape. I don't perform "the voice surgery". I do not believe it is possible. They're still speaking like me.'

On the other side of the city was Dr Preecha, widely regarded as Thailand's pioneer of modern-day sex-change procedures. Almost every legitimate surgeon in the country who conducted these operations had studied under him – close to eighty plastic surgeons over the past thirty years.

Preecha ran his clinic out of a slick, air-conditioned facility called PAI (the Preecha Aesthetic Institute) on the main road of Sukhumvit 55, a trendy area of restaurants and boutiques popular with Bangkok designers, expats and cashed-up tourists. Its reception also resembled the suite of a luxury hotel. Preecha's staff looked like they worked for *Vogue*, with their perfect skin, tailored clothes and asymmetrical haircuts. I waited for Preecha on suede sofas so deep that my feet didn't quite touch the floor. Opposite me, there was a framed certificate of appreciation from an organisation named the Houston Transgender Unity Committee.

Preecha was one of the most expressive people I had ever met. Everything he said was accompanied by the hand movements and facial expressions of a primary school teacher reading to children. He pretended to be scared when he talked about fear, pointed to imaginary things when telling a story, and even changed positions in his seat when he re-enacted conversations between two people.

When he found out I was Australian, Preecha told me that he had studied plastic surgery in Melbourne for a year in 1976. There, a plastic surgeon asked him to observe and assist with a male-to-female genital sex-change procedure. It was the first time Preecha had seen anything like it. Then, when he returned to Thailand, he started seeing patient after patient who, desperate for a sex change, had been horribly mutilated by unqualified surgeons. Throughout the '70s and into the '80s, Thai surgeons were basically improvising sex-change procedures, making it up as they went along. Surgeries across the country became butcheries.

'Some would just cut off the penis!' Preecha exclaimed, making a snipping V-shaped motion with his finger. 'Cut off their balls, sew it up! That's it!'

He pretended to throw something over his shoulder like garbage, disgusted.

'What happened is,' he said, 'they have no *hole*. Some just look like an *animal*. See? So we have to do a lot of reconstruction. Really difficult! We had to do lots of corrections with very limited amounts of tissue.' He put his fingers together in a pinching motion as if to say: *only this much.*

Local psychiatrists told Preecha that when they diagnosed someone as being transsexual, they didn't know who to trust for their referrals. So Preecha got to work and started training surgeons around him, based on the sex-change procedure he'd observed in Melbourne. It was revolutionary work but marred by controversy. Many of his clients were lower-class transsexual women with little money, who mainly earned their living through sex work. Other surgeons even criticised him to his face.

'Why do you spend your time operating on these people?' they would ask. 'It's crazy! You operate on them, then they just go out and sell sex.'

But Preecha saw his work as a social project as much as a medical one. The more successful were the operations he and his team performed, the easier it would be for these women to integrate themselves into Thai society and climb the social ladder. He saw a direct link between performing successful sex-change procedures and improving his patients' social standing.

'First higher education starts to come out, then you start to have beauticians with their own television show!' he said. 'Now we have medical students, bankers, lawyers, all kinds of professions. We have many high-class families in the country who have the sex change. The families have started to accept.'

As with Pichet's, most of Preecha's patients were now from overseas: Australia, America, Canada and Europe. Still, that didn't mean only rich Thai ladyboys had sex changes.

'No, that's not true. See? The rich: they can *choose* the surgeon. Haha. The poor, they will go to the medical centre. They get the student, but under supervision, the same as in any city hospital in the world.'

I showed Preecha a picture of Miss Tiffany's Contestant #8 – Nadia – on my digital camera. He looked impressed and nodded thoughtfully, the way art dealers do when they're inspecting a particularly fine sculpture.

'I imagine a lot of work has gone into her,' I said.

To get this result, Preecha explained, Nadia would have had to start on hormone therapy from a young age, ideally before puberty. The reason why Thai transsexual women all looked beautiful was because they had access to the hormones at an early age, since they could buy them over the counter, no prescription needed.

'So these women aren't just beautiful because Thai people are more feminine, or because Thai surgeons are better,' I said. 'They're beautiful because they're getting hormones when they're kids?'

Preecha nodded. Nowadays, he said, you could venture into Thai schoolyards and find kids and teenagers who had an encyclopaedic knowledge of the types of hormones they could score at chemists, the doses you should take and the results they'd produce.

'They know which hormones make the breasts enlarge, the hair full, the voice more feminine. They even teach *us* how to choose the hormone!' Preecha exclaimed, slapping the table and laughing.

Some of the Miss Tiffany's finalists had told me they had felt female from childhood, while others felt it more when they hit puberty. Most of them counted themselves lucky that hormone pills – oestrogen, puberty arresters, testosterone blockers – were traded around Thai schools in the way other kids around the world traded baseball cards or Pokémon. Twelve-year-old kids asked older kids for pills, then took them often without their parents knowing. There was an entire underground playground racket going on. Even kids understood that you needed to get onto hormone treatments quickly. The last thing any of them wanted was to be fourteen years old and have a moustache.

Preecha had heard terrible stories of Westerners who couldn't get on the drugs until they were seventeen or eighteen, by which time their pituitary glands had betrayed them. Fuelled by the brute, pumping force of naturally produced testosterone, their body hair, broad shoulders and facial hair had burst out. Many of Preecha's overseas male-to-female clients were in their forties or fifties, and some were married with children. 'They've tried to be a man, you see,' he said, shaking his head in pity. Fighting the broad shoulders and masculine facial structure of a fully developed adult male was always going to be an uphill battle.

Thailand's underground trade in teenage hormones wasn't exactly legal, but Preecha said its existence reflected a kind of Buddhist live-and-let-live attitude towards sex and gender in Thailand. 'The Thai community is very easy to adjust to any new phenomenon. They adjust to anything. They're very easy to accommodate the new thing. We're very free and open-minded. Now, they not really *agree* with this kind of phenomenon. Many families are against. There is still discrimination. It's getting better because of the social acceptance, not because of the law. In Thailand, *society* accepting.'

'So, it's not like Thailand necessarily has any more ladyboys than other countries?' I asked.

'No! Not true,' Preecha said, hands flailing about. 'It's just society *accepts*. They want to show off; come out in the public. You can see in America, you don't even see transsexuals in the *cabinet*! But actually there is some, just hiding!'

To demonstrate, Preecha drew his arms close to his body and looked around, pretending to be frightened – like, I guess, someone trapped in a cabinet. 'Not because Thailand has more, no. Because the Thai *allow* you! "Okay, come out, come out!" See?'

Then Preecha mimed opening a door, stepping outside and suddenly spreading out his arms. He changed his facial expression from frightened to beaming with happiness. This was what it looked like to finally climb out of the cabinet. I smiled and applauded softly.

*

Back at Miss Tiffany's, the girls were preparing for the swimsuit round at Central Beach, a towering multi-level mall in Pattaya. Made of white concrete and what seemed to be kilometres of glass, the mall proclaimed itself the world's largest beachside shopping centre. It loomed over the ocean like a shiny monolith.

An entire section of the mall had been sealed off for Miss Tiffany's. The swimsuit round was a special source of anxiety for some of the girls. It was a sensitive issue whether contestants had or hadn't retained male genitals. No photographers or reporters were let inside the dressing rooms where girls were changing into their bikinis.

'What's going on in there?' I asked Pear, pointing to the closed door.

'Some of the girls are taping themselves up,' she said.

'Does it matter to the judges whether they still have ...' I trailed off. 'You know?'

'No one knows,' Pear said. 'It's not a part of the judging process.'

I nodded. 'What's actually involved in taping yourself up anyway?'

'I don't know,' Pear said. 'But apparently it's quite painful.'

From the taping rooms, the girls came out for hair and make-up. It was easy to tell how much money was behind each contestant. Like any competition, there was no such thing as an even playing field. Some of Miss Tiffany's contestants had come from Thailand's outer regions and had only a single friend, sister or self-trained beautician-slash-second-cousin doing their make-up. Those contestants – like the startled, doe-eyed #6, or the terminally shy #24 – were always the quiet ones. Noon was perched in her corner with her hair in curlers, while a butch-looking female relative stoically applied make-up to her face.

Nadia, on the other hand, had a glamorous entourage attending to make-up, costume, hair and styling. She had money behind her and was already on an agency's books. Even putting aside her looks, there was something fundamentally magnetic about her. Some of it, I think, had to do with that primal instinct to align yourself with the winning team. After a group of men helped strap a massive pair of angel's wings to Nadia's shoulders, she walked back and forth as everyone closely analysed her movements. When she sat back down, a plump, squat man with a belly bursting out of a too-tight shirt expertly applied eyeliner and mascara, while a swarm of young gay men twittered around her taking photos and sending MMSes to friends. They wore leather hats, studded belts and screenprinted t-shirts with slogans like 'HOT GUY FROM MYSPACE, FACEBOOK & OTHER', and shoes in colours like chemical-fume purple and blue-black fuchsia that existed only outside the natural world.

Jung, a young guy in his early twenties, had dyed his hair

blond and grown it long, covering his face. When I asked him whether he thought Nadia had a chance of winning, Jung and his friends said Nadia wouldn't just win tonight's round but the whole competition.

'What makes you so confident?' I said, grinning.

He put his hand to his mouth and laughed bitchily. 'I mean, don't *you* think he's a handsome girl?'

I stopped grinning. Nadia sat still for the make-up artist but shot Jung a look.

'That's horrible,' I said. 'Nadia's a *she* – a beautiful girl.'

'No, no! Handsome boy, handsome boy!'

Jung cracked up and shrieked shrilly, prompting the other guys to start clapping and make whooping noises. I tried to ignore this.

'Are you willing to put money on her?' I asked.

They all laughed. 'No, we are just his friend,' Jung said.

'Why do you still refer to Nadia as *he*?'

Jung sighed dramatically like I'd killed all the fun. 'Okay,' he said. '*She, she, she.*'

Outside the mall, I ate an ice-cream and watched the sun sink into the sea like a slowly poached yolk. By now, hundreds of people – supporters, onlookers, curious tourists – sat on concrete tiers around the open-air catwalk erected in Central Beach's courtyard. The evening's five judges took their seats in front of the stage, a motley crew of academics, former models and urban professionals. In a brown jungle-inspired outfit, Sorrawee arrived wearing her crown to sit alongside last year's Miss International Queen, an adorable Japanese woman named Haruna Ai. All big smiles and bubblegum cheeks, Haruna had won the title of world's most beautiful ladyboy the year before, even though she'd come from Japan: a country that had only legalised sex-change procedures in 2004. She was now a huge mainstream television and pop star back home.

People started calling out, 'Sorrawee, Sorrawee!' To Haruna Ai, they cried out, 'Hello, hello!' Both women smiled, waved and posed for their photographs, before giggling with each other. Sorrawee didn't speak Japanese, Haruna didn't speak Thai and neither woman spoke much English, so they communicated by taking photos of each other with their smartphones like high school kids on some marvellous UN-sponsored beauty exchange.

It was dark now and the catwalk lights burst on. Cabaret ladyboys appeared on the stage in skyscraper-high crowns and Thai silk dresses, posing in tableaux. Male dancers leaped into action with choreographed, jerky dancing and the speakers began to pump out a brand of European house music I'd wrongly assumed had become extinct in the mid '90s. The male dancers somersaulted and spun their forearms around with big cruise-ship smiles as the women started to lip-sync to a song about 'flying so high' to 'make you believe in me' because 'it's my destiny'.

At the song's finale, the lights went off dramatically. When they came back on, the Miss Tiffany's contestants appeared in swimsuits. The crowd roared their approval. The girls stormed the stage in groups of three, pounding the catwalk with their heels before posing in trios for the dozens of photographers at the front of the catwalk. The audience ate it up, applauding and wolf-whistling.

'You just can't tell, can you?' clucked an elderly British man behind me.

Each of the girls wore bikinis, stilettos and theatrical stage props, a unique combination of apparel and accessories that belonged in no other worldly situation except on this catwalk, right now. Some of the props were heartbreakingly literal (Contestant #6: 'I am carrying a blow-up flotation device because I'm in a *bikini!*') while others were patently bizarre (Contestant #11: 'I have come dressed as a hybrid of a wedding cake, an arrangement of oriental lilies and one of Tolkien's Ents! *Behold!* I have ceramic doves glued to my body!')

Nadia nailed it with her outfit, though. She walked out in her plain white bikini with the confidence of a Milan Fashion Week veteran, making burning eye contact with the judges, her angel wings folded discreetly behind her. Halfway up the stage, she spread the wings out. The two girls who shared the stage with her disappeared almost entirely. It was a brilliant move. The crowd went apeshit. Nadia's gay mafia posse stomped the ground with their feet and howled like jackals. I found myself hollering and whooping at the stage too. There was something contagious and electric about what was happening. The noise was deafening and drowned out the electronic music. In response, the judges started laughing too, enjoying the racket.

If Nadia doesn't win the finals, I thought, *I'll eat my shirt.*

*

Several years ago, there were actually two ladyboy beauty pageants in Pattaya, both of which were equally famous and broadcast nationally. One was Miss Tiffany's. The other was something called Miss Alcazar, which folded in 2005. There weren't too many differences between the Tiffany and Alcazar pageants, except that Alcazar had talent rounds where the contestants had to show off special talents, such as comedy, acrobatics, public speaking or ballroom dancing. Instead of winning a car, Alcazar winners scored 100,000 baht (over 3200 US dollars) and a diamond ring.

Alcazar's winner in 2005 was a woman named Yollada Krerkkong Suanyot, who introduced herself to me by her nickname, Nok. At thirty, Nok looked obscenely young (she could easily have passed for eighteen) and had the lithe body of Audrey Hepburn combined with the height of Uma Thurman. On her black top, she wore a gold pendant with diamonds crafted in the shape of a woman's silhouette. If she had been a contestant in this year's Miss Tiffany's, I would have put money on her above the other girls. For Nok, it was bittersweet that she had won the last Miss Alcazar title before it closed for business.

'Basically, you'll be Miss Alcazar forever,' I said.

Nok burst out laughing in wild hoots. 'Yes, the last one!'

Dr Preecha had told me to get in touch with Nok, mainly because she was smart – the most impressive transsexual woman he knew. Nok had co-founded and managed a successful brand of jewellery named Carat & Secret, which was predominantly sold through TV infomercials, and she was also in the middle of a PhD examining quality-of-life issues for ladyboys in Thailand, whom Nok referred to as 'trans females'. In between work and study, Nok ran the Trans Female Association of Thailand, a sort of community activist group and sharing circle whose members ranged in age from ten to their late forties. Members exchanged stories in an online forum and also met every month in Bangkok.

'We just come and talk-talk-talk,' Nok said, making quacking movements with her hand. 'We formed our group, how do you say? By *destiny*.' She laughed.

We met on Nok's lunch break at Carat & Secret headquarters, an office space in the back corner of the 24-hour cable channel that sold the jewellery. We looked over photos of Nok growing up in Thailand's northern province of Nan. One childhood snapshot showed two cute schoolboys posing with a severe-looking male teacher standing between them. Both boys wore blue shorts pulled up high over their waists. The one on the left was Nok.

'And you know,' Nok said, pointing to the boy on the right, '*she* is a trans female too!' She laughed delightedly. In the photo, the two boys were only six or seven years old, but Nok remembered the two of them exchanging notes about not feeling male even back then. Another photo showed a teenage girl, her face smooth with the soft puppy fat that comes for a lot of girls at that age.

'That's me,' Nok said.

The girl looked nothing like Nok.

'That's *you?*'

'When I take hormones, it made me fat.'

Nok was thirteen or fourteen in this photo. She had already been taking female hormones for two years. Her father was a macho guy, a policeman who ran a Muay Thai boxing school. He'd resisted the idea of Nok becoming a female at first, but Nok's strategy was simple: don't argue, stay quiet and simply demonstrate who she was.

'Both my parents just tried to treat me good, but they didn't think I was going to have SRS,' she said, referring to sex-reassignment surgery. Nok went ahead with a genital sex change when she turned seventeen, paying the 80,000 baht (2600 US dollars) fee herself, helped along by an education scholarship. Nok went to a hospital and was intially examined by Dr Preecha, but had no idea who actually operated on her.

'I'm not sure if Dr Preecha was the "knife person" or not.

Maybe he just only stand and watch the students.'

'You seriously don't know who operated on you?'

'No, I don't know!' she said, laughing.

Things weren't funny when Nok turned twenty-one. At that age, Thai men are obliged to enrol in a conscription lottery that determines whether they will serve in the military. Thailand doesn't allow people to change their sex on any official documentation, which meant that Nok was still considered a man. She was forced to put her details into the lottery too. Just like that, her number came up.

On her first day in the army, Nok stood alongside all the male recruits and, like everyone else, was told to take off her shirt. By that stage, she had fully developed breasts and female genitals courtesy of hormones and surgery. Surrounded by shirtless, snickering young men and intimidating army commanders, Nok stood and stared at the ground, fully clothed, hugging herself. The officers looked at her coldly.

'You say you've had a sex change already,' they said, 'so you'll have to show us. *Prove it.*'

Nok was almost relieved at the thought of an examination, assuming she would be taken to a private room with a doctor. But after being led to a toilet, the officers told her to disrobe on the spot. Dozens of eyes were trained on her, some watching with disgust, others with gleeful, sadistic curiosity. It was the first day of a long military stretch for many of them and they were grateful for the entertainment. Shaking, Nok took off her clothes slowly, doing her best to cover her breasts and genitals, and started to cry.

'I cannot say anything,' Nok said now, quietly. 'Just only cry. When you're twenty-one, you're still young, right?'

When they finished ogling her, they told Nok she could put her clothes back on. They discharged her with a medical certificate saying she suffered from a 'mental perversion'. That medical certificate was a mixed blessing. On one hand, she was officially excused from the military. On the other, it was a permanent stain on her record that meant she'd never be able to get a government job, say, in education, health or the public service.

That Thailand banned its citizens from officially changing their sex might seem a minor oversight, but Nok's situation was only one example of how it could often give rise to nightmare scenarios. For instance, until 2007, Thai law didn't recognise male-on-male rape as a crime, which meant no laws protected transsexual females from rape either. Noon – the chipmunk-cute Miss Tiffany's contestant with the broken heel – said that every time she flew to the United States, she had to carry a male Thai passport with an English letter from her doctor explaining that she was transitioning sex. That was humiliating enough, but one time she forgot to bring the letter and had a wretched, nerve-racking 24-hour plane ride. When she finally got to the US airport, the immigration officers took her aside and gave her a full body inspection.

'I was so upset,' Noon said. 'Because I forgot my certificate, I could only stay for three weeks. I had to go back and get another certificate.'

After being dismissed from the military, Nok obtained a fake ID that showed her as female, as a giant fuck-you to the world. With her new under-the-counter identity, she entered a mainstream beauty pageant without declaring she was transsexual. No one could tell she wasn't a genetic girl. Suddenly, she was on the books with the agency Elite Models and posed in big corporate pageant events like Miss Mitsubishi. She also studied like a demon, finishing degrees in food science and broadcast and television.

Then she did Alcazar. Nok and I laughed and cooed now over photos of that pageant. One showed her receiving the title in a beautiful gold gown, pinned with the number eighteen. For the talent section, Nok had dressed as a clown: not exactly sexy, she realised, but it worked with the judges. Nok said pageants like Miss Tiffany's and Alcazar were necessary for trans-female visibility, but said she also had reservations. She paused to think about how she could phrase it so she didn't sound conceited.

'When I go somewhere,' she said slowly, 'and they know and respect me, they think, "Oh wow: *pretty.*" But I have much more than being pretty. You have to focus on other parts of us too. And there are people who were born in bodies that *aren't* pretty. You know?'

I knew. For every conventionally beautiful Miss Tiffany's contestant, there were dozens of trans women in Thailand who had difficulty 'passing' as female and were still saving up thousands of dollars for surgery. If beauty pageants were the only way these women could be seen and heard, it wasn't surprising that most Thai ladyboys still felt invisible or shunned.

Just before her fake ID expired, someone – Nok still didn't know who – told the police her card was counterfeit. It not only ended her modelling career but took her to court. She was sentenced to prison for a year, but this was lessened on appeal to good behaviour for two years. Nok couldn't risk getting another ID, so her official ID now said *Nai,* or 'Mister'.

A few years ago, Nok tried to mobilise Thai transsexuals to lobby the government into allowing them to change their official sex from *Nai* to *Nang-Saww* (Miss). Knowing trans women were such a tiny minority, she formed a coalition with divorced married women who wanted the right to change their name from *Nang* (Mrs) back to the unmarried *Nang-Saww*. Despite the combined power of fierce divorcees and transsexual women, the proposal was rejected.

'They say, "It's a very little problem. It's a *tiny* problem." They said, "You are a man who wants to live as a woman? But you're *not* a woman!" They agreed for us to be a freak or a third gender, but it's not the same. It was not a success.'

'Thai people *like* ladyboys, though,' I said stupidly.

Nok smiled. 'You know, Thai society is like ...' She paused to think of an appropriate analogy. 'You know pad thai, right? You know pad thai ho kai?'

I nodded. I had seen the dish: a thin, delicately crafted egg crepe parcel, stuffed with glistening pad thai noodles.

'When you see pad thai hok hai, it's beautiful,' Nok said. 'But when you open it, you see the pad thai is very ...' She made a face, like something had died.

'Like it's full of worms,' I said.

Nok pointed at me and smiled. 'That's Thai society. On the outside, people say, "Oh, they accept us!" But when we said, "We have this problem," they say, "It's *your* problem."'

We changed the subject and gossiped about boys. Like teenagers, we pored over photos of Nok's current and ex-boyfriends and rated them all with commentary. One photo showed Nok in the arms of a toned blond man, a handsome Scandinavian who looked like a poster boy for the Aryan Nations.

'Peter, the Finnish guy,' she said. 'He didn't know.'

It was a delicate thing, deciding how – or if – to break the news. The first thing Nok told potential boyfriends was that she couldn't get pregnant. When they asked why, she would sit them down and make a few things clear.

'When I tell my personal secrets, I have to make sure they know: *I am a girl, and you are a boy*. I must make sure the guy understands that I'm female. I confirm, "I am a female and I am a lady. I can be your best girlfriend, but I cannot get pregnant." And I have to confirm to him too, that he is not a gay. Because a guy is afraid that he'll become gay – I don't know why!'

'Why do they think that?' I said, thinking back to my conversations with Kristian the photographer.

Nok shrugged.

'What about your boyfriend now?' I asked.

Nok rummaged around on her hard drive until she brought up a photo of a handsome, baby-faced Thai guy.

'Oh, he's cute!' I said.

'He's fat now,' Nok said sighing, flicking through other photos on the monitor.

'Nok, you can't say that.'

She giggled conspiratorially. 'He's *fat*.'

'He's not fat, Nok. Jesus.'

*

To win Thailand's biggest transsexual beauty pageant, you needed to fulfil a number of contradictory and near-impossible criteria. It helped if you were tall, but big hands and feet were a minus. You needed to look 'natural', even though judges often pulled losing contestants aside and consoled them by saying they should undergo more surgery for next year's round. Above all, the judges wanted you to look like a 'real girl', even though the competition's entire premise was that you were originally born male. 'The whole idea,' a Miss Tiffany's publicist told me, 'is that these "boys" look like girls. They just have to be beautiful, that's all.'

On the night of the finale, the media were tightly controlled and quarantined from certain areas. An hour or so before the broadcast began, photographers and journalists were herded into the upstairs area of the auditorium and allowed exactly thirty minutes to interview, record or photograph the girls, who were stationed at their hair and make-up banks. With their blue ribbon numbers on their wrists, they recalled the bovine section of a royal agricultural show. At a signal, the reporters rushed them. Camera flashes exploded, people talked over each other and the place became more zoo than show.

'Sawadee-*krap*!' a male TV journalist yipped at one contestant.

'Nadia, Nadia!'

'Hello! Big smile for me!'

Flashes went off.

'What would it mean if you won tonight?'

'Are your parents here tonight?'

'What do your parents think of this?'

'Do you have a boyfriend?'

'What is your secret weapon?'

'What does this *mean* to you?'

'Who did your hair?'

'Who did your *surgery*?'

Some girls got no attention while others were lavished with it. There was something sad about the whole thing. Overlooked contestants smiled broadly, standing silently at their banks with big pleading eyes darting around the room for a journalist – *any journalist* – to come up and talk to them. In the far corner of the room, Bank – Contestant #1 – was working the crowd. She was still the odds-on favourite to win, having surprised everyone by narrowly edging out Nadia in the swimsuit round at Central

Beach. Earlier in the day, I'd already put money down that either Bank or Nadia would win. Everyone agreed it was neck and neck.

'This is the stage of such honour,' Nadia would later say. 'Whoever stood here before me, it has not been easy for them, either.' It struck me as a beautiful, poignant sentiment. All the women who'd ever competed in this pageant were beautiful, but were also bound together by a shared and specific pain. Most were barely in their twenties (some were *teenagers*, I had to remind myself) and had only reached this point through a process of upsetting their loved ones, before raising towering amounts of money to slice, cut and bruise themselves into this shared idea of beauty. Unlike most beauty pageants, Miss Tiffany's in some ways had less to do with ego and delusion, and more to do with personal obligation and familial responsibility.

'If I win tonight,' Bank told me backstage in Thai, through a translator, 'it would really be a chance to upgrade my gender. I want to be an example for younger generations, change minds and laws, so maybe one day we can get married.'

'Upgrade my gender' was a catchphrase I'd heard a lot over the course of the competition. Earlier in the evening, I'd talked to a publicist from an agency that worked for the Miss Tiffany's pageant every year. 'It used to be that only make-up artists, dancers or costume designers would enter,' she said. 'But now, 80 per cent of the contestants are studying in college or university. We've had a contestant trained in fire fighting. Last year, we had a nurse, someone who studied civil engineering, an accountant, and students of international business and law.'

The media scrum was over.

'Okay: out-out-out,' someone said, ushering us out to a media-only balcony that overlooked the audience and stage.

The auditorium below was packed. Television cameras warmed up, ready for live broadcast in minutes. Across the country, Thai families watched Miss Tiffany's opening credits while VTR tech-heads with clipboards gave sharp hand signals to camera men perched on cranes to go live any second.

Finally, the stage lights came on. Frozen and posing at the top of a steel pyramid staircase, Sorrawee appeared, surrounded by other transsexual dancers from the Miss Tiffany's nightly cabaret show, all of them wearing tuxedos. The opening beats to 'I Am What I Am' pumped into the room. When they reached the climax of the song – *I AM WHAT I AAA-AAMMMMMM!* – Sorrawee and the dancers grasped their crotches firmly, and in one swift action tore their tuxedos off to reveal sequinned gowns. Up in the balconies, journalists hollered along with the crowd below.

I shoved my way into the audience seating downstairs so I could get a better look. Down here, the air was thick. The air-conditioning was working against a 32-degree night-time heatwave and everyone's recycled oxygen. It smelled and felt like the locker room of an all-male gymnasium. The cameras rarely panned out into the audience. Home viewers would have seen us crammed into our chairs with our knees up, often with two people to a seat.

After the commercial break, the Miss Tiffany's contestants strutted the stage in full evening gowns while a cabaret performer lip-synced to a Thai recording of Madonna's 'Frozen'. Acrobats in white unitards interpretive-danced their way across the stage alongside a giant transparent plastic ball, while two other dancers cartwheeled *inside* the ball. It was the most breathtakingly ridiculous thing I had ever seen.

After endless posing, catwalking and close-up staring into cameras, the judges culled the twenty-eight women to a final ten. Announced one by one, the finalists looked euphoric as their names were announced. Nadia and Bank were both called. Noon missed out. The lights dimmed to black on the eighteen eliminated women. They walked quietly off-stage during the commercial break, all of them with fixed smiles that were heartbroken and horrible to behold, as if some cruel dentist had set them with cement.

After a quick costume change, the top ten returned to the stage for the questioning round. This would be the first time the girls' voices would be broadcast. Contestant #21 was first.

'What,' the male host asked, 'is the most serious problem for Thai teenagers at the moment?'

Contestant #21 – a girl with the easy-going demeanour of a lifestyle TV host – responded immediately. She spoke in the triumphant tone of a student who'd been given the assignment question for which she'd prepared all night.

'Drugs!' she said in Thai. 'Teenagers are so important to Thailand. If they get addicted to drugs, Thailand will suffer. We've *got* to help!'

Everyone applauded. The hosts moved on to Contestant #5.

'If you could change one thing about *yourself*, what would it be?'

'I wouldn't change anything!' she declared. 'Because truth is the truth! And you have to live with the truth forever!'

The crowd ate it up. The hosts moved on to Contestant #24, the Nervous Wreck of the competition. She was cute, but had the shy mannerisms of an overlooked sister. Out of everyone, I noticed she had spent a lot of the competition wearing minimal make-up and keeping her eyes to the ground.

'What is the biggest goal in your life,' they asked her. 'And why have you set this goal for yourself?'

Though she looked barely out of her teens, the voice that came out of her fine-featured face was both masculine and low with the occasional squeak. It reminded me of my voice as a fourteen-year-old.

'My biggest goal is to earn money to help my mother,' she said. 'My mum sacrificed a lot for her children, so I'd like to earn money to help my mother when she's older.'

More applause. Finally, they reached Contestant #2, full name Siripahawarin Mongkhonphanmani. She was a mousy-looking girl in a knockout green gown, with long eyelashes like a cartoon deer.

'If you could change one law in Thailand,' the female host asked, 'what would it be?'

Siripahawarin smiled into the camera widely. Already, I could sense something was wrong. Siripahawarin moved her mouth a little, but no words came out.

'If I could change one law ...'

Siripahawarin stared out into space as dead air was beamed live to 15 million homes around the country. Across Thailand, people squirmed.

'If I could change one law in Thailand ...'

The audience leaned forward in their seats. Some people covered their faces, groaning softly, unable to look. Even though I didn't know Siripahawarin, I felt like an anxious parent watching a daughter forget her lines in a school play. The silence was excruciating. I wondered whether Siripahawarin had experienced a seizure and needed medical attention. Finally, Siripahawarin relented. It was as though a valve had been released in her brain.

'Every law in Thailand,' she finally said, 'is okay.'

Everyone in the auditorium sighed with relief. People

applauded purposefully and slowly, the way people do when an ordeal is over. Smiling with pity, the hosts moved onto the far side of the stage, when, out of nowhere, Siripahawarin continued speaking, desperate to claw back ground.

'What would I like to change?' she asked in Thai, speeding up. 'I would change the age people can drink and go to night-clubs. Yes! I would like to change it to twenty and twenty-two. Because eighteen and twenty is too young!'

We had all moved on. The hosts were already addressing the cameras to introduce the next segment. I watched Siripahawarin register the fact that she had blown it. Her mouth continued smiling, but her eyes held the truth. Any last traces of hope flickered briefly before being finally snuffed out.

It was only much later, after the pageant was over – after Siripahawarin was knocked out; after the ten finalists were culled down to three; after Nadia communicated her answers in sign language to wild, feral applause; after Contestant #26, a short, cute-as-a-button nineteen-year-old named Nalada Thamthanakorn, came out of nowhere to secure the winner's crown and a car she was barely legal to drive – that I thought about it properly: Siripahawarin had been given an impossible question to answer. As a transsexual woman, what laws did she think should have been changed in Thailand? The obvious answer would have been to give women like Siripahawarin proper legal recognition as, well, women. But it was an issue that no one cared about, and it would have taken all night to detail the finer points of that legal mess.

The next day, Bangkok's newspapers ran stories about the pageant. Reuters syndicated dramatic photos of Bank – who came second – being hauled off-stage unconscious after fainting from dehydration, with Haruna Ai and Sorrawee Natee trailing in her wake. Costumes were packed away, hair exten-sions and wigs were sealed up and make-up poured down the drain. The girls retreated back to their hotel for a final night together, consoling each other and congratulating the winner, bracing themselves for the return to their regular lives and jobs. Besides Nalada's, no one's life would change. Not really. Back at the auditorium and across Thailand, all the lights on these women had been dimmed. They'd had their evening. It would be another year before the lights came back on or anyone even thought about them again.

CHINA

In which we discover a parallel universe version of the internet and a parallel universe version of marriage where gay men marry lesbians or unwitting straight women (who become understandably upset). Key quote: 'In China, homosexuals don't have any kind of publicity, apart from websites. So when you say "homosexuals", it's like a ghost. Something that doesn't even exist.'

*

IT DIDN'T TAKE LONG to get used to the pollution in Beijing. On good days, it was barely noticeable. On bad days, I'd ride my bike from Peking University past Google's Beijing head-quarters, cutting through fumes that hung in the air like a white cataract of fog. The effect was like looking at the world after too many hours in an over-chlorinated pool. After a while, you just lived with it. The snot I blew out of my nose at the end of the day wasn't *always* black.

On a good day like this one, I could head to Liufang subway station, walk a block and look up through clear skies to see a permanent rainbow. It was formed by the curtains of Beijing's LGBT centre, thick vertical blocks of red, orange, yellow, green, blue and purple that – when pulled right across – formed a pride flag. You'd think a giant gay rainbow would be conspicu-ous in a grey cement city like Beijing, but rainbows were only a beacon if you were looking for one, and most Chinese people weren't aware a local pride movement existed, not knowing that rainbows were used to represent it.

Beijing's LGBT centre sat on the twenty-first floor of Xian-TianDi Plaza. Like a lot of apartment blocks in the area, the building's corridors didn't let much sunlight in. The floors were sticky. Apartment 2108 stood out from the others only because of four coloured paper squares discreetly stuck onto the door. One was a rainbow, another was a blue square saying 'No Smoking' in Chinese and English, and a third square said, 'Free Wi-Fi.' The last simply said, 'One Coin, One Join.' I checked my jeans pocket to make sure I had coins, then knocked on the door.

Inside, it was less like the headquarters of an underground gay resistance I'd been expecting, and more like a bachelor pad styled by IKEA – bathed in light with blond wooden panels and shiny new appliances. A choir of young gay men was warming up, singing *doo-baah, doo-baah, doo-baah, doo-baah* in an ascending scale. Other young men lounged on the sofa reading novels while women typed energetically on laptops in the kitchen. They looked up briefly to smile at me. It was like walking in on a friendly sharehouse where no one knew you, but no one minded you being around. If you pulled aside the rainbow curtains, the 21st-floor view was impressive: you could see the scalps of Beijing's buildings and a rooftop basketball court where teenage guys had stripped out of their tops to shoot hoops. If you were a young gay dude in this city, I could see a few reasons why you'd want to spend time here.

A woman with a no-nonsense haircut, thin-rimmed glasses, a big smile and a large black t-shirt that said 'San Francisco' came out of a meeting to greet me.

'You must be Xian,' I said, extending my hand.

'And you must be Benjamin.'

Xian was in her late thirties, one of the city's most prominent lesbian activists and coordinators, and among the first
people in China to have gone online. She was also possibly the
first Chinese woman to have made contact with other lesbians
using the internet.

Xian and I went out for lunch and talked over a meal of
steamed river fish that was full of bones. She worked full-time
for Common Language, a lesbian group she'd co-founded,
which ran summer camps and a phone hotline, conducted
research and lobbied for legal changes. Like most queer groups
in China, almost all of Common Language's funding came
from overseas organisations, as Chinese government grants
weren't available for sexual minority groups. In its five-year history, Common Language had scored only one grant from
inside China: a domestic violence initiative, where the funding
was used to address violence against lesbian and bisexual
women, mainly inflicted by their parents.

'Wait, these women get assaulted by their *parents?*'

Xian nodded. It was a pretty common thing. 'The highest
rate of violence towards gay women is from their parents. In
China, parents punishing children is a common practice. If
your parents think you're doing something bad, they think it's
totally reasonable for them to punish you. On gay issues, sometimes the punishment can be really absurd. Parents will use
extreme ways trying to stop their daughter from being bad.'

'How extreme?' I asked.

Xian remembered one woman in her late twenties, whom
I'll call Lucy, who lived in Beijing and worked in a professional
job. Like most Chinese adults who'd moved to the city for work,
Lucy would wire money back to her family. In Beijing, Lucy had

a live-in girlfriend, but she was closeted to her parents, who were pressuring her more and more to marry. On the phone, her parents' questions intensified. So did the nagging. In the Spring Festival, when people from all over China travel back home to their families, Lucy dropped two conversational bombs on her folks. First: she never wanted to get married. Second: she already had a partner – a female *lover*, she took pains to emphasise. Her parents were aghast. Who had ever heard of such a thing?

Lucy's conversations with her parents alternated between awkward questions and heated arguments, tear-streaked pleading and hostile silence. On Chinese New Year, Lucy returned to Beijing, shaken. She had no idea that her parents were following behind her. When her parents arrived in Beijing, they moved into her apartment. Together they drove Lucy's lover out and, after they'd dusted off their hands from that task, sat Lucy down and laid down the new rules. Number one: Lucy was to cut off all communication with her girlfriend. Number two: Lucy had to meet boys – with the intention to marry within a year.

Lucy contacted Common Language, distraught. What Xian and her team of phone counsellors could offer was pretty limited. They gave her legal advice, like calling the police to protect her and her girlfriend.

'Also,' the counsellors said, 'if the apartment was paid for by you and your girlfriend, your parents have no right to drive your girlfriend away. Parents can't *force* their daughter into certain behaviours.'

They also emphasised communication. In Western countries, Xian said, it might be an option to sever all ties with your family or even bring your case to court. In China, your identity was completely bound up with your family. And when you were an only child – like most young Chinese people born under the one-child policy – your parents were the only family you had. In Chinese culture, it wasn't possible to turn your back and run.

'In the West, when children become financially independent, they don't really have to care about the parents. If the parents don't like the lifestyle, they can just go separate ways,' Xian said. 'That rarely happens in China. Mentally, for the children, they will feel strange. They can't cut off that relationship. There are social traditions. So it remains a very challenging issue for us.'

Eventually, Common Language lost all contact with Lucy. Xian had no idea what had happened to her. Common Language still ran its phone counselling service, but it kept encountering a fundamental conundrum: people rang the hotline to discuss their options, but Common Language often had to concede that there weren't any.

It was even harder when Xian was a young woman. She sought out books about lesbianism before the arrival of the internet, but found that such titles scarcely existed in China. In college, she'd found a few books in the library but they were pretty obscure. One was an oral history book on lesbian nuns in the United States. She also found literature reviews of feminist writers and a copy of *The Well of Loneliness,* an infamously bleak and suicide-inducing 1928 lesbian novel by Radclyffe Hall, in which lesbians dressed as men and led miserable lives that ended in either solitude or death.

Then in the late '90s, towards the end of Xian's college degree, the internet arrived in China. Modems were a rarity, even in universities, but her campus's computer lab had managed to score the latest gear. The internet Xian logged onto was unrecognisable by today's standards, a still-developing slug of a thing called the Gopher protocol: a text-oriented system of cascading information where people could contribute to common-interest newsgroups.

'The worldwide web – the three Ws technique – was still under development or something,' Xian said. 'So I joined a newsgroup, and a newsgroup could also search. "Search" is such a powerful tool.' For me, trying to imagine the internet before its "search" function existed was as difficult as trying to imagine the boundaries of the universe. It felt as if my brain would melt from the effort.

Xian would stare into her university's small, bottle-thick glass monitor, and it didn't take long to find a newsgroup for lesbians. Her heart beat faster. Without even thinking, she posted an English message, shooting out a single bleating request into the abyss:

I'm in China and I'm looking for LGBT information. It's so isolated here.

She had no idea whether anyone would respond. 'I wasn't really asking for help,' she said, 'but communication.' To her surprise, people from around the world started replying. One American publishing house specialising in queer titles posted her books, which Xian devoured. But on reading those American titles, she found a disconnect between Western perspectives on lesbianism and her life in China. How could something like the Stonewall Riots happen in China, where there were no gay bars to shut down? How could a vocal queer rights movement start here, when no one even spoke about gays or knew what they were? It's one thing to be actively persecuted, another to feel that you don't even exist.

So Xian started looking for real people in her country. Through Gopher newsgroups, expatriate Chinese lesbians and gays gave Xian contacts for people back home who were probably as lonely as her. Nervous and giddy, Xian phoned them, wrote to them and arranged to meet in Beijing's bars. For most, it was the first time they'd met other people who were gay and lesbian. And here they were, having lived in the same city all along. For Xian, it was mind-blowing.

At that stage, the Chinese government hadn't yet started to censor the internet, presumably because it didn't know there was anything *to* censor. Then, around 2000, the internet took off throughout the country, and with it, gay and lesbian websites and message boards. People found quiet corners in internet cafés, logged on and started finding each other, answering and posting personal ads for romance and hooking up for casual sex. They listened to each other's stories and formed support groups.

'The real turning point in my life,' Xian said, 'was the internet.'

It was the last thing I expected to hear: that in a country renowned for its draconian web-monitoring regime, it was the internet that had given birth to modern gay consciousness.

*

In 2008, China quietly leapfrogged the United States to become the world's biggest internet-user population. At last count, 420 million people were regularly online in China, about a third of the entire population. By the time you read this, that figure will be well out of date: China's growth in internet use is far too rapid to pin down in something as static as a book.

With that many people online, monitoring and censoring the internet – in its sprawling, multi-tentacled mutant glory – required the resources of fourteen government ministries and an estimated 30,000 state employees to keep watch around the clock. Workers were charged with different tasks, from creating automated software that scanned blacklisted search terms to logging into chatrooms and posing as regular citizens to steer online conversations back to government-approved lines. It was a blend of the high-tech and the comically primitive, or what the *New York Times* once bitchily described as 'part George Orwell, part Rube Goldberg'.

Here was the surprising thing: most people in China were *in favour* of internet censorship. When surveyed, over 80 per cent of Chinese internet-using respondents said that they thought the internet should be managed or controlled in some way. Roughly the same number thought the government was the body that should be responsible for the task. When I spoke to university students and young translators, they thought that the current level of censorship was definitely too restrictive, but believed the internet had to be censored somehow. 'If you live in a country without any censorship at all,' one young woman told me, 'it would be chaos. Or just lots of porn.' Thinking about the internet back home, the logic was difficult to refute. Censorship in China might have been a problem, they said, but what would the internet be like without it? It would be wild and chaotic, overrun with smut, perversion and subversive ideas. When you let people do whatever they wanted, what did you get? Anarchy.

So in China, the internet operated in a parallel universe. Running Google searches inside the country for China's taboo 'Three Ts'– Tiananmen, Tibet and Taiwan – yielded completely different results than would the same search outside the country. When I typed 'Tiananmen' into Google's image search, it was as though those iconic images – bloodshed, protesters, tanks – didn't exist. I just got touristy images of the square as it looked now. YouTube was blacklisted, but hey, there was no need to worry when you could watch clips on *Youko*. And sure, Facebook was banned, but there wasn't any need to get upset: Chinese language social-networking site *RenRen* was everywhere. It didn't matter that MSN was blocked when everyone had their personal *QQ* account. For every website that was cut off, there was a government-approved Chinese version that was often just as good and, in some cases, arguably better.

Recently, though, internet censorship had become especially intense. A few months before, the government had silently geared up for the twentieth anniversary of the Tiananmen Square massacre by vacuuming up online references to it before they reached Chinese computer monitors. Resolved and ready, the network of internet censors embarked on a vast cleansing campaign, blocking access to major sites like Twitter, Flickr and Bing, and news sites like BBC, CNN and the *New York Times*. Facebook and Wikipedia had already been blacklisted, and now Hotmail mysteriously disappeared overnight too. Knowing all this, I signed up for a VPN – a virtual private network that allowed me access to banned sites for a fee – in a spirit of adolescent resentment: *Why did the Chinese government hate the internet so much? What exactly was their problem?*

Around the same time, the government's State Council Information Office released its first ever white paper on the internet, officially outlining the nation's attitude to online connectivity. On first read, it seemed that I (and most of the Western media) had been mistaken. The Chinese government didn't hate the internet at all. In fact, the internet, the white paper announced, in vaguely Buddhist tones, was 'the crystallisation of human wisdom'. The paper also assured people that the Chinese government would 'unswervingly safeguard the freedom of speech on the Internet enjoyed by Chinese citizens'.

Reading that made me disorientated. Wasn't this the same government that operated 24-hour surveillance systems and enforced filters to sift out activism and dissent? I was confused. It didn't take long for the white paper to return to familiar territory, though. Soon, the paper started to focus on issues like 'effectively protecting Internet security', 'protecting state security' and how the Chinese government refused to tolerate anything that would subvert state power, jeopardise national unification, damage state honour and interests, instigate ethnic hatred or discrimination, jeopardise ethnic unity or state religious policy, propagate heretical or superstitious ideas – the list went on and on. The section explaining what was and wasn't allowed went on for pages and pages, too. But there was nothing about gay and lesbian content. At least not explicitly.

Still, everyone was careful. Young gay men told me that every time there was a huge internet crackdown, dozens of popular gay websites would disappear without a trace. No one knew whether it was the gay stuff that made the site a target, though. Gay internet porn – like all porn – was technically banned in China, but sites still existed; they were just well hidden and required membership. You needed to know the rules, but you also needed to know what you were looking *at*, because these websites didn't look like gay porn sites at all. Instead, an innocuous homepage was the first step in a long obstacle course.

If you were accepted, you had to become an active member in the discussion forum. By posting the required (and secret) number of messages in the forums, you scored points on your profile. Once you got enough points, the site unlocked, and you could suddenly gain access to the gold: videos of dudes having sex with each other. This arduous process was the price you had to pay without a VPN.

It was a complicated system, but perfect for getting around China's censorship infrastructure. If you were a government-employed censor, you wouldn't have time to leave messages in the forums. You definitely wouldn't be aware of a points system. The ministry's automated bots would never find these websites either, since there were no keywords or images to scan, filter out and destroy.

When I met Jeff – a well-groomed 29-year-old IT specialist – he had just launched *Feizan*, a kind of Chinese-language version of Facebook that catered exclusively to gay men. In its first half-year *Feizan* had already racked up an average of 1000 new members each month. Jeff and his friends looked like friendly members of a high school AV club. Allen – a 23-year-old online games designer, dressed in skatey clothes – wasn't openly gay with his family, but regularly organised social activities through *Feizan*, like movie and reading groups. Suan, a bespectacled string-bean of a 27-year-old, worked full-time for an internet company and helped Jeff maintain the website. Over dinner, Jeff recalled how he had come up with the idea of *Feizan* during a holiday in Thailand.

'I'd log in to some gay sites overseas and found they were very professional and commercial,' Jeff said in Mandarin. 'When I saw the sites in China, most of them were out of date and not professional. I wanted to make a site that was professional and represented the real life of gays. Because I have some gay friends – some couples – that have been together for a very long time. Some are musicians, lawyers, architects, and they are very "colourful". Sex is not the entire life of gays. They want to communicate with each other too.'

Nearby, a sloppy-looking middle-aged man with a massive gut eavesdropped on the conversation, pricking up his ears when he heard the word 'sex' come up. Whenever I turned to him, his eyes darted to the ceiling.

When he wasn't working full-time, Jeff spent most of his waking hours maintaining *Feizan*. Even at work, he'd constantly maintain the website in the background and would keep going until past midnight. This constant monitoring was one of the most important aspects of his work with *Feizan*. If he slipped up on any 'rules' – rules that weren't exactly clear – the entire site could disappear without any warning. Everyone in China's queer community knew that LGBT websites regularly disappeared without any explanation from Chinese censors. Jeff hosted *Feizan* on foreign servers in Kuala Lumpur, a decision that had its pros and cons. On one hand, it meant Chinese censors couldn't ever take down the site entirely and it could always be accessed from overseas. On the other, running a Chinese website without a government-issued licence risked having the government find it and block it off on the grounds that it wasn't properly registered.

'I actually *want* to register the site with the government,' Jeff explained. 'I want the licence. Because if you don't have a licence, the government can easily block you by using the excuse: "You're not registered, so you're illegal."'

'Do you think the government has anything against gay websites, though?'

Jeff shook his head. 'No,' he said.

Technically, Jeff was right. For the Chinese Communist Party, homosexuality fell under what was termed 'the three nos': no support, no prohibition and no promotion. Its official stance on homosexuality was supposed to be completely neutral. Yet some webmasters argued that homosexual content existed in a grey zone of acceptability. In 2009, the Ministry of Industry and Information Technology had installed filtering software on all new PCs sold on the mainland, which ended up blocking any references to homosexuality altogether, including non-pornographic sites. It might have been a bug, though. This was the same filter that infamously blocked photos of pigs from web browsers when the software mistook pig skin for naked human skin.

So rather than waiting to be taken offline, Jeff did what all Chinese webmasters did: he self-censored vigorously. Internet commentators often argued most of China's censorship didn't come from the central government agency, but from the web moderators themselves, fearful of being shut down. As Suan and Allen passed a large bottle of Sprite to share around the table, Jeff showed me how he moderated *Feizan* remotely from his iPhone.

'I'm like the government,' he said, laughing. He scrolled through the website's back-end and showed me how it worked. Every time users uploaded new photos, Jeff manually scanned through them to see whether they violated *Feizan*'s user policies and China's anti-pornography laws. Naked photos were an obvious no-no. Jeff tapped and flicked through some photos until he found something that made him chuckle. It was a photo someone had tried to add to his *Feizan* profile. When Jeff passed over his phone, I barely registered what I was seeing before the pixels came together –

('Oh, Christ.')

– to form an extreme close-up of a young man bent over in a red jockstrap, pulling his arse cheeks apart to reveal a tightly knotted purple anus. It was one angry-looking arsehole. For a microsecond, my female translator caught a glimpse of the photo, then darted her face back to me with big bug eyes, suppressing a shocked laugh. It's difficult to get an eyeful of a stranger's anus at the best of times, but it was worse when you were trying to eat.

'What would happen if you *didn't* take these photos down?' I asked.

'Well, there are two kinds of trouble. First, if I don't self-censor, then maybe it will break the Chinese wall,' he said, referring to China's censorship firewall. 'Second is that it might become something *I* don't want. I want the site to *not* be like that.'

'But you already have 5000 users and the website's only getting bigger. How will you keep monitoring this stuff?'

'Actually,' Jeff said, grinning as he showed the jockstrap photo to Allen and Suan, 'people who do this are not very common to see on *Feizan*.'

The bloated man in the singlet next to us tried to sneak a look at Jeff's iPhone too, but before he could, Jeff fished it back from Allen and Suan and removed the picture with a single tap. For the time being, *Feizan* had slipped under the radar. It hadn't crossed any lines, as far as Jeff could tell. But in its five months of existence, it had already managed to stir up some controversy, at least among its users. In its early days, it had asked intensely personal questions during the registration process, stuff you'd expect from gay dating and cruising websites but not a social site like Facebook: 'Are you circumcised? Are you a top or a bottom?' Both of those questions were gone now.

'We didn't want to send the users a message that *Feizan* was only for people to find boyfriends. But for a while, we had some questions that weren't quite … *right*. For example, when you registered, you were asked whether you were more like a "guy", or more like a "girl", but it's the wrong question. We're *gay*. You cannot look at gay people from a straight person's perspective.'

Still, the most howlingly controversial question remained on *Feizan*'s registration page: 'Do you plan to get married?' And Jeff didn't mean married to someone of the same sex. That wasn't legal in China. Rather, the question was asking you: *As a gay man, do you plan to get married to a woman?*

'Why did you put that question up there?' I asked.

'It's a fun and, well, provocative question,' Jeff said. 'I think most gay people in China feel they have to get married and have no other choice. People around me – my gay friends – are either already married to women or are concerned with the issue of getting married.'

It took me a moment to process what Jeff was saying.

'Wait: so out of *Feizan*'s 5000 users now, what option are they choosing with the marriage question?'

'Well, *I've* ticked "No,"' Jeff said. 'Most people will choose *not sure*.'

There was also an option you could check called 'fake marriage', which meant finding a lesbian for a sham marriage, an increasingly popular practice. On paper, it made sense. Gays and lesbians needed exactly the same thing: the freedom to pursue relationships with same-sex partners while proving to their parents they were fulfilling their filial duties.

Allen, the youngest of the group and still in his early twenties, stared down at the table when I asked him what he'd ticked. 'I prefer not to marry, but I'm not sure,' he said. 'I'm young and not at the age to consider this question. But I think, maybe not? Now, I think about it: *no*. But I don't know whether I'll change my mind in the future.'

'I chose "No,"' Suan said. 'No, I will not get married.' But then there came a pause as he thought about it more. His bravado slipped a little. 'Maybe I will do the fake marriage thing later,' he added, trailing off.

For a moment, everyone stopped eating. Only moments ago, we had been giggling at the photo of a stranger's butthole and now we were strangely solemn. Nearby, the fat eavesdropping guy in the singlet had grown bored of our conversation and turned his attention to the restaurant's television. For the first moment that evening we were all quiet, thinking about what each other's futures held, which boxes we would check in the end.

Say you're a gay man in China looking for a lesbian to marry. What you'll need is an account with a website like *Tianya.cn* or an LGBT group on *QQ* that specialises in these kinds of *homo seeks lezzo* classifieds. Imagine a Chinese Craigslist for homosexuals, where everyone's after a fake wedding. One afternoon, a gay male couple showed me these websites on my laptop and explained the process.

'It's like renting an apartment,' they said. 'You have to have both parties satisfied on the terms.'

'And what were your terms?' I asked.

'As simple as possible. Just a wedding. No marriage certificate. No kids. No shared properties.'

'Some of them want *kids*?' I asked.

I'd met the Baos through my friend and translator Silvano, who had told me about this monogamous gay couple who'd been together for eight years. One of them had recently married a lesbian to calm down his parents. Doock was thirty-five years old and looked like a former athlete. He had cropped hair, a high hairline and the tanned face of someone who enjoys the outdoors. Dressed in a white North Face t-shirt and exercise shorts, Doock was the more rugged-looking but quieter of the pair. Eric was the same age as Doock, but had a completely different build. He was short and bookish-looking with spectacles on his friendly, doughy face, and had a dry, ironic laugh that showcased rabbity teeth.

Both of the Baos were big on the outdoors, and Eric showed me photos on his mobile phone of their camping expeditions together. Throughout the conversation, Doock slapped Eric's thigh gently and massaged it without even thinking, the kind of things couples do when they've been together for nearly a decade.

'Our story has not that much drama,' Doock said. He said this out of humility, in case I'd find them both boring. *Not much drama.* Here was a couple who'd constructed an elaborate set of lies, cast a lesbian as Doock's fictitious bride, and got married in front of her mother, before staging another wedding for *his* parents. If this wasn't drama – or, at least, a pitch for a B-grade sitcom pilot – I didn't know what was.

Doock had only started questioning his sexuality after an incident with his best friend from high school, whom I'll call Lee. After school, Doock and Lee were both accepted into colleges, but their institutions were at opposite ends of the country. On a break during their second year of college, they reunited back home and got, as Doock puts it, 'physically intimate'. In their minds, Doock and Lee weren't homosexual or what Chinese people called *tongzhi*. At that stage, they didn't even have a vocabulary for what they were doing or feeling.

The next morning, neither Doock nor Lee mentioned what had happened the night before. For Doock, what happened became almost a philosophical question: If you experienced something with another person, but neither of you ever spoke of it again, could you be sure it had ever happened?

After returning to their colleges, Doock and Lee kept writing letters, heartfelt messages that would take four days to reach the other. Neither of them mentioned what had happened on semester break. Whenever Doock sent a letter off, he'd wait around, pacing with nerves, finding it difficult to concentrate because all he could think of was how Lee would reply.

Then one day, Lee's letter came back with big news. He was getting married. To a woman.

'I didn't realise my feelings for him were beyond friendship,' Doock said. 'But when he said he was getting married, I felt very sad and I wondered why. I thought, *If he's a friend, I should be happy for him.* So this was a sadness I couldn't articulate.'

Doock wrote Lee an epic letter – about eight pages long – finally outlining his true feelings, saying he felt caught in an emotional trap. He sent it so that Lee would receive it just before the wedding in their hometown. Doock hadn't been invited.

Doock never got a response. He never saw or heard from Lee again. By this stage, Doock was twenty-five and had never been in a relationship with anyone. By Chinese standards, he was getting old. Nearly all his friends were either married or engaged, and Doock started wondering whether he should do the same. At night, lying in bed, he asked himself to be honest: had he *ever* liked girls? He tried to imagine what it'd be like dating one, holding one, having sex with one, spending the rest of his life with one. If he was really honest, the answer to his question was 'No'. He liked other guys. So he went on the internet.

Finding men online was both heartening and painful. Before this, Doock said, he hadn't had to consider the possibility of living 'a life beyond norms'. Still, it didn't take long to find someone Doock clicked with, and they quickly became boyfriends. Doock also registered with a chirpy-sounding website called SunHomo, which connected gay guys in China who had similar interests like badminton, swimming, volleyball and singing. It was all very wholesome, and it was how Doock met Eric. Eric immediately found Doock attractive, but knew Doock already had a boyfriend.

('But I wanted him to become *my* boyfriend,' Eric mock-whined now.)

If Doock and Eric's love story was ever novelised, it would be less *Love in the Time of Cholera* and more *Love in the Time of the 2003 SARS Outbreak*. Doock's then boyfriend lived in a separate city when the descending epidemic forced people to stay indoors, rushing out to the grocery stores with disposable medical masks strapped onto their faces only when supplies ran low. Hospitals swelled with wheezing, frightened patients, who knew they were infected with something mysterious and deathly. Families quarantined themselves in their apartments, glued to the TV news as they watched the death toll climb.

For several months, it was impossible for Doock and his boyfriend to visit one another. Maybe it was the distance or all the time he had to himself, but Doock soon realised he didn't have much in common with his boyfriend at all. He called the relationship off. Eric saw his opportunity and made his move. And that was that. After a few months, when they were both twenty-seven, Eric and Doock moved in together.

Although he wasn't physically imposing or conventionally handsome, Eric had the winning confidence that came with being very self-assured from an early age. He had been dimly aware of being gay since he was a kid and had started having sex with other guys during college. ('I'm precocious,' he said, laughing.) It took him years before he came out to his parents, though. After he moved in with Doock, he formulated a plan whereby he'd slowly drip-feed his parents information about gay culture and drop strong hints about himself. He'd erode their expectations over time, rather than coming down on them with a revelation like an anvil.

Part of Eric's plan involved having his parents live with them for a year. I was appalled.

'They lived with you for a *year?*'

'We had two bedrooms,' Eric said. 'My parents had one; we had one. Every night, we'd lock the door before going to bed. My mother was very curious. "Why do you do that?" she asked. I said it was Doock's preference, that he was a child raised without a sense of security.'

We all laughed, because the story was lame on so many levels. Still, Eric's parents weren't totally dumb.

One day, while eyeing off Doock, Eric's mother leaned over and said to Eric: 'Don't be too close to him.'

Eric's brother and cousin already knew he was gay, but they'd each warned him that his mother would commit suicide if she ever found out the truth. But Eric went ahead anyway, sitting his mother down one evening while Doock was in another room. His mother was crying so much that it was difficult for her to say anything.

'My gay identity cannot be changed,' Eric told her. 'Research has proved that. And I've been with Doock for so many years. I'm not going to separate from him, and it's not something you can choose. The only option is to accept our relationship, because that's what makes us happy.'

The next morning, everyone pretended that nothing had

happened: the traditional Chinese approach. Eric's mum had filled in his father about the situation. Her eyes were swollen from crying. Before she left, Eric said to her, 'You have to convince yourself of our happiness.'

Eric's relationship with his parents wasn't perfect, but he could stand it.

At that point in the story, Doock stretched and casually changed the subject.

'As for *my* parents?' he said, looking quite pleased with himself. 'Well, I'm married to a *lesbian.*'

I laughed. His declaration had come out of nowhere. I suspected Doock had rehearsed that line in English just to impress people, because he repeated it when he saw my reaction.

'I'm married to a *lesbian!*' he said in English again, slapping his thighs. He looked up at the ceiling, like someone who could barely believe what he'd got away with.

Doock came from Henan province. Because of timing and geography, his parents weren't subject to the one-child policy, so Doock had a little brother, whom I'll call Leung. When Leung announced he was getting married, Doock's parents were horrified, since it was traditional for the eldest sibling to marry first. To them, siblings getting married in the wrong order was shameful. It would have been enough to scandalise the entire village. When Doock's mother heard that Leung was engaged to marry, she cried every day down the phone line, begging Doock to marry someone first. It was pretty intense. Doock's main concern was his little brother. He didn't want to make Leung wait forever, so he turned to his gay friends for advice.

'What you need to do,' they told him, 'is marry a lesbian.'

Doock stared at them.

'Well, what are your options?' they said. 'You can postpone

it, but your younger brother's already engaged. You don't want to make him wait, so the only option is to just get married. Find a lesbian who wants the same arrangement as you. Everything will be fine.'

Doock and Eric were wary. They'd both heard bad stories – and even seen firsthand – how these sham weddings could get out of hand. At one, the gay groom had made the mistake of inviting his gay friends. They'd gotten completely smashed on booze and treated the whole thing like a joke. One of them had climbed onto the lazy Susan and asked another guy to spin him around and around, cackling and hooting while everyone looked on in horror.

In the end, though, Doock and Eric agreed with their friends. There wasn't another option. They set up an account with *Tianya.cn* and started searching for lesbians.

As it turned out, finding lesbians for a fake wedding was a little like going on a game show to see who's behind the mystery door. First up: Lesbian Couple #1! *And what did these lesbians want? An official marriage certificate, shared property and a relatively wealthy husband!* Looking back, Doock and Eric felt Lesbian Couple #1 were too aggressive in their demands. 'The requirements were more strict than if you were choosing a *real* husband,' Doock said. Lesbian Couple #1 were quickly ruled out.

Lesbian Couple #2 weren't interested in shared property, but did want a legally binding marriage certificate and children. For Eric and Doock, both of those things were out of the question, especially the kids. It was a shame, because Lesbian Couple #2 and the Baos got along really well and shared the same dry sense of humour. Lesbian Couple #2 wished the Baos the best and referred them on to Lesbian Couple #3.

'Ah, the third couple,' Doock said now, bowing his head.

'One meeting determines a lifetime.'

Lesbian Couple #3 lived in Tianjin, China's third biggest metropolis behind Shanghai and Beijing. Eric had already been scheduled to go to Tianjin for work, so Doock booked tickets to come along for the ride.

The Baos met the lesbian (I'll call her Linda) and her girl-friend in a hotel lobby. Like the organisers of any decent crime, everyone thought it would be best to chat in a public place. Doock showed me a picture of Linda on his Nokia mobile phone. She was a handsome, bespectacled, broad-faced woman with a square jaw and a sensible haircut, dressed in a fuschia blouse.

'She looks nice,' I said, passing the phone back to Doock.

'Very butch,' Doock said, nodding.

Doock, Eric, Linda and her girlfriend broke the ice by talking about their hobbies, backgrounds and jobs, before moving on to their relationships. Linda and her partner, whom I'll call Susan, had been together for a decade and were childhood sweethearts. Susan had already fake-married a gay guy in Beijing; now Linda's parents were pressuring her to get married too. Though Doock and Linda barely knew each other, it was obvious that their needs matched up perfectly. That's all it took. The marriage was on.

From there it was all amateur theatre, complete with wed-ding costumes and fudged lines. Doock explained Chinese parents didn't care how couples had first met, but he and Linda concocted a story anyway, something about having a mutual friend. 'If I forgot my lines,' Doock said, 'I'd look to Linda for help and she'd cover for me.' It helped that Doock bore an uncanny resemblance to Linda's late father. His future mother-in-law took an immediate shine to him.

There would be two weddings: one for Linda's mother and

another for Doock's parents, since they lived so far from one another. The in-laws would never meet. For both weddings, neither Linda nor Susan invited anyone who knew they were lesbians. To be safe, Doock and Eric didn't invite any of their gay friends either. The only people who knew the true identities of the couples were the celebrants, who were actually actors the couples knew. No one could risk anything. None of this was about fun.

At the Tianjin wedding for Linda's mother, Linda's relatives gave Doock *hóng-bau*, traditional red paper packets stuffed with money that are given at Chinese weddings instead of gifts. Doock refrained from drinking, mainly because he didn't want to get drunk, but also because he needed to drive. It made for a long evening. After the wedding was over, Doock drove his new mother-in-law back home, then drove with Linda to the entrance of Tianjin's superhighway. Eric and Susan were waiting for them by the side of the road. The couples exchanged partners and Doock took all the *hóng-bau* money out of his trousers.

'Here,' he said to Linda and Susan. 'This isn't mine.'

Together, they drove to Doock's home province of Henan and hired two hotel rooms: one for Doock and Linda; the other for Eric and Susan. In the middle of the night, under cover of darkness, the couples opened their doors, crept down the corridor and, giggling like high schoolers on camp, exchanged partners again.

'We really didn't have any other options,' Doock said. 'It's hard to say whether we have chosen the best course, because it was the only one available. But since then, the people around us – the parents, the relatives – they feel satisfied. They're pleased with the marriage. In the end, we think it was worthwhile taking the trouble.'

'You don't feel any guilt?' I asked. 'Towards your parents, I mean.'

Doock looked into the middle distance, thinking. 'A little.'

Nowadays, the official story was that because Doock worked in Beijing and Linda worked in Tianjin, they were a 'weekend couple', an increasingly common phenomenon for young couples in China who worked in different cities. They told their parents they lived in Doock's Beijing apartment whenever they could. There had only been one occasion when Linda's mother announced that she wanted to visit Beijing to see where Doock and Linda lived. They put up photos of Doock and Linda and removed the ones of Doock and Eric. They removed Eric's clothes from the shared wardrobe and replaced them with Linda's outfits. Eric left the house, effectively forced out of his own home.

'It's just for one day,' Eric said, shrugging. 'She's only made one visit in three years, so that's no big deal. There was some tension, but only because we were afraid we'd blow it.'

Doock and Eric knew at least twenty other gay couples who'd found lesbians to fake-marry. Sometimes they'd all get together and laugh over shared war stories – the partner-swapping, the botched logistics, the close calls and the sham ceremonies – but they acknowledged it was less of a romp and more of a grim necessity.

'Fake marriage is not so good,' Eric said. 'We are lucky to have suitable girls to play along with us. But I would prefer a gay marriage if possible.'

Since then, Doock had heard that Lesbian Couple #1 had undergone a dramatic breakup. Lesbian Couple #2 had ended up finding a gay man to marry, but they didn't have children together in the end. And now, even though they had made it clear that they didn't want children, both Doock's and Linda's parents were pestering them about the possibility. Doock told everyone he was too busy. Linda told everyone she wasn't physically strong enough.

Recently, Doock had taken Linda back to Henan to visit his parents. It was one thing real marriages and fake marriages had in common: the mutual obligation of visiting each other's parents when you really couldn't be bothered. On the train ride there, Doock and Linda talked about the conundrum of children.

'Maybe you should still give me a kid,' Doock said to Linda. 'I'll pay 15,000 yuan.'

Linda thought about it – the sum was close to 2400 US dollars – then raised an eyebrow. 'Make it 16,000,' she said. Then, after a moment of terse silence, they burst into laughter, neither of them quite sure where the joke began and where it ended.

*

Most gay men in China were married: either in sham marriages like Doock's, or in marriages where the wife was unaware of the husband's preference for guys. If such men needed a quick fix, a lot of them went online to search for anonymous fuck-buddies, while others cruised in parks for fervent sex in the shadows. In Beijing, the best place to find other men for quick sex was Mudanyuan Park. At a glance, you couldn't tell it was the city's hotspot for man-on-man action. In the day, it was one of Beijing's loveliest family outdoor areas, a tidy public garden with a narrow canal running through it like a cement artery. This waterway was lined with boxy shrubs that led to lush lawns, while a giant spindly transmission tower loomed in the distance. Old men and women came here with their grandkids to fly kites so high that they trailed out of sight and all you saw were taut cords being pulled into the atmosphere.

If you ventured away from the families, walked from the canal up the park's sloping hill, you'd find an open-air section thick with bushes, which operated as a kind of sex terrace for horny men. Trees were planted at arm's length from each other, and between these trees were large wooden benches in clearings where people – mainly men – could gather and chat. On the day I went exploring, one clearing was occupied by a fierce-looking drag queen who was performing a feisty monologue in front of skinny, mincing gay men. Some lay down and rested their heads on their lovers' laps, trying not to move in the heat. One stretched out on a ratty tarpaulin on the ground, wearing a singlet artfully shredded to reveal his nipples. Older men quietly did embroidery, murmuring to each other in low gossipy tones. It was an outdoor queer stitch and bitch where men could happily gossip the day away.

Further back, the shrubs grew thicker and well-worn human tracks snaked their way between dense six-foot bushes. Some of these bushes had been hollowed out, as though dwarves had hacked their way through the branches to create discreet spaces specifically for men to fuck inside. Inside the hollows was debris: disposable tissue wrappers, single-use lube packets, crumpled cigarette boxes, mint wrappers, decaying wads of toilet paper and layers of dried-out condoms from long-forgotten sex. Lawn mowers had recently charged through the park, shredding the toilet paper and strewing snowy white dandruff over the grass. As I wandered through the bushes, young urban professionals in starched work shirts made intense eye contact with me. A lot of them wore wedding bands.

After a while, I was less interested in the men. Instead, I started to wonder about their wives.

He Xiaopei was an academic who specialised in Chinese wives stuck in marriages to gay men. There was even a name for them: *tongqi*, or 'homowives'. Xiaopei was in her mid fifties, looked like an old-school dyke – shaved head, thin-rimmed glasses – and ran a women's organisation called Pink Space. In late 2007, Xiaopei went to a conference of gay Chinese men discussing how they could make use of the law to protect themselves. Men got up and presented their stories, with testimonies about being harassed by police and bullied by their family members. Out of the blue, a woman raised her hand and asked if she could share her story. He Xiaopei and the men turned around in their chairs to face her. They had seen this woman on the way in, but no one knew who she was. She had arrived at the conference alone.

'I'm not sure if I should speak,' she said. 'I'm just a standard heterosexual woman.'

Xiaopei and the others laughed to themselves. What was a 'standard heterosexual', anyway? And if such a thing existed, what was she doing here in a room full of non-standard homosexuals?

The woman's eyes darted around nervously, but she persevered. 'After I was married to my husband,' she said, 'he would beat me. And after our child was conceived, there was a year and a half without any sex whatsoever. Afterwards, my husband wouldn't even touch me. He didn't even look at me in the eyes! So when I discovered he is gay, of course it made sense ...'

The woman kept talking, about how her husband would fuck men, about how when she complained, he would beat her.

One of the key speakers at the conference – a female sexologist who was relatively famous in China, but whom Xiaopei declined to name – interjected from the stage.

'I'm sorry,' the sexologist said, 'but I've done a lot of studies into gay men and what you're saying just isn't *represented* in the research. It's not in the literature. There have been no such stories of domestic violence.'

Emboldened, a male gay activist joined in. 'And this is a *gay* meeting,' he told the woman. 'This is not an appropriate place to tell this kind of story!'

'I'm sorry,' the woman said, 'I didn't mean to –'

Other men called out, joining in the chorus, telling the woman to be quiet and sit down. Stunned, the woman took her seat. Xiaopei felt sorry for her. And, although she didn't say this to anyone at the time, she strongly disagreed with the sexologist.

'Obviously, it's "represented",' she told me. 'No matter whether straight or heterosexual, domestic violence happens in one-third of all families in China. Why not gay men? Gay men have *more* reason to beat up their wives: they don't like them! I felt like this woman was being told she didn't exist.'

During the interval, the conference organiser approached Xiaopei, worried about what had happened. 'Was it a mistake, allowing that woman to come to the conference?' he asked quietly.

'Of course not,' Xiaopei said.

When the meeting was over, Xiaopei introduced herself to the woman and asked whether she could interview her. Xiaopei travelled to her hometown, met her child and spent hours talking about her case. It was the first time Xiaopei had heard anything like this, but she suspected there were other cases.

Xiaopei decided she would start a *tongqi* phone hotline that would operate every Wednesday. Advertising something like this was a little awkward. Xiaopei placed advertisements in gay newspapers, hoping married gay men would pass the details on to their wives. *Marie Claire*'s Chinese edition rang a story on *tongqi* with all the details for the hotline, but because only middle-class, rich or expatriate women in China tended to read the magazine, Xiaopei knew it would not reach women in regional China. Still, women somehow kept discovering the hotline. When the calls came, they lasted for hours, and the women were prepared to pay. It wasn't a cheap service, since all calls were handled over a standard mobile phone line, which was incredibly expensive by Chinese standards.

'When people call, *they* pay a lot,' Xiaopei said. 'Lots of people will call for two hours.'

Because of the volume of calls, Xiaopei arranged a face-to-face meeting just for *tongqi*, the first of its kind in China. Some heard about it through the hotline; others found out about it through friends or the internet. They travelled by train and bus to get there, mainly solo, except for one married couple: a gay man who'd tried to commit suicide, and his wife. In total, there were ten people. It was going to be a full-day session, and when everyone arrived that morning, they were nervous. Some of them left their sunglasses on, trying to shield their identities.

In the first few minutes of the meeting, nothing much happened. Someone started weeping, then it became contagious, with everyone in the room breaking down. One woman in her mid fifties couldn't even speak, she was crying so much. She spent the first couple of hours releasing intense, heaving sobs, as though someone were tugging a deeply anchored rope out of her. Like any good lesbian organiser, Xiaopei eventually focused on workshopping everyone's feelings. What emotions were being expressed? What were people's needs? How did people feel? Everyone gathered around and brainstormed, writing on a large sheet of butcher's paper. The main thing these women needed, Xiaopei discovered, was someone to talk to.

All of them said the same thing: that after they discovered their husbands were having sex with other men, they couldn't talk to their parents or friends about it. Xiaopei was curious.

'What's the difference?' she asked the women. 'Lots of husbands have affairs with *women*, so what's the difference if your husband has an affair with a man?'

'If your husband has an affair with a woman,' one woman said, 'you could talk to your friends and family. If your husband has an affair with a man, you can't talk to anybody.'

The group kept exchanging personal stories. When they got to the sole man – the one who'd brought his wife along – he talked endlessly. Sitting next to him, his wife remained resolutely silent. Patiently, listening to the man dissect the difficulties of being a gay man married to a woman, Xiaopei gently interrupted.

'We've only heard from you so far,' Xiaopei said to the man. 'Can we hear from her now?'

'She can't talk,' the husband said. 'She has nothing to say.'

'Maybe if you're quiet,' Xiaopei said, 'and really don't interrupt, she'll talk. We want to hear from her.'

The wife looked around at the other women, opened her mouth, then meekly started talking. After a stumbling start, she ended up talking non-stop too, barely taking a breath, like someone who had developed circular breathing. It was a monumental outpouring, an avalanche of bitterness, accusations, anger and hatred towards this husband of hers, rambling on and on until, finally – as though the idea had only just occurred to her – she turned on her husband, pointed an accusatory finger in his face and demanded a divorce. Xiaopei looked on, quietly thrilled.

She couldn't help but laugh when recounting the story now. But in China, she explained, divorce was rarely the best option for such women. If you were a married woman, you had the support of both your husband and your family. If you were divorced, the stigma meant your own family often wouldn't associate with you. And then there was the financial shock of divorce, especially if you were a non-working woman, and especially if you had a kid. A lot of *tongqi* weighed things up and stayed in the marriage.

Tongqi weren't unique to China. All over the world, closeted gay men married women to fit in, repress their sexual desires, or because they didn't have a choice. It was why Western people referred to these women as *beards*: they were something to hide behind. But in China, everything was compounded by an irrefutable expectation of marriage, a government-enforced one-child policy that placed pressure on young people to reproduce, and a lack of public knowledge.

'Do you feel this is unique to China?' I asked Xiaopei.

'In a way,' she said. 'In China, homosexuals don't have any kind of publicity, apart from on websites. In newspapers, television and books, homosexuals can't appear. So when you say "homosexuals", it's like a ghost. Something that doesn't even exist.'

*

David was twenty-six years old but looked younger. He was short and lanky, and wore a combination of board shorts, screenprinted t-shirt and Converse sneakers, like a teenager in a boyswear catalogue. Around the eyes, though, David looked far older. He had a haunted look about him, and there was always a slight delay when he smiled. Afterwards, I concluded that this was probably what happened when psychologists tried to reverse your homosexuality with self-harming aversion therapies and an over-prescription of Prozac.

David grew up in a small rural village called Shi Qiao in the north of Hubei province. Between his home and school was a large creek where local farmers bred freshwater fish. As a young teenager, David would pass the creek four times every day: to get to school, come home for lunch, head back to school, then finally come back home. David couldn't swim himself, but in the summer boys his age would strip off and swim there naked. David would find himself hiding behind bushes, unable to take his eyes off their bodies. It was the first time he suspected he was different somehow.

When David eventually went to university in Shenyang, he didn't find any information about homosexuality in the library. Some of his classmates had shown him how to use the internet, but only students studying courses in technology and design were allowed access to university computers. For everyone else, there were public 'computer bars', or internet cafés.

'I'll be frank,' David told me. 'When I began to use the internet, the first thing I looked for wasn't information about homosexuality or whether homosexuality was abnormal. It was to look at pictures of males. A lot of websites had very hot pictures, and it was all about that.' Every time he visited the internet café, he would sit in the same strategically placed seat: pushed up against the corner with a wall directly behind his back for privacy.

Horny and confused but unable to jerk off there, David would rush back to his college dorm. But, as in most Chinese universities, it was difficult to find any personal space. Communal shower blocks were entirely without walls and only open for set hours every day. Dorms housed triple-decker bunk beds against every available wall without any personal study areas. On rare occasions, though, David got back to find that all his roommates were out. Because it wasn't possible to lock the room, he had to seize the opportunity to come quickly and furtively in his hand.

Every time he went to the internet café, though, David felt more and more guilty, sensing he was doing something wrong. He didn't talk to anyone about his feelings and suspected no one else was like him. In 2004, he started looking for help on the internet. In the Chinese search engine *Baidu*, he typed in the word for 'homosexuality' in Chinese (*tong zhi lian*) as well as 'treatment'(*yiliao*).

David found two sources of information. One of them was a website named *Aibai*, an online gay education resource with a question and answer service. He also found an advertisement for a university's psychology department that said they were able to assist with disorders like depression. It seemed legitimate.

But by the time David got there, he was so nervous that he couldn't speak. The psychologist had to guess his problem for him.

'Okay,' the psychologist said. 'You're a man, so I think I know your question! A lot of people your age come to me for help. Your question or problem is about … *love*! Have you separated from your girlfriend recently? Maybe you don't feel good? I'm here to help. I see many such examples, you know.'

'No,' David said shakily. 'My problem isn't about this.'

'Then speak to me,' the doctor said. 'What is your problem?'

David started to stammer, but he was frozen with nerves.

For him, homosexuality was almost impossible to talk about. It was a condition so embarrassing, so unheard of, he may as well have had another head growing out of his neck. Bemused, the doctor told David to come back after the holidays, before referring him on to another specialist.

This next guy set David at ease. He was an elderly psychologist who reminded David of an affable grandfather. He was good at making small talk and asked David questions about his studies and his hometown, getting him to speak. As soon as he asked David what was wrong, it all came spilling out of him.

'I have this problem, I like boys, I don't like girls, what's happening to me – what's *wrong* with me?'

The psychologist smiled and tried to calm David down.

'Other people like you come here for this kind of problem,' he said. 'It's *very* common and is something that can be changed. If you want to change, it can be changed.'

To prove his point, the psychologist told David about a couple of lesbians who had come to him for help some months before. They were romantically involved, but couldn't stand feeling abnormal and guilty any longer. For David's sake, the psychologist cut out the details of the treatment and skipped straight to the happy ending. After he treated them, he said, both women found boyfriends and lived very happily with their new partners.

David was pepped up by the idea, so he was given some homework. First, he would have to buy some sexy posters of women, stick them up on his dorm wall and think about them whenever he masturbated.

'Look at the posters and learn to appreciate the beauty of females,' the psychologist said.

And even though China's medical standards weren't as high

as those in the United States – they didn't have those fancy electric-shock machines for this kind of treatment just yet, the doctor explained – David could just as easily invest in some thick rubber bands to place on his wrists and thighs. Every time he thought of boys in a sexual way, he simply had to snap them. Hard. This would train and reshape his brain, the psychologist explained.

Finally, the psychologist wrote out a prescription.

'Take this medicine,' he said, tearing it off for David. 'It will help you relax.'

It was for a drug called Prozac. David didn't ask what its purpose was, and the psychologist didn't really explain.

'I just thought, *I believe in this old specialist so much, I will follow everything he tells me*,' David said now. 'I had no doubt about the medicine at all and spent the money.'

It wasn't cheap. Four sheets of Prozac cost more than several hundred yuan, and David had to take money from his college scholarship to buy enough.

When his roommates were out of the dorm, David tried masturbating to the beautiful girls in the pin-ups to see whether he could make himself aroused. Pleasingly, he found he could do it. It was working! After a couple of weeks, David was buoyant. Things seemed to be getting better, just as the psychologist had said they would. Every two weeks he'd see the same shrink, and every time the psychologist told David he was doing well.

'If you persist in this,' he said, 'you will be successful in changing yourself some day!'

After a few more weeks, though, David wasn't sure. He still thought about guys all the time. His wrists were badly bruised from the rubber bands and seemed permanently purply-green. Every time he snapped the bands, they hurt more and more, because there was no time for the bruises to heal before the next round of self-flagellation.

For David's next appointment, his friendly grandfather-like psychologist was missing, having gone to a conference. A younger male doctor was in his place. This shrink had read David's files and discussed David's case with the older doctor. He had a different perspective.

'David,' he said, 'if I told you sexual orientation was something that *cannot* be changed, what would you do?'

David hadn't considered this before. He took the question very seriously.

'If I couldn't change myself,' he said matter-of-factly, 'I would kill myself.'

The doctor nodded slowly. He was careful with his words.

'Maybe you can think about this from another perspective,' he said. 'Say sexual orientation is part of you? You could try to accept it.'

David thought this new shrink was trying to catch him out somehow. Maybe he knew less about David's condition because he was younger and less educated. Sensing David wasn't ready for a big change, the doctor advised him to keep following the same medical regimen as before.

In the meantime, David had started logging in to the gay resource website *Aibai*, the one he had originally found when he was looking for treatment options for his homosexuality. One of *Aibai*'s writers was a man named Damien, an agony aunt who ran the website's Q&A section. After David emailed Damien, he got a response quickly that detailed how the older generation of Chinese psychologists, educated during the Cultural Revolution, were years behind the rest of the world. The World Health Organization, Damien told David, had held conferences about homosexuality that confirmed it wasn't a disease at all. Even China hadn't officially regarded homosexuality as a disease since 2001.

Upset with Damien's response, David went back to the hospital and confronted the young psychologist with his newfound knowledge.

'I know about the World Health Organization,' he said. 'And I know that in 2001, China eliminated homosexuality as a mental illness. Why did you keep giving me this kind of treatment?'

The psychologist looked at David evenly.

'David,' he said, 'do you remember how I asked you a question? I asked, "If you couldn't change yourself, what would you do?"'

David stared at the psychologist, remembering.

'You told me that you would kill yourself. The reason I kept giving you the treatment was not because of homosexuality itself, but because you refused to accept that knowledge.'

David was stunned. *Aibai*'s Damien had been right.

*

Damien was a Chinese-American guy in his early fifties. He lived in Los Angeles, but had been the advice writer for *Aibai* for more than eleven years. In that time, he had personally answered around 60,000 questions from angst-ridden guys desperate for advice. Some were gay men living in heterosexual marriages; others wanted to come out to their parents but didn't know where to start. Some days, Damien would receive only a few questions. On others, he'd get over thirty. To date, he had answered every single question, including David's.

'To be honest, David's was one of the more benign cases,'

Damien said. 'All the doctor recommended he do was use rubber bands. He did, incidentally, get bruised terribly around his wrists. But that's the extent of it. I've encountered much more grievous cases.'

The worst was when Damien had travelled to Beijing for an *Aibai* meeting in 2004. A young guy in his mid twenties, whom I'll call Perry, had travelled over 1300 kilometres from Hubei province to meet everyone and tell his story. When he was a teenager, Perry's parents had found out he was gay and immediately taken him to a paediatrician for examination. The doctor prescribed Perry five psychotropic medications (like Prozac and Xanax) simultaneously – medications that, even taken individually, warranted close supervision, especially in young people. Perry's doses were insanely high. After a week, he was unable to walk. The doctor increased the dose, but, upon inspecting Perry a few weeks later, had to make an admission to the parents.

'I don't really think I can successfully cure him of his homosexuality,' he said. 'It's possible I could make him *asexual*, though.' To be honest, he said, all of this was really about trial and error. Still, the parents were willing to do whatever it took. Together, the doctor and Perry's parents agreed to increase the dose again.

Eventually, Perry had to stop taking the drugs, not because they were physically disabling him as such, but because they were imported and oppressively expensive. His parents became bankrupt after spending all their savings. When Perry told his story at *Aibai*'s meeting, everyone started crying quietly. From the stop-start, slurring way Perry was now speaking, it was clear he had suffered irreversible neurological damage.

'When he talked to you,' Damien told me, 'he was like a drug addict. His eyes couldn't even focus on you. He was never able to go to college or hold a job. This is common now: the first thing parents do when they find out their kid is gay is go on the internet, look on websites and try to find cures. But the mental health profession in China is somewhere between fifty and sixty years behind the West. There are still many people – licensed clinicians – who are stuck in the 1950s and 1960s who offer "cures", which are sometimes very inhumane and cruel types of treatment, claiming to be able to cure homosexuality. Electroshock therapy and drugs that induce vomiting are routinely used.'

It was cases like Perry's that kept Damien answering every question he received on *Aibai*. Because of the sheer volume of correspondence, Damien kept responses short. There was a section on *Aibai* dedicated to frequently asked questions, but that hadn't stopped the same questions from coming through.

'From Day One, the question I'll always get is: "I'm like *this*, and *this*, and *this*. Am I gay?" That question continues to persist, non-stop,' he said. 'But some questions have certainly changed. Ten years ago, more people were asking where they could get condoms. In some parts of China, if you wanted to buy condoms from a drugstore, you had to show a marriage certificate. It was thought that if you weren't married, you shouldn't need it, right? Today, nobody asks that anymore.'

Massive numbers of questions centred on marriage. In Damien's experience, there were four types of married homosexual men in China. Type #1 was men who didn't know they were gay when they married. Type #2 was men who suspected they were gay, but believed – or at least hoped – that getting married to a woman would cure them of their homosexuality. Type #3 was men who instinctively knew they were gay, but felt it was morally wrong and wanted to get married.

'Then there are a large number who are the fourth type,' Damien said. 'They're *really* the problem. These are people who *know* they are gay, who fully intend to break their marriage vows even before they get married and completely use their spouse to cover themselves. Before, during and after the marriage, they have homosexual relations. They might have a boyfriend, get married to a woman, and continue to have that boyfriend or several boyfriends.'

Damien said it was common for these guys to have unprotected sex with other men, transmit diseases – including HIV – to their wives and still be unapologetic. Partly it was due to a particular brand of ingrained Chinese misogyny, he thought. Men often believed that so long as they provided for their wife financially, they could do whatever they wanted in their own time. Many married men – gay and straight alike – saw their wife as simply someone who could produce a child for them.

Despite the constant barrage, Damien said his job with *Aibai* wasn't too difficult. He fit answering the questions into three daily sessions: one in the morning, another in the late afternoon and a final one late in the evening before he went to bed. But despite Damien's discipline, there had been times where readers hadn't been able to access his responses. There was one particularly bad patch in 2005, when the entire site was blocked without explanation for a year. It was definitely the Chinese censors at work; the only question was why.

'No one from government has ever told us we could not operate,' Damien said. 'We were never able to verify whether it was a deliberate shutdown of *Aibai* or not. We just don't know.' Since then, authorities had occasionally contacted *Aibai* about specific content they wanted removed, such as a short story someone had posted about Tiananmen. But for the most part, *Aibai* played it safe.

'The Chinese government is somewhat schizophrenic on this,' Damien said. 'I don't think they consider us a threat, and some portions of the government – particularly in health – are much more friendly to gays. But the propaganda branch is still stuck in the '70s. The Chinese authorities have put out very clear directives to mainstream media saying positive portrayal of homosexuality and homosexual culture is not allowed.'

After talking to Damien on the phone, I went for a walk back through Mudanyuan Park to have a think. This time, I stuck to the areas where the families were gathered, although I knew dozens of men would have been covertly groping each other only metres away, over in the bushes. A couple of months later, twenty police cars would descend on this site at night, catching eighty men in the middle of sex acts and dragging them out of the bushes to detain and question them. After the police mandated blood tests and forced the men to produce their ID cards, it would be revealed that many of them were married. For some of the wives, the arrest wouldn't come as a surprise. For others, it would. A couple of wives might find Xiaopei's *tongqi* hotline in the end, but most would stay quiet, not knowing whom to turn to or how even to describe this development in their marriage.

People had to manage their sexuality in the same way that webmasters in China administered their websites: by necessity it was about constant self-censorship. Outsiders always pointed to the government or China's legal system as being the biggest issue for gays and lesbians, but it cut far deeper than that. It was social, cultural and personal. It was *internal*. The young men cruising in the park right now weren't getting any younger, and the unmarried ones would have to make their choice eventually. *As a gay man, do you plan to get married?* Some would find their answers on the internet, or they'd find a gay pride centre, or they'd find a woman to sham-marry. Some would go online because they felt lonely and lost, while others would be led to weird places and given terrible doses of drugs. And sometimes they would just disappear entirely. This was what it was like to be a ghost in this country: a person who was entirely invisible, even to yourself.

JAPAN

In which we discover that drag queens, camp gays and transsexuals are popular on television. (Lesbians and non-camp homosexuals: not so much.) Key question: 'Why is Japanese television so gay?' Key quote: 'Sure, there are gay characters on TV, but they are only characters.' Celebrities approached for this story: twenty-two. Celebrities actually spoken to: four.

*

IT'S TRUE: YOU WILL find the most breathtakingly messed-up porn in Japan. From outside, the gay sex shop looked innocent enough – decorated with cartoon motifs of Popeye with his muscular, vein-bulging forearms (the perfect icon for hardcore gay porn, I later realised) – but inside, it housed some of the most dizzyingly intense examples of filth I'd ever seen.

Fisting was a given. So were blow jobs, anal sex, muscled gods, twinks, interracial stuff, locker-room fantasies and transsexuals. I had expected all that. But because Japan specialised in catering to super-specific niches, the until-now-unheard-of (at least to me) genre of Fat Men Masturbating in Business Suits took up an entire shelf. So did DVDs of predatory gay men sucking off kidnapped and rope-bound 'straight' boys, and videos of boys so young, feminine, fine-featured and hairless that the images on the covers veered close to underage lesbian territory. There was also the infamous *guro* (gore) porn, an umbrella category of nightmarish stuff that involved blood, disfiguration, beatings, urine, enemas or faeces, as well as a generous and diverse *bukkake* selection, one of Japan's more successful international exports.

Just metres away from the entrance, a DVD played in a loop showing two guys going to town on each other. Twisting themselves gymnastically into a 69 position, each reamed the other's butthole with the enthusiasm of a diner at an all-you-can-eat buffet. Although Japanese law dictated that below-the-waist orifices were to be pixelated out of pornographic films, you didn't have to work your imagination to make out what was happening. All you had to do was blur your eyes and your brain filled in the blanks.

After browsing around the sex shop, I reeled outside and almost ran into a primary school kid, skipping along with his mother after finishing the day at school. It struck me as both impressive and appalling that the only thing separating this kid from a widescreen hardcore homosexual rim-job video was a semi-sheer plastic curtain.

Welcome to Shinjuku Ni-Chome – 'Shinjuku, Second Block' – Tokyo's premier gay hub. Shinjuku is an engine of human activity, the beating heart of Tokyo's megalopolis. Its train station is the world's busiest, with 3.5 million commuters coming through its automated turnstiles every day. At night, the district throws an epileptic fit of neon light and colour. In the midst of this fluorescent wonderland sits Ni-Chome, tiny, low-key and relatively dim, despite its international reputation as a gay enclave. Even with its clubs, bars and the famous 24-hour Kaikan male sex sauna, Ni-Chome is unassuming: a cluster of narrow grey buildings with ropey tangles of power lines stretched between them like old vines. During the day, the place is quiet and sleepy. After lunch, fast-talking salarymen and slow-moving elderly women stroll through, seemingly oblivious to the parallel world of gay hotspots.

You had to look up. The only way you could tell Ni-Chome was any different was by the small square signs that jutted out like fins on buildings, advertising gay bars on the upper levels. These were pokey places with names like BLOKE (all caps; men only) and BAR (women only), tucked away so that you had to climb stairs and knock on the right door to get in. Because of Tokyo's insane rental prices, the bars were small and restricted their clientele by type. In Ni-Chome, there were bars for guys like me – *garisen* (skinny guys) – as well as places dedicated to *fukesen* (old men), *gaisen* (foreigners) and *debusen* (fat men). And then there were the lesbian bars, most of which banned men entirely on the basis that they usually came to ogle.

Taq's Knot was one of the oldest bars in Ni-Chome, a rare place that welcomed most gay men and even the occasional woman. It was roughly the size of an economy-class cabin on a cruise ship and could barely fit ten people at a time. The bar itself was sunken, which meant the barman looked as if he had fallen into a ditch. Behind the bar were big acrylic paintings of muscled men with giant cocks, and instead of branded match-boxes Taq's Knot offered free condoms, the wrappers featuring works by local artists. Two computer monitors played '80s music videos on repeat.

Taq Otsuka started Taq's Knot in 1982, the year I was born. Over the course of my life, Taq had seen not only Ni-Chome change, but Japan's entire gay scene evolve. Taq looked like my dad with a goatee, which was to say he looked like a 62-year-old version of me: slender, wispy-haired and boyish despite his age.

He wore a striped blue-and-white shirt over athletic cargo fatigues and sported grey hair in ruffles, giving him the appearance of a retired gay Phys Ed teacher.

When Taq was a kid, he'd read magazine articles about the fabled bars of Ni-Chome, with journalists reporting wild stories from an underground world where men dressed as women and worked as prostitutes at night.

'I didn't have television when I was a kid,' he said, 'so the only images I could get were from these magazines. But the impression of Shinjuku Ni-Chome itself was really negative. It was represented as abnormal, as *hentai*.'

'What does *hentai* mean?'

'Sort of like "queer". But, like, the bad meaning of queer, before gay liberation. Sometimes queer is used with a positive meaning nowadays, but beforehand, queer was – how do you say? Everyone feared the word. So *that* meaning of queer.'

It wasn't like homophobia in the West. Japanese attitudes were more ambivalent, more evasive and unspoken. Throughout the country's history, there had been cultural precedents for sex between men, specific relationship dynamics to which our modern-day notions of 'homosexual', 'gay' and 'transgender' didn't much apply. Centuries ago, adolescent male prostitution took place around kabuki sites in Kyoto, while sexual relationships between samurai masters and apprentices, and priests and page boys had occurred since the eighteenth century. One famous poem featuring same-sex male longing – *Iwatsutsuji* ('Azaleas on the Cliffs') – dated back to the ninth century. It wasn't anything new.

'Japanese people see gay people as shameful, but not *sinful*,' Taq said. 'There has never been anything against gay people. As long as they're invisible, they'll be tolerated.'

When Taq first encountered television as a young adult, there was hardly anything gay to be seen. Then in the 1990s, Taq noticed big changes. In fact, the Japanese media was suddenly caught up in an intense public fascination with gay men on screen, which became so noticeable that there was even a special term for it: *gei būmu* – literally, a 'gay boom'. Viewers loved gay characters. Movies and TV programs showcased them, and plotlines in comedies and dramas saw gay men accidentally marrying women (whoops!) or women becoming their fag hags. It was all very festive and family-friendly. On television, gay talent – *gei tarento* – was suddenly everywhere. Still, Taq felt something was missing.

'They're characters, like men dressing up as women. But there's no *real* gay people who behave like men who say, "I really like men."'

'Only a very specific type of gay person is seen on Japanese television?'

Taq nodded. 'Colourful, feminine and over-acting. It's a kind of like – how would you say?' Taq searched his mind for an English term, but came up with a Japanese one instead: *onee*, pronounced 'oh-neh-eh'. It meant 'older sister'. Sassy drag queens, camp gay men and giggling transsexuals, they were all *onee*: camp, feminine, hilarious and weirdly sexless. They presented themselves as happy little eunuchs, like Japan's first gay celebrities, Piko and Osugi, twin brothers who declared themselves gay back in the 1970s, but insisted they were celibate to make everyone comfortable.

'From a Western point of view,' Taq said, 'there seem to be a lot of gay characters on Japanese TV, right?'

I nodded.

'You must think, "Good: Japanese gays are on TV!" So you

are gay and entertain me? Okay! But if you are gay and insist on changing the legal system? No. It's vague what Japanese society is willing to do. Japanese culture tries to avoid conflict.'

Sure, homosexuality was legal in Japan, Western-style homophobia wasn't rampant and TV programming was relentlessly faggy, but coming out as gay or lesbian in real life was still very difficult. Talking about sexuality – actual queer sexuality, what being gay actually meant – was generally taboo. Seen in a bigger context, the situation struck me as slightly sinister: queer celebrities going on-screen to have millions of viewers laugh at them, but knowing viewers couldn't care less once the TVs were off.

When I asked Taq to list the most famous gay people on Japanese TV right now, he laughed and pretended to be overwhelmed.

'Oh, there are so many!' he said. 'There's Ikko-san, Matsuko-san, Bourebonne-san ...'

Taq had to say Bourebonne-san, of course. Bourebonne-san was an old friend who worked at Taq's Knot when he wasn't appearing on television or rehearsing for his live drag queen variety show. Bourebonne-san's star was on the rise, Taq explained, and he also had a powerful friend and mentor in Matsuko Deluxe, a gloriously obese 140-kilogram drag queen who was one of the most renowned TV personalities. A self-described 'fat transvestite columnist', Matsuko Deluxe was loved for her luxurious silken-tofu fat rolls and ability to shoot off rapid-fire jokes and double entendres. She was currently everywhere as part of Fuji TV's autumn marketing campaign and also advertised pizza, a mobile phone company, Nintendo games and her own chocolate-filled biscuits that came imprinted with a cartoon image of herself. If Bourebonne-san wanted to be famous, having Matsuko Deluxe on call would help enormously.

'So is Bourebonne-san becoming really famous now?' I said.

'Mmm ...' Taq said. He laughed teasingly. *'Becoming.'*

After talking to Taq, I took myself to a local 24-hour *sento*, a traditional public bathhouse where men and women separated before soaking in communal mineral baths and broiling their skin in the sauna. Although surrounded by naked, sweating Japanese men, I kept my attention focused squarely on the encased flatscreen television. It was tuned into a format that dominated the airways: variety-news shows. These followed a simple formula: the news of the day with a panel of celebrity guests. As raw footage reeled off – plane crashes, disgraced sports stars leaving court, political speeches, baby animals being born in zoos – a small box in the corner of the screen stayed on the celebrities' faces for their reactions: Nodding Concern, Startled Delight, Breathless Laughter, Muted Shock, Considered Listening, Silent Crying over Something Very Moving and Poignant. The celebrities' reactions provided a sort of emotional laugh track for the audience: when to feel sad, when to chuckle.

As always, there was one ultra-camp gay man on the panel. It was almost a prerequisite to have at least one *onee* on board. They were on morning shopping programs and late-night variety shows, or advertising dolphin-shaped toilet cleaners and demonstrating the latest in flower-arranging techniques. All this visibility had to be a good thing, I thought. In a nation of fickle viewers, *gei būmu* seemed here to stay, having outlasted the TV fads for fatties, women with massive tits, washed-up popstars and lawyers-slash-comedians. But it seemed odd that real-life queer rights hadn't grown with this trend. I decided to track down the gay stars, one by one, and find out what they thought: whether they saw themselves as offering a sort of gay minstrel show, or whether there was more to them than that. I took out my dictaphone and notepad and started calling people, knowing I was out to violate an unspoken rule: *gei tarento* won't speak about their private lives, and journalists don't ask, to save audiences from extending their imagination in that direction.

As the weeks went on, I realised I'd seriously underestimated the difficulty of my assignment. One problem was my utter lack of written or spoken Japanese. I would scour celebrities' official websites for contact details and forcibly mash the Japanese script through Google Translate, only to get not-quite-right translations that I'd have to squint to read, such as 'Cultural Tours pre-Haruna love and go!' and 'For inquiries, Avex Entertainment, Inc. Medium and delivered in record straight!' When a couple of translators came on board, they made phone calls and sent countless emails on my behalf, while I prepped for interviews and pored over the bare details of these celebrities' private lives. It felt as though we were running a gossip rag.

We approached Akihiro Miwa, the beloved TV drag queen in her mid seventies, who was always accompanied on-screen by flowers and a Barbara Cartland glow. There was also KABA. Chan (real name: Eiji Kabashima), a choreographer, member of the music group DOS and contestant on Japan's *Dancing with the Stars*. We tried accessing Shogo Kariyazaki, the famous gay TV florist (a Japanese speciality), and someone named JONTE'★Moaning, an American drag queen modelled after Grace Jones who had somehow made it big in the Land of the Rising Sun.

Our requests were met with radio silence.

*

I decided to just go ahead and visit Bourebonne-san when he was at work. On the night we met, he was working in Taq's Knot, pulling beers from the sunken bar and dressed as a regular guy. He wore a loud checked shirt with ironed-on scout's badges displaying words like MAXIMUM and CALIFORNIA. He was handsome, and tall by Japanese standards.

As a kid, Bourebonne-san hadn't seen many images on television of what he wanted to be, but as an adult, he watched RuPaul and the Australian film *Priscilla: Queen of the Desert.* Something clicked.

'Priscilla and RuPaul changed my heart,' he told me in English, putting his hands to his chest and fluttering his eyelashes.

The music system had been playing Lionel Ritchie's 'All Night Long', Culture Club's 'Karma Chameleon' and Frankie Goes to Hollywood's 'Relax', but when Bourebonne-san discovered I was Australian, he clapped his hands, squealed and flicked the system to Kylie Minogue's 'I Should Be So Lucky' in my honour. Businessmen in their spectacles and ties surrounded me and my translator, curious and eager to chat.

'So Otsuka-san told me you were becoming famous!' I told Bourebonne-san, recalling my conversation with Taq.

Bourebonne-san beamed at the news, delighted.

'*Nooooooo,*' he said with typical Japanese modesty. 'But you want to see me on television?'

He stopped the Kylie song and loaded YouTube on the monitor. We all watched as the opening credits for a daytime talk show called *You Wanted to Know!* came on. The male host introduced three apparently female guests who sat alongside each other in carrels, as in a game show. Bourebonne-san was unrecognisable. In this episode, he wore a long brown wig, a flowery black ribbon in his hair, a long dress in autumnal colours and a flowing pearl necklace. It wasn't a conventionally outrageous drag outfit, but rather something you'd expect a classy aunty in her fifties to wear. Bourebonne-san told me he got most of his clothes from a costume website in the United States, though some pieces were made to order. Unlike many other drag queens, he chose to dress with class.

On the show, the three guests watched rolling news footage before making quips or offering their sympathetic take on the news. The camera loved Bourebonne-san. He was the most striking of the women – probably because he was a man – and offered the most arch jokes. But he was also very pleasant, polite and feminine, not vulgar or overly sexual like most drag queens on American TV. In the commercial break, the show cut to an advertisement showing a deliciously fat Matsuko Deluxe, seemingly pregnant, reclining in a white gown and breathing hard. I had no idea what the advertisement was for, but later discovered it was a teaser for Fuji Television's new season. Matsuko Deluxe was pregnant with the TV schedule, telling the audience it was due any day now.

When the video clip ended, the Taq's Knot clientele offered a smattering of applause.

'Is it easier to be a drag queen on TV than an ordinary gay guy?' I asked.

Bourebonne-san thought about it. 'Well, it's much easier to work with make-up and dress-up. Because you have to be – how would you say? – "catchy" to get work. You know?'

'Is there a difference between this Bourebonne-san,' I said, pointing to the TV, 'and the one I'd see at your drag show?'

'Perhaps I'm less funny on this,' he said, pointing to the monitor. 'There are less dirty jokes. Because this is a nationwide TV show, the whole country is watching, you know?'

I nodded, understanding.

'The good jokes come,' he said, 'when you're talking about sex.'

Several days later, Bourebonne-san pulled some strings and invited me to his drag queen extravaganza *Campy,* which was taking place in the basement of a seven-level entertainment complex called the Loft/Plus One: Talk Live House. Underneath the Loft's flashing green sign, someone had stuck a child-like, hand-drawn sign in big blobby texta letters saying, '*Campy!* Vol. 8.' Everyone in line was in good spirits as they clutched their tickets, content in the knowledge they had scored entry to a sold-out event.

The line seemed to be chiefly gay men who had arrived in hordes, teasing and slapping each other good-naturedly. My translator pointed out a prominent TV news anchor who was known to be gay in queer circles but wasn't open about his sexuality in public. Lesbians had come in small groups or couples. And surprisingly, there was a contingent of straight people, who had come in couples or rowdy packs. Macho straight men stood in line, hand in hand with their girlfriends.

A short, compactly muscled Japanese man with a beard took our tickets. He was naked except for a fake tiger skin that wrapped around his crotch and ribboned over his shoulder where it was attached to a plush tiger's head. After collecting our complimentary *Campy* DVDs, we were greeted by five drag queens.

'Benjamin!' one of them said, putting his open palms by his face as a hello.

There was no mistaking Bourebonne-san's broad shoulders.

Tonight, he was dressed sleekly in the outfit of a chic First Lady, complete with Jackie O wig.

'Bourebonne-san,' I said, planting a kiss on his cheek.

Another drag queen wore giant heart-shaped glasses like Lolita. A third had the hard, pumped body of an elite swimmer poured into a tight blue cocktail dress. When I reached out to shake his hand, I accidentally dropped my notebook. When I went to stand up, he'd shoved his arse right in front of my face. The queens hooted with laughter.

The Loft was a grungy parlour that had the look of an old strip club with exposed wiring and lights hanging off banisters. Seats filled quickly and people crammed in around small tables the size of lazy Susans. My interpreter and I made friends with a table of raucous straight men and women who'd come just because they thought drag queens were a scream. We shared snacks and ordered rounds of beer and Japanese lemon sours.

It didn't take long for the entertainment to become a blur: partly because I didn't understand the Japanese jokes, but mainly because I was drunk. Most of the jokes, my translator told me, were saucy and foul but the puns were so linguistically and culturally specific that they were nearly impossible to translate. From what I could gather, no topics were off limits. They joked about eating disorders and how ugly they all looked. Bourebonne-san delivered a sordid monologue about going to a love hotel with a guy he'd met while still in drag. When they discovered the love motel only played boring straight porn, Bourebonne-san had to use gay porn on his iPod to get his lover into the mood, by which time the man had fallen asleep. One of the drag queens made a really graphic joke about hanging a shit so big it wouldn't flush down the toilet. I didn't need a translator for that one. Let's just say it was all in the miming.

When it was all over, Bourebonne-san came up to me, sweating through his make-up.

'People love you guys!' I said.

'Yes, drag queens are getting very popular!' he said, dabbing at his face.

The audiences left the Loft grinning stupidly, *Campy* DVDs in their bags. Bourebonne-san said I was right: a chunk of the audience tonight were straight. Most were gay or lesbian, but about a third were heterosexuals who loved seeing drag queens, camp men and giggly transsexual women on their televisions and stages. Still, I felt there was an obvious missing element.

'What about lesbians?' I asked.

Bourebonne-san nodded, as though he'd given this some thought.

'Oh, being lesbian is harder than gay,' he said. 'For gays, it's much easier to be seen as funny. Boys getting dressed as women? That's already entertaining. For ladies, it's a different story.'

*

Ayaka Ichinose responded to my interview request pretty quickly. Perhaps she needed any publicity she could get. If Ayaka had a business card, it would have said something like 'model/actress/writer' or simply 'Japan's first celesbian'. Ayaka was blessed with the kind of looks Japanese women would kill for: soft, long hair and flawless skin, like a teenage boy's fantasy avatar for a video game. Though she had recently turned thirty, she still looked like a high-school student.

Ayaka had started out as something called a 'gravure model', which wasn't exactly nude modelling, but posing in just enough clothes to give the *impression* you were naked. She was also smart enough to know that modelling got you only so far in Japan. To be successful, you had to diversify. Lately, Ayaka had been branching out into writing a thirteen-episode manga series called *Real Bian*, lesbian comics based on her own experiences. She had also produced and starred in *SekuMai*, a gravure modelling DVD that combined footage of her in skimpy, barely-there gear with a discussion of issues pertinent to lesbians in Japan. In between sequences of Ayaka posing in her underwear, she talked about what it was like to live as a lesbian, recounted the history of the Ni-Chome district and interviewed other queer women. Her work was sexy *and* educational. *Sexucational.*

I met Ayaka in a ground-level café in Ni-Chome that was around the corner from the DVD porno shop of horrors. Though I had seen photos in which Ayaka was topless and bent over in a G-string, on this occasion she was dressed conservatively in a beige zip-up dress. Accompanying Ayaka was her manager, Nakazawa-san, whose weathered face made him look like a Japanese Tommy Lee Jones.

'The majority of lesbians in Japan don't come out,' Ayaka explained. 'So the interviews in my DVD were trying to address those issues. *What are lesbians really like? What are they interested in? What do they do in their spare time? What kind of fashion are they into?*' They may as well have been fantastic and mythological creatures, such as hydras or mermaids: mysterious and vaguely heard about, but rarely seen in everyday life.

'I get the sense that seeing gay men, drag queens and transsexual women is really common here,' I said. 'But not lesbians.'

'Yeah-yeah-yeah,' Ayaka said. She got this question a lot. 'It's true: you don't really hear about lesbians in Japan, mainly because it's still a man's world. In the gay scene here, the majority of the venues – the saunas, the bars – are targeted at men. A lot of females aren't as interested in that. Or they try to hide it. When I was young, I knew I had feelings for girls, but didn't actually *know* I was even a "lesbian". There was no point in coming out, because I didn't even know I *was* one.' No one spoke about lesbians, so Ayaka hadn't realised that such a thing existed.

In her twenties, Ayaka worked part-time at a mixed-sex bar in Shinjuku Ni-Chome. Very quickly, her looks attracted the attention of local glamour photographers. Modelling scouts approached her and she picked up gravure modelling easily, as well as minor acting jobs and TV appearances. About two years into her career, her prospects were looking good. Then she decided to come out as a lesbian. It wasn't an easy decision.

'There had been no lesbians that had come out in this industry,' she said. 'So it was like, "Oh my god, should we be doing this?"'

Part of the probem, Ayaka said, was that a lot of Japanese people didn't actually understand what a lesbian was. Even her manager hadn't suspected.

Nakazawa-san laughed now, thinking about it. 'Oh, I was *shocked*,' he said. 'She was the first lesbian I had ever met.'

They knew her coming out was a risk, but neither had any clear idea what the consequences could be. There weren't many precedents. In the 1970s, there had been a hugely popular pop-folk singer named Naomi Sagara. Her chaste and memorable songs were family-friendly hits across the country. Then a woman claiming to be Sagara's scorned lover went public with the news that they had been a couple, which caused a minor scandal. The news was talked about in hushed tones, but it was enough to cut short Sagara's career. She had more or less disappeared from the music circuit.

'But that was thirty years ago,' Ayaka said. 'And thirty years ago, they didn't really have the kind of gay vocabulary that exists now, like "LGBT". I mean, there weren't even many *men* who were gay back then.'

Ayaka said she hadn't wanted to make coming out a massive drama. In any case, she wasn't yet a household name. In the end, she took a low-key approach. 'It wasn't a big deal. People would ask whether I had a boyfriend and I'd just say, "No, I have a girl-friend."'

Where it was a big deal was in Japan's close-knit lesbian scene. Even now, she stood relatively alone. When we tried to list other women in Japan in the public eye who were openly gay – not just entertainers, but *anyone*: athletes, artists, news anchors, musicians, actors, directors – the only person either of us could think of was Kanako Otsuji, a now-retired politician who had been a member of the 110-member Osaka assembly.

In a sense, there was also the manga artist Takeuchi Sachiko, whose work focused on lesbian romances. Sachiko was open in her professional life but closeted to the extent that not even her parents – with whom she still lived – knew the nature of her work. Rather than tell her parents about her lesbian romance manga, Sachiko told them she wrote pornographic manga instead, because writing explicit comic book smut was apparently more acceptable than loving the ladies. When Sachiko appeared on television to talk about sexual minorities, she came on stage with a paper mask attached to her face.

'Do you ever feel a burden of responsibility, because you're the only lesbian out?' I asked Ayaka. 'You know, the burden to represent *all* lesbians? To be a good role model?'

'*So des ne,*' she said, agreeing. She paused, then added brightly, 'But because I'm new and the only woman who has come out, it's easy in another way. People don't really have any expectations.'

I'd originally read about Ayaka Ichinose on a website called Tokyo Wrestling, which was pretty much Japan's only source of queer news for women. Because Tokyo Wrestling's coverage of Ayaka had gained her a cult following, Ayaka returned the favour and posed in skimpy Tokyo Wrestling–branded gear on her DVD. Even though I wasn't exactly Tokyo Wrestling's target demographic, I'd become a fan. It was both serious and playful, with a sexy, muscular, 1980s neon-maritime aesthetic that spoke to me.

I contacted Tokyo Wrestling's founder, Yuki Keiser, the daughter of a Swiss father and a Japanese mother, who looked like a Eurasian version of the British actress Carey Mulligan. Yuki was in her thirties, with fingernails painted baby blue and a bold Susan Sontag streak of white in her short brown hair. Yuki told me she understood where Ayaka was coming from, but added that Japanese people, or at least horny Japanese men, *did* have expectations of lesbians.

'Lesbians are associated with porn,' Yuki said simply. 'You just don't see any lesbians on normal TV, though. We have no faces. We don't have a lesbian media. We have lesbian blogs, but that's not the same. When Ayaka Ichinose came out last year, that was news among Japanese lesbians, but I wouldn't say every-body knows her. If I switched on the TV, I'm not going to see her. You can't say there's a lesbian icon or role model on TV now. If you go into the streets and ask, "Do you know any lesbians?" they would say no.'

All this made being openly gay hard for Japanese women, even for someone like Yuki. Although she was the editor and public face of Tokyo Wrestling, she wasn't always open about her sexuality either. Once, when she had been interviewed on television about the website, she had used her real name and allowed her face to be shown. Then, at her daytime workplace, a colleague said they had seen Yuki on television and asked about the interview. Yuki became evasive. You could never anticipate other people's attitudes and Yuki didn't want to broadcast her sexuality at work. Recently, she had been dining with her colleagues and a Japanese client, when people started asking Yuki whether she had a boyfriend or was married.

'I'm not interested in marriage,' she'd said, honestly. And that was where she left the conversation.

This was probably something familiar to most gays and lesbians: everyone had ways to mislead people without it descending into outright lies. 'No, I don't have a wife (because I have a boyfriend).' 'I'm not interested in marriage (because marrying my girlfriend isn't possible).' Yuki never referred to her girlfriend as 'he' or 'him' at work, but she never denied her existence either. She was vocal and visible within the queer scene, but made her queerness invisible in the workplace. I got the sense that Yuki was someone who refused to turn her sexuality into a show for spectators.

*

Eventually, some celebrities' managers started returning our calls. This was excellent, except that I had started to develop a wheezing cough, which was getting more intense as the nights wore on, and wouldn't help me during my interviews. Locking these interviews in was important, but obtaining sufficient time was crucial: relying on a translator meant interviews usually took twice – sometimes three times – as long as speaking to someone in the same language.

One gay celebrity who agreed to an interview was Maeda Ken. Everyone I'd talked to – Yuki Keiser, Bourebonne-san, Taq Otsuka, Ayaka Ichinose – said Ken was different to other *gei tarento*. Sure, like all the others, Ken had started out as a TV drag queen, so flamingly camp he may as well have been on fire, lapping up the applause and hoots on set before retreating backstage to take off his make-up and become anonymous again. But recently, he had also become the only gay man on Japanese television who appeared as ... well, himself. No wigs. No schtick. No fake tits. Yuki Keiser told me Ken was more or less the only openly gay man on Japanese television who wasn't constantly presenting himself as *onee*.

Initially, Maeda Ken was difficult to track down. He was famous to the extent that most Japanese people knew his name, partly because he worked like a dog. As well as being an actor – about to star in a suspense telemovie called *The Seven Suspects* – Ken had written a book, performed as a stand-up comic and directed films, with his next project being an adaptation of his short-story collection, due for release in the spring.

Eventually, I was told to meet Ken after hours in the building of his management agency. His staff led me and my translator into a conference room, where Ken was waiting for us like a company chairman across a large wide table. He had the wide, friendly face of a kid plonked on an adult's body. Despite being almost forty years old, he dressed like a teenager. Or maybe it was more that he dressed like the *idea* of a teenager, wearing a baseball cap turned on an angle, a bright-red baseball jacket and a t-shirt screenprinted with a teddy bear playing an electric guitar. To begin with, he wasn't in the mood to talk.

'Thanks for making the time. I know you're in very high demand at the moment ...'

'No, I'm not.'

'Really?' I said. 'What's a typical week for you right now?'

'There's no certain schedule to what I do.'

'Are you working on anything right now?'

'I'm going to do dramas.'

'What sort of drama?'

'TV drama.'

I figured it had been a long day, or maybe he was wary of me probing where I shouldn't. Ken warmed up when we started talking about his career history, the early days, where he scored his first breaks on TV by excelling at *monomane* – the type of hammy, queeny celebrity impersonations everyone loved so much in Japan – doing brutally hilarious impersonations of J-pop singer Aya Matsura, made even funnier by the fact Ken had a super-masculine face: big cheeks, strong eyebrows and a five o'clock shadow, like a giant otter in women's clothes.

Ken had come out to his family and friends long ago, well before he achieved national fame, but it took him a long time to come out publicly. He didn't want to make a big deal of it. After he released a book, during his promotional tour someone had asked if he was gay, like one of his book's characters. Ken simply said yes and people nodded politely. He hadn't chased publicity, but soon there was a buzz in the press about it. Emails and letters from fans poured in saying things like, 'Through listening to you, reading your book and hearing you on the news, you've given me the courage and made me more brave to come out.'

'That was a big boost,' Ken said. 'It made me really happy to know I had that impact. The best thing about coming out is helping other people – particularly in rural areas of Japan – to get the confidence and the courage to come out.'

In terms of Ken's job prospects, nothing had changed too

much. The only thing it had affected was his private life. Once he had come out publicly, he found it harder to pick up boy-friends.

'Why was that?' I asked.

'I don't know,' he said. 'A lot of people in Japan aren't open and gays don't come out, which actually makes it *easier* for them to pick up. But because I've already come out, I've written a book, I'm on TV ...'

'Because being gay in Japan is about discretion, right?'

'Exactly.'

As his career flourished, Ken branched out into projects where he didn't have to be flamboyant or camp, at least not all the time. Still, he had fun with being known as gay. Recently, he had starred in *Yurusugi Kogi*, a quasi-mockumentary that fol-lowed him as he dated men in an effort to find love. One of Ken's dates was at an aquarium, another was getting Japanese waffles, another was hanging out in an *onsen* sauna. The show was aimed at families, so it was played for laughs. Audiences knew Ken was gay, and that the men he was 'dating' were straight male comedians playing a character. That struck me as sad, somehow.

'How do you think people would have responded if it *wasn't* played for laughs?' I said. 'Like, if it had been a straightforward documentary about a man looking for same-sex love?'

Ken raised his eyebrows. 'It's difficult to imagine,' he said. 'If we were to have done it for real?' He trailed off, thinking. 'Peo-ple would have been a lot more shocked.'

As much as Ken presented himself as an ordinary guy, he had no problem with acting camp on screen. Even now, he was asked to do TV appearances where producers would tell him to be more flamboyant and girly. It was what audiences wanted from their gay men and Ken was more than happy to amp up the camp. ('If they want me to play camp, I can do it,' he said. 'I *am* an actor.')

Still, Ken wanted to expand Japan's idea of what a gay man could be. In 2009, he appeared on the TV program *Haato O Tsunago* ('Heart to Heart') on Japan's national public broadcaster NHK to talk frankly about life as a gay man. *Haato O Tsunago* had first focused on what it was like to come out as an LGBT person in 2007.

Several nights later, I met the program's founding producer, an efficient-looking man who introduced himself to me as Mr Miyata. Originally, Miyata-san said, the idea of the show was to get people to talk about any issue Japanese people felt they couldn't discuss in everyday life. *Haato O Tsunago* featured three hosts and a large panel of eight guests, who sat in an Alpine-themed set of mountains and pine trees, everyone inexplicably surrounded by replica woodland creatures, plus a random camel. The three hosts of the special LGBT episode – the pop musician Sonim, the writer and actor Ira Ishida and the news anchor Yoko Sakurai – all had different levels of knowledge and friendships with LGBT people beforehand, which is exactly what Miyata-san wanted.

'They were almost representatives of what viewers at home would be like,' he said.

After filming, the female hosts Sonim and Sakurai compared notes. Both were struck by the fact that while they had gay male friends, neither of them had met a single lesbian until the show's filming. Miyata-san felt he was onto something, put the episodes to air and watched as viewer feedback rolled in.

'Viewers said a lot of things, but mostly they said they felt alone,' he said. 'Not all of them, but most of them. Some of them are very happy people. They had come out to their families already, had good, accepting parents and friends. But especially in regional, rural areas, they felt terribly isolated. Some of them were trapped in families that didn't accept their situation at all. They didn't have anyone to talk to and felt extremely alone, like no one was like them. Some people wrote in, talking about how much they disgusted themselves, that they could barely admit it to themselves that they were gay.'

It wasn't common for *Haato O Tsunago* to touch on the same topic again soon afterwards, but Miyata-san knew immediately they had to do another show on LGBT issues. It was the kind of viewer response you couldn't ignore.

Something else unexpected started to happen. Young people from Tokyo and beyond began to make treks to sit in the NHK studio audience on the days of filming. Some were members of queer campus groups from nearby universities, but a lot were young people who came by themselves. Some even allowed themselves to be interviewed on camera, though they asked to have their faces blurred and their voices altered, in case their parents or bosses recognised them. In time, *Haato O Tsunago* became synonymous with LGBT issues. One of the country's most stuffy and conservative TV stations found itself a driving force in disseminating information about queer sexuality. Slowly, things were starting to change.

*

Let's put it crudely. If there was a hierarchy of queer visibility in Japan, lesbians would be at the bottom, nowhere to be seen. Very camp gay men and drag queens were everywhere. But ruling over everyone, with her recently won beauty pageant sceptre in her hand, was someone entirely different: the undisputed reigning queen of Japanese television and pop music, post-op transsexual woman, bubblegum princess ... ladies and gentlemen, the one and only Haruna Ai!

I had met Haruni Ai briefly while trailing the Miss Tiffany's pageant in Thailand. In Japan, I tried getting back in touch with her, only to discover that she was a huge star, like, absolutely-impossible-to-interview huge. Besides her weekly TV appearances across several stations, she also had a major recording deal and was the CEO of a chain of successful restaurants, popular with artists, media types and young cigarette-smoking hipsters.

Among queer people in Japan, opinions were split on Haruna Ai. Most loved the fact that one of the most famous TV personalities in Japan was a transsexual woman. In a country that had only legalised sex-change procedures in the past decade, her rise to become an adored mainstream darling was startling. Others had reservations.

'With people like Haruna Ai,' Maeda Ken told me, 'the audience generally likes them because they're easy to understand. They're soft and fun, friendly and happy.' I got the sense his feelings toward her were ambivalent at best. Yuki Keiser didn't mind Haruna Ai, but felt *tarento* like her weren't challenging anyone's perception of sex or gender roles. If anything, she reinforced them.

'Gender binary pressure is very strong in Japan,' Yuki said. 'If you want to generalise, women in Japan have to act in certain ways. Transsexuals are more accepted, because they fit into those ideas. Haruna Ai is very feminine and wants to please men.'

For instance, Yuki told me about one TV segment where Haruna Ai told the audience that she never put her right earring in with her right hand, or her left earring with her left. Her tip: it was more elegant and appealing to men to ensure your arms crossed over at all times: right hand inserting the left earring; left hand inserting the right. 'She puts them in crossways because it's cuter for men,' Yuki said, shaking her head slightly.

For weeks, I emailed Haruna Ai's management trying to lock in an interview, but my butchered quasi-Japanese emails got me nowhere. 'Please respond to this email with a simple question mark (?) if you cannot read English,' I wrote at the bottom of emails in pre-translated Japanese. 'I will arrange a Japanese translation of the email as soon as possible.'

Then someone told me to get in touch with a man called F. Kasai. I sent Kasai-san a long and respectful interview request in English, and his reply came back. It was short and blunt, haiku-like in its succinct beauty:

> *i say your order for HARUNA AI office*
> *but she is very very busy TV star*
> *she can not return soon*

My heart sank. I sent more emails to Kasai-san and left messages on his phone. I pursued Haruna Ai's TV station reps, producers and Japanese record label. My translators made phone calls on my behalf. Everything I did encountered dead ends.

Walking through Tokyo's autumn-chilled streets, Haruna Ais hovered around me, peering out from magazines on newsstands and CDs in record shops. I was getting sick and coughed violently into my fist, feeling stupid for having even tried contacting her. Her face was everywhere, like a Sanrio cartoon character in human form. Friends and people I met in Tokyo – journalists, translators, expatriates and exchange students – all squealed when they found out I was trying to track her down, before skeptically wishing me good luck. Then one day, out of nowhere, Kasai-san yielded and gave me a phone number.

> *ai chans manager say your interview ok*
> *maybe he call you*
> *his name is MR KAZAMA*
> *please talk with him*

Several phone calls later, and we were in. The only problem was, my cough was getting worse. A couple of weeks later, a doctor would diagnose me with whooping cough.

Usually I had only one translator with me, but both my translators – Aya and Simon – insisted on coming together. It was Haruna Ai, they said, and nothing else mattered. That we'd scored the interview at all was some sort of miracle. The three of us headed to the TBS network headquarters in freezing conditions with cold rain spitting on us, my hacking cough mimicking the sound of a cat being kicked. On arrival, a female assistant came out to the foyer and greeted us with a lot of bowing, before leading us to level 4F where the magic happened. Simon, Aya and I waited in a small cafeteria-like space, from which two doors led to different TV studios.

'Look!' Aya said, squealing and pointing. 'That's her!'

The monitor showed what was being filmed in the left-hand TV studio. A pug-faced man with a giant white meringue of hair was running through a news story about a junior baseball player wanting to make the big time. The baseball player was crying and so were his family members. As the footage ran, the small box in the screen's corner showed Haruna Ai expressing a combination of Nodding Concern and Heartfelt Sympathy. She was nailing all the facial expressions. Tonight, she was wearing a white dapple-patterned dress with Disney princess puffy sleeves and a big red bow in her hair. I got excited and started coughing again.

'She's only a few metres away!' I said.

'Oh my god, this is *so* exciting,' Simon said.

Recording of the show wrapped up and the audience filed out. For a moment, Haruna Ai sailed past us towards her dressing room. Simon and Aya both made bug eyes at me and we all mimed silent screaming.

'She will be with you in a moment,' her assistant told us.

Then we heard a troubling, high-pitched sound, a squeal that sounded distressing and animal-like. We realised it was coming from two girls. Just being in Haruna Ai's orbit made people in Japan emit this sound. The girls were in their twenties, dressed in monochromatic, wildly patterned and weirdly tailored Harajuku outfits, bouncing from foot to foot and bowing at Haruna Ai almost spastically. She paused, laughed, grabbed their hands and squealed along with them, as if *she* was delighted to meet *them*. One of the girls started crying. With anyone else I would be rolling my eyes, but the excitement was contagious.

Later, Haruna Ai came out of her dressing room wearing loose pyjama bottoms and a bright orange hoodie that said 'Mississippi Ridgeland Football Club'. With glittery moisturiser still on her face, she grabbed our hands to greet us one by one, offering us chilled green tea and water. As Simon made the introductions, Haruna Ai said she remembered me from Miss Tiffany's. I stood there grinning like an idiot, coughing into my elbow. Concerned, Haruna Ai demanded cold tea for me.

Haruna Ai's voice was feminine – ultra-girly, even – but impossible to place. It was high-pitched with a slight gravelly quality, as though she was a twelve-year-old girl with a smoking problem. Unexpectedly, it made for a great broadcast voice.

As one of the only transsexual women on Japanese television, she was in great demand. But her fame was encumbered with the pressure that came with anything one-of-a-kind, a burden of responsibility to ensure she was a good role model.

'It's really hard,' she said. 'There aren't that many people on TV like myself who have changed from a man to woman, so it's difficult. It's very hard for people in Japan to relate to me and to understand what I've been through. Japan's very behind in this area. Japanese people can't seem to understand why you'd want to change your sex. So in order to educate people – but in a fun way! – I do a lot of comedy and talk shows to help Japanese people understand. Nowadays, most people look at me as a person, instead of being a Person Who's Been Through a Sex Change, which is good.'

That week alone, she had done product promotions in Tokyo and Hokkaido, had her regular appearances on TBS and NTV, had worked on a music video and released her second major CD single, 'Crazy Love', a song that – like most J-pop – was maddeningly stupid and infuriatingly catchy. Her voice was autotuned and low in the mix and the video was sexy without being *sexual*. It showed Haruna Ai, with four back-up dancers, first in a gown made of silver with head jewels, then a cheerleading outfit, then a pants-and-hat tomboy outfit, then finally a pink cocktail outfit made of feathers. It had no narrative and made no sense. The edits were annoying and epileptic, and the song immediately bored into my brain like some terrible parasite:

I'm so crazy
Crazy crazy for you
Need you baby
Baby baby
It's you

Sweet lord, the song was hideous. Even so, no one could hold this against Haruna Ai.

Recently, she had raced a charity marathon after the public nominated her as the person they most wanted to see run.

'The marathon was thirty-five kilometres, they could only choose one person, and I was selected to do it!' Haruna Ai said, squealing. 'In high school, I tried not to exercise a lot, so this was a big challenge for me.' By the end of the race, Haruna Ai's make-up had completely melted off and it looked as though someone had taken a blowtorch to her face. Yet for a woman whose fame rested mostly on her appearance, she didn't seem that bothered – sweating and ghoulish, she was still giggling and pumping her fists in the air. And nor did other people seem to care.

After an hour, Haruna Ai apologised for having to leave and handed us complimentary copies of 'Crazy Love' before posing for photos, then made some phone calls. Dinner would be waiting for us at one of her restaurants, she said. After a series of giggling bows and hand-clutching, she disappeared out of the studio, into her private life, and I knew I'd never see her again, except on television.

It was only later that I'd listen to our interview and realise that it had gone awfully. When we weren't giggling like idiots, I spent most of the time apparently trying to hack up my lung. We didn't talk about anything important whatsoever. Haruna Ai skimmed over her love life and ducked any questions that were overtly political. But I also realised that I didn't care. Haruna Ai wasn't about serious conversation. She was about fun.

'Educate people,' she had exclaimed, 'but in a fun way!' She came off as sweet and lightheaded, but perhaps that was her gift: you never forgot she was transsexual, but by being so captivating, so lovable, so friendly, her sexual identity ceased being her sole gimmick. That, in and of itself, was kind of genius.

*

In Japan, there is one TV set for every 1.2 people, making it one of the most dense television-owning populations in the world. Despite the country being at the forefront of technological wizardry and craft, television remains by far the most influential and popular medium. Even on subways and trains, people watch vodcasts of their favourite shows on phones and MP3 players, while some remain resolutely old-school and watch live TV on analogue portables the size of small bricks, antennae stretched and hovering over fellow train passengers like giant praying mantises.

For me, bedridden with whooping cough, it was a beautiful thing to know that at any moment of the day, I could flick through the channels and discover some of the most flamboyantly mincing personalities this fine country had to offer. After the morning news, there was my friend Bourebonne-san, providing his snappy, tongue-in-cheek commentary about the day's events. Prime time took us to Haruna Ai, dancing and chatting and giggling away. On the nights when I was coughing so hard I thought I'd vomit, I'd while away my insomnia by watching the delightfully hammy sprite KABA.Chan, who told me about the best handbags, vacuum cleaners, portable GPS devices and slimming tights Japan's premier home-shopping program had to offer. From Japan's helmet-haired transgender make-up artist Ikko to gay aerobics instructor Chris Matsumura (think Japan's answer to Richard Simmons), no one ever needed to have a boring straight moment with Japanese television: it was just one big, exploding rainbow poof of colour!

I didn't really have a problem with this. For a start, it was stupidly entertaining, and a lot of gay men out there just *were* that hyper-camp. Still, I worried about the absence of anything else. No lesbians, no transsexual men and no gay men out of drag. No LGBT people taken seriously. All the men were wacky, but never sexual. What happened to people's headspace when they saw gay men only as camp drag queens on TV, or read about them only as aliens and wizards in comic books? And what impact did this have on young queer Japanese teenagers? So much of queerness in Japan seemed to be a performance for straight people. When the televisions were finally turned off, most straight people went about their business assuming that they didn't know any queer people themselves. For the country with the most colourful television in the world, Japan felt like it was only just coming out of the black-and-white era.

MALAYSIA

In which we meet Christian and Muslim
fundamentalists who treat homosexuality as an
affliction that can be cured. Key quote: 'Don't tell me,
"It's okay for women to be with women, for men to be
with men." It's not okay. It's in the scriptures. It's
against nature.' Time spent singing while researching
this chapter: forty-five minutes.

*

IS IT POSSIBLE TO stop being a lesbian? Get straightened
out? Un-gayed? De-faggoted? I've met people who say it can be
done. If you're struggling with unwanted same-sex desires –
and the key word is 'unwanted' – you'll be relieved to know that
it's possible to become an ex-homosexual, walking proud and
straight down the path of hetero-righteousness. They've seen it
happen to others and it's happened to them. All you need, they
say, is willpower. Willpower and faith.

They didn't hate gays or lesbians. How could they, when they
had been one themselves? And no one was born homosexual,
they told me. People *became* gay. No one knew how, exactly, but
there seemed to be a lot of different factors: traumatic childhood experiences like abuse, parental neglect, divorce, teasing,
the time you accidentally shat your pants when you were nine,
and that other time when you were six and that girl chased you

around the playground and kissed you on the mouth – which was, you now realise, actually a form of sexual molestation. There was no need to worry, though, because just as people became gay, anyone could become ex-gay too.

It's possible, my friends. *Believe.*

*

At ten o'clock on a Sunday, the canal-lined streets of Melaka were unusually quiet, but the Real Love Ministry had already started its morning service. On the walls of the building's stairwell, glittery craft letters spelled out 'REAL ♥' and 'www.r-l-m. com', and Hillsong soft-rock melodies wafted through the building. I took off my shoes, opened the doors and was immediately knocked back by the force of song.

'We wanna see Jesus lifted high,' people sang, 'a banner that flies across this land!'

There were just twenty people in the room – mostly adults, some kids, a couple of elderly ladies – who all smiled, still singing, as I entered. A small band led the hymns on electric guitars, drums and bass, while a rosy-cheeked Chinese-Malaysian woman named Judith sang into the mic.

We wanna see [clap-clap-clap]
We wanna see [clap-clap-clap]
We wanna see Jesus lifted high!

Usually, I was uncomfortable with public singing unless I was drunk, but this song was infuriatingly catchy. Any song that featured prominent handclaps tended to win me over.

RLM's church was the size of a standard classroom.

Ambience-wise, it was more like a corporate call centre than a sacred place of worship. The hospital-grade fluoro lighting made it feel antiseptic, but the smiles and songs warmed the place right up. As I shuffled into one of the back seats, four kids sitting up front turned around to wave to me excitedly. One curly-haired mop of a girl giggled with sugar-rush excitement.

'Hi!' I mouthed, waving.

She turned to her friend and mimed squealing. This was Pastor Edmund's seven-year-old daughter, Angel. Next to her was her six-year-old brother, Ethan. He waved too, showing off white teeth and squeezable baby gopher cheeks.

It was easy to spot Pastor Edmund and his wife, Amanda. They were standing in the front row, dancing to the music and singing the loudest. I recognised them from a *Malaysian Women's Weekly* profile I'd read online, branded with the headline: 'TRUE CONFESSION: My Husband Only Liked Men until He Met Me. Is this Malaysia's most controversial marriage?' The story's lead read: 'Until twelve years ago, Edmund Smith led a homosexual lifestyle. Now he's happily married and a father of two. Here's the story of his remarkable journey.'

And it *was* a remarkable journey. Edmund's mother had wished for a daughter and sometimes dressed Edmund in girls' clothes. Looking back, Edmund told the magazine reporter, this completely messed up his sexual hard-wiring. Things got worse after Edmund was sent to an all-boys school at the age of twelve and found like-minded company.

'I found ten other boys who were just as girly,' he said. 'By the time I was thirteen, I was already leading a wild life with sexual escapades on stairways and at the homes of my lovers.'

Later, Edmund told me that until the age of twenty-four, he was what you would call a rampant homosexual, involved in gay cruising and gay clubs and gay sex and gay orgies and gay prostitution (generally just being super-gay, really), before a bad break-up led him to decide he'd had enough of the whole gay thing. He sought religious therapy through Choices, an ex-gay ministry in Singapore, and soon after married Amanda, who'd been his best friend since they'd taught together at a school for disabled kids.

Edmund hadn't turned back since then. In fact, he'd gone on to build his career around his story of sexual brokenness, travelling throughout Malaysia and preaching his good news of sexual metamorphosis, insisting anyone could change. He had no less than three Facebook pages dedicated to his work. On his personal Facebook page, Edmund used the 'relationship' feature to list all his friends as his brothers, sisters, cousins, 'spiritual children' and 'spiritual grandchildren'. He also listed his favourite shows: *American Idol, Glee, Desperate Housewives* and *Oprah*. In his bio, he wrote:

I am a Child of God. I am a real man. I love Jesus & Jesus loves me ... no, more than that. Jesus is crazy about me. I am happily married to the most beautiful woman in MY world. I am blessed with 2 gifted kids. I have a great spiritual family! Highly Favored! Deeply Loved! Greatly Blessed!

Now at his church, the Hillsong hymn was finishing as a lone guitar continued to strum gently. Amanda came on-stage to lead us through a loud, ecstatic prayer. An ethnically Indian woman with thick black curls, Amanda had a maternal beauty, the kind of comforting face you'd want by your bedside if you were a kid with a tummy ache.

'Thank you, Jesus!' she said, eyes closed, microphone to her mouth. 'Thank you, Lord! We worship you this morning, O Lord!'

People raised their hands as if testifying. In the front row, Pastor Edmund bowed with both hands held up by his face, mumbling incoherently.

'*Shak-arajabel-ahshukelasol ... ekajabelahshuk-elasshak.*'

It took me a while to realise he was speaking in tongues.

'He is the peace and light,' Amanda said, looking ecstatic. 'He speaks to us. Jesus! Jesus! *Jesus!* You know our hurt. You know our disappointment!'

'*Thank you, Jesus!*' Edmund whispered.

'You *know* our desperation,' Amanda said.

'*Your grace, Looooord,*' sang Edmund in falsetto.

'You know secrets nobody knows! You know, Lord. You *know.*'

The band picked up speed again, reinforcing the lone guitar and growing in volume until they hit a riff that sounded vaguely like Nirvana's 'Smells Like Teen Spirit'. With horror, I realised the guitar had been only a bridge between songs. The entire morning was a *medley* of hymns.

Dear God, I thought.

'WHOO!' someone said.

In the end, we sang for forty-five minutes straight. It was intense. It was a hot day and I supported myself by holding on to the plastic chair in front of me. Edmund showed no signs of slowing down. His energy was relentless, his dance moves hypnotic. During one song, he placed an open palm over his heart and balled his other hand into a fist, pumping violently as if he were angrily milking an uncooperative cow. In the upbeat songs, he thrust his flattened palms in unison to the rhythm, doing swift push-ups against an invisible wall. His face, sweating madly, swung violently from left to right as though he was being slapped.

'WHOO!' someone said again.

When the songs finally ended, we stood there panting and exhausted. Smiling blissfully, Amanda told us to sit down.

'*Shalom!*' she said.

'*Shalom!*'

'I'd like to welcome our visitors here,' she said. 'Firstly, I'd like to welcome Ben from Australia.'

People turned to me and clapped. I smiled back at them and waved.

'I hope you have a blessed time in Malaysia,' Amanda said, smiling.

'Thanks!' I said brightly.

Edmund turned around, a big welcoming grin on his face. His features were broad, elegant and vaguely feline. Today he was wearing a purple vest with matching purple trousers, and his white leather belt matched his lightly embroidered white shirt. On one of his immaculately manicured fingers was his wedding ring.

Now it was time for the sermon. On stage, Pastor Edmund spoke with an intense theatrical cadence, moving from soft whispers to intense bark-like yelling without warning, which kept everyone on their toes. His preaching voice lay on the spectrum between the American comedian Gilbert Gottfried – the guy who voiced the parrot in Disney's *Aladdin* – and a Brooklyn drag queen with hearing damage.

'We want to hear from you, O God!' he said. 'You and you *alone! For you can transform our hearts,*' he said, whispering. 'FOR YOU CAN SET US FREE!' he said, screaming. 'Only you can heal our SEX-U-A-LI-*teee*, O God!'

He gestured to us.

'Every one of you,' he said, 'whether you're sexually broken or not, you are sexual beings! So this service today is for *everybody*. Look at your friends and say, "You are a sexual being." Go on!'

I turned to the man next to me. Lionel was a tall, handsome guy with a Sri Lankan background who wore glasses. I had watched him during the hymns, dancing awkwardly in the way tall men dance, keeping their hands close to their body as if they're worried their limbs might cause a scene.

'You are a sexual being,' I said to Lionel, laughing awkwardly.

'You are a sexual being,' he said back, in a deep, British-inflected voice.

Two frail white-haired ladies behind us turned to each other.

'You are a sexual being,' they said sombrely.

'Some of you *used* to be sexually regular,' Edmund said. 'But then things began to happen and you became *sexually different*.'

Being 'sexually different' was bad. 'Sexually regular' was the ideal, and there were only two ways to achieve it: heterosexual marriage or celibacy. Everything else was 'sexually different', a sin in the eyes of the Lord. 'Sexually different' behaviour included – it was a long list – sex before marriage, homosexuality, bisexuality, adultery, bestiality, paedophilia, promiscuity and polygamy. If you masturbated, you were sexually different. ('If you are a man having sex with yourself, it means you are mas-tur-ba-*ting*,' Edmund explained. 'YOU ARE NOT SUPPOSED TO HAVE SEX WITH YOURSELF!') Watching pornography was also sexually different. ('WHEN YOU WATCH PORN, it means you are HAVING SEX WITH THOSE *IMAGES*. Then when you MASTURBATE, you are HAVING SEX WITH YOURSELF.')

There was another category of people who were 'sexually

broken'. These were sexually different people who wanted to change. This was better than being sexually different, because God could only put you back together once you admitted you were truly broken.

Edmund pointed out it wasn't our place to judge sexually different people. He had dealt with homosexuals, people who masturbated and people who frequently watched porn. He didn't judge any of them. He even had friends who, to this day, remained gay.

'I even have friends who are *paedophiles*,' he told us. 'REAL PAEDOPHILES! I'm not like, "Ew, ew, ew. Don't do that."'

Jesus, I thought.

'Because we should be sexually-different-people *friendly*,' he said. 'We should be able to stand with them, pray for them' – his voice descended into a whisper – '*and guide them*.'

There were murmurs of approval and agreement.

Edmund leaned forward, gazing into our eyes.

'Now, *I* have no right to judge you,' he said. 'But I'm also supposed to tell you the truth: that based on God's standard, you are *sexually different*. Don't tell me, "Oh, it's okay for women to be with women, for men to be with men, for adults to be with children sexually." It's NOT OKAY. It's in the SCRIPTURES. It's *against* nature,' he whispered. 'ARE YOU LISTENING?' he hollered. 'MAN marries WOMAN. *Period!* There's no other way! Can you say Am-eh-en?'

Edmund pronounced Amen in the same three-syllabled way Californian girls said 'Heh-loooo-*oooh*?'

'Amen,' we said.

'Men has sex with men, it is shameful,' Edmund said. 'SAY "SHAMEFUL".'

'Shameful,' we said.

'Now most of you know my story,' he said. 'I never thought I would get a CHANCE to get married. I never thought I'd get a CHANCE to become a father! I thought I'd always be gay and look for Mr Right. I tried that for *eleven years*. It never worked. I was so BROKEN! If I imagined myself being with a woman, sexually' – here he started to dry-retch – 'I started to get nausea! *Oooooh*, I feel like vomiting. *Disgusted*, you know?'

Some of the congregation laughed, maybe in recognition.

'So I could not imagine that today, I would be enjoying what God gave Adam and Eve.'

Amanda looked at him with devoted, helpless love.

'*It's a wonderful thing*,' he whispered. 'IT'S A WONDERFUL THING, I SAID. SAY "AMEN!"' he screamed.

'Amen.'

'Now, I've had all kinds of excitement!' he said. 'I've had *orgies*; I've had *sex for money*. I've had sex with teenagers; I've had sex with seventy-year-old GRANDPA!' He grinned. 'Yes! I've had sex with all kinds of people and I'm not proud of all this. I had all kinds of excitement! I tell you: before becoming ex-gay, *I slept with a man every night*.'

I was impressed, then remembered children were in the audience.

'But when you open the word of God, our hearts begin to beat faster. There will be a *su-per-nat-u-ral* experience for each and every one of us. Let's get *excited*! Not just in church but in your own homes. When you open the word of God, *GET EXCITED*. Some of you have not ARRIVED THERE YET, so start asking: "GOD GIVE ME AN EXCITED HEART!"'

'God, give me an excited heart,' we said.

'Say it! "I WANT THAT EXCITEMENT, JESUS!"'

'I want that excitement, Jesus.'

'"MAKE ME EXCITED, JESUS!"'

'Make me excited, Jesus.'

'Some of you know, your favourite movie is coming out soon,' he said. '*Glee* 3D. *Glee* movie! In 3D! In the cinema, *wah*! You know, I get so excited about the *Glee* movie! I love *Glee*! I'm excited about that. But trust me-*lah*: I'm *not* more excited about that than the *word of God*. Who can say Ah-meh-en?'

He winked and waved a cheeky finger at us.

'Amen,' we said.

*

After the service, Edmund came over to me, with Amanda and the kids in tow, giving me a big hug and kiss on the cheek.

'*Shalom*, Benjamin! You made it.'

Angel, Edmund's daughter, squealed excitedly.

'Why are you so excited, Angel?' I said.

'Because you're here, you're *here*, you're really *HERE*,' she said, then released a groan. 'This is the first time in my LIFE we're meeting! You're here and I'm meeting you and I'M SO *EXCITED*! Argh!'

I laughed. 'Argh!' I said.

'Argh!' she said again.

Edmund then invited me to join them for lunch. Amanda, Angel, Ethan, Angel's best friend Isabelle and Edmund's mother – a regal woman who wore her grey hair in an elegant perm – were already in the family's eight-seat car.

When I opened the door, Angel started squealing again, jamming her fists into her mouth. She had not expected me to ride with them.

'Argh!' she squealed.

'Argh!' I said.

Smiling, Edmund started the engine. I asked Angel, Isabelle and Ethan what they wanted to be when they grew up. Ethan wanted to be a professional football player; Angel and Isabelle wanted to be fashion designers. I stuck my head between the front seats to speak to Edmund and Amanda.

'Your kids are pretty adorable,' I said.

Amanda and Edmund smiled, proud parents who'd scored good kids.

'Praise Jesus,' Edmund said.

At the eatery, other members of the congregation joined us, including the singer Judith, Sri Lankan Lionel and a butch-looking girl, Ally, whom I'd mistaken for a teenage boy at the service based on her thick eyebrows and short hair gelled into a mohawk.

Over lunch, Edmund passed over his business card that said he was part of something called Rafohs Creative Entertainment. It was a company he ran with Jerry, who was both his assistant pastor and professional manager. When he wasn't preaching, Edmund worked as an MC, actor and singer, and had recently been in a Singaporean feature film. ('You must look it up on YouTube!' he told me.)

There had been a small glass case back at RLM headquarters that displayed Edmund's merchandise. CDs for sale included his debut album, *Wake Up* – a collection of self-penned Christian songs – and the limited edition EP, *Perfect*. There was also a VCD of one of Edmund's cable television appearances called *It's a New Day: Homosexuals Can Change ... If They Want To*.

Later that afternoon, I met Edmund and Jerry again in a canal-side café. They came wearing outfits very different from those they'd worn at church. Jerry was now dressed in a muscle top paired with above-the-knee denim cut-offs. Edmund was a vision in white: low-cut white V-neck shirt; white beach trousers; white Kangol-style cap; giant white vinyl carry bag large enough to fit a small child. He was dressed like a fabulous retired gentleman on a tropical holiday, the kind who drinks chilled white wine served by handsome waitstaff.

'So, how exactly do you stop being gay?' I asked.

Edmund sighed, and Jerry started taking photos with a digital camera. When I gave him a puzzled look, he explained they were going up on RLM's Facebook page.

'It's a *journey*,' Edmund said. 'It begins with a decision. I mean, if you *come* from a gay background, you *might* know what I'm talking about ...'

'Okay,' I said, playing dumb.

'Because if you come from that background, you can empathise better. You can be a better shoulder to cry on.'

I asked Edmund whether he felt he'd been born gay and he shook his head emphatically. 'I *felt*,' he said, emphasising the past tense. 'I don't feel that anymore. I don't *believe* that anymore.'

Edmund recalled those heady gay days between the ages of thirteen and twenty-four with a smile. He brought friends along to cruising spots and hooked them on the thrill of anonymous sex. Edmund didn't speak of anything with disgust or shame – the group sex, the late nights, the anonymous fucking. Instead, he was smiling, even laughing, reminiscing as if those were the good old days.

'Well, in a way, it *was* the good old days!' he said, laughing. 'Of course, I've done certain things I shouldn't have done, definitely. But I don't believe in *regretting*. I've repented for the things I believe are sins today, but those are things that have happened already. You can't do anything about it.'

In the last three years of his gay 'phase', Edmund pursued three year-long relationships with three different guys. He was looking for long-term monogamy by then, but each relationship ended badly. Incidentally, his last boyfriend's name – the one, he said, who really broke his heart – was Benjamin.

'Oh!' I said.

Edmund laughed, but said he was shattered at the time.

'I gave him my most. But it's the same old story you hear: gays *cannot* be trusted. At the end of the day, they can be your friends, but they cannot live with you happily ever after.' He then added quietly: 'I think I loved him more than he loved me.'

But there were gay couples I knew who had been together for years, even decades, I said, conveniently failing to mention that I belonged to one of those couples.

'There *are* people who've been together for twenty years,' he said. 'Yes! They *claim* they're like married couples, blah-blah-blah. They have a house, three dogs – and then, when their partner's not around, they flirt with me! So what does *that* say? To me, it's scary!'

'Heterosexual people do that too,' I said.

'I know *thaa-aat*,' he said, singsong. He shrugged. 'Maybe I've not seen enough gay people? I don't know.'

Heartbroken after his bust-up with Benjamin, Edmund decided he'd had enough. It seemed logical that his gayness was holding him back from happiness. He found Choices in Singapore, which promised to help rid him of homosexual desires once and for all. Edmund travelled to Singapore with Amanda, his best friend from the age of twenty-one, when he was still living as a gay man. For Amanda, it had been love at first sight.

'And for you?' I asked.

'No, I was gay!' he said, laughing.

After Choices, Edmund felt a change. He still looked at men
– 'Of *course* I did' – but said that they ceased being important to
him. Instead of pursuing men, he started pursuing Jesus. And
that's when he and Amanda decided to get married.

Edmund conceded he wouldn't encourage other people to
do what they did, but said it made sense at the time. Amanda,
Edmund told me, was 'sexually broken' too. She wasn't a lesbian,
no-no-no, but had experienced sexual abuse from a young age
and as a result wasn't comfortable having sex. Edmund didn't
want to have sex with Amanda either, so the whole arrangement
seemed perfect.

Right, I thought. I tried to phrase what I wanted to say delicately.

'I've got female friends I'm very close to,' I said, 'but I don't
want to have *sex* with them. I see them as friends. And that
seems like a reason why I *wouldn't* marry them.'

Edmund stared. 'The theme for our marriage was, "Today I
Married My Best Friend." Does that tell you anything?'

I looked at him blankly.

'We didn't marry for sex, obviously. We married because we
realised we were each other's soul mates. We wanted to grow
old together. We got married as best friends, not as husband
and wife. At that time it was such a win-win situation for both
of us. Today she's my wife, in every respect' – Edmund gave me
a look that clearly implied marital sex – 'but back then, it was a
mistake –'

Edmund stopped and backtracked, putting up his hands.

'– no, *not* a mistake. But I would not encourage people to do
that.'

This was disingenous: Edmund's entire life *was* encouraging people to do that. Week after week, Edmund used his marriage to Amanda as an example of what you could achieve if you committed to the journey, and now he was telling me he regretted the decision? It was kind of creepy. But not as creepy as something he'd said at the sermon.

'I was sort of shocked when you said that you were friends with someone who was a paedophile ...'

'Why are you shocked?' Edmund said evenly. He sucked his drink through a straw silently, not breaking eye contact.

'If you're saying all these things – homosexuality, having sex outside of marriage, masturbation – are perversions, then surely paedophilia is worse.'

'Why?' he said.

'Because,' I said slowly, 'you're talking about the abuse of a child.'

'Hold on,' he said, smiling. 'When *you* talk about paedophiles, you're talking about a sexually *different* paedophile. A sexually *broken* paedophile? That's a different story altogether.'

'Okay.'

'A sexually *broken* paedophile is someone who wants to change; someone who seriously wants out. So yeah, they still *can* be dangerous, but they are crying out for help! And if we don't help them, who's going to help them?'

One man, Edmund explained, had come to RLM with uncontrollable sexual desires for young boys. He had already molested some, Edmund said, but it hadn't gone 'too far'. (When I asked him to define 'too far', Edmund said, 'No penetration.') The man had become part of the RLM community, but didn't finish the RLM 'journey' to heal himself.

'He started the journey, but didn't go far,' Edmund said.

'Because of his sexual brokenness, he was emotionally very unstable. He was struggling with depression. It affected his career; it affected his journey of recovery, which we call JOR.'

'JOR,' Jerry echoed, nodding and taking another photo.

Edmund didn't know what had happened to this man. He had disappeared from RLM.

'You never thought to report him to the police?' I said.

Edmund gave me a look. It said: *And why would I do something like that?*

*

On Tuesday evening, RLM held its monthly V-Meet for sexually broken members. The 'V' stood for victory. It wasn't just the sexually broken who turned up, though. Others were there for moral support or because they'd signed up to be a 'befriender' to the 'befriendees' (similar to the Alcoholics Anonymous sponsor system).

Edmund addressed us from the podium, reading from notes on his Toshiba laptop. I was sitting next to Sri Lankan Lionel again. Edmund told all the befriendees – the sexually broken among us – to stand up. Five men stood up, including Lionel. At well over six feet, he loomed over everybody else.

'Let me speak to the befriendees,' Edmund said, peering over his laptop. 'If what I say applies to you, say, "That's me." The more "that's me" you're saying, the better it is. It shows how serious you are as a struggler.'

Edmund recited the checklist, call-and-response style.

'The befriendee admits to be struggling and desires help,' he said.

('That's me.')

'The befriendee is an individual who chooses recovery and freedom by going through the journey of recovery.'

('That's me.')

'The befriendee partners with a befriender, who walks side by side in the journey of recovery.'

('That's me.')

'The befriendee is completely honest and accountable to the befriender.'

('That's me.')

It was a long checklist. It felt as though they were new employees at a particularly uninspiring call centre, pledging their allegiance to a communications company whose slogan was, 'That's me.'

When Edmund finished, he told the rest of us to give them a clap. We offered encouraging applause, like parents cheering on a potty-training toddler.

'We *love* you!' Edmund said, smacking his hands together enthusiastically. 'Everyone, look to a person who is a befriendee and say "I love you." Come on!'

I turned to Lionel. 'I love you,' I said.

Lionel smiled sheepishly.

'Mean it!' Edmund said.

'I love you,' I said again.

The befriendee–befriender partners split off into corners to update each other on their progress. Lionel talked animatedly with his befriender while an Indian-Malaysian guy confided in his.

'The befriender,' Edmund explained, 'is a counsellor *and* a friend, and commits to walking with the befriendee for one year.'

Despite the year-long commitment, three befrienders hadn't

shown up. One of the stranded befriendees was a spectacled Chinese guy who was one of the saddest-looking people I'd ever encountered. He looked completely, well, 'broken'. He dressed like an IT guy: shirt checked like a spreadsheet; plain slacks the colour of old paperwork. His teeth were concertina crooked and he had a faint adolescent moustache. He looked despondent that his befriender hadn't showed up, but not particularly surprised. His eyes gave off a medicated sheen.

When we re-gathered, we sat in a big circle as Edmund led us through conversational ice-breakers to foster trust among us.

'Are you ready to SHARE?' he said.

Edmund's first sharing exercise involved each of us telling the group something no one knew about us.

'For instance,' he said, hands fluttering, 'my favourite author is Enid Blyton! I still read her books to this day. Also, I wear earplugs to sleep every night!'

The Indian-Malaysian man to Edmund's left, who had a bit of a belly protruding, tried to think of something.

'I like food?' he said.

'You like food, I know that,' Edmund said. Everyone laughed. The man chuckled, a little embarrassed.

Jerry offered that he had just joined a sixty-day program he had found on the internet to help him with his sexual brokenness. It was different to RLM, but also reinforced the work he was doing here.

When we got to the sad-looking Chinese guy, he just shrugged. He looked at the floor, unable to think of anything to share.

'Hmm,' Edmund said, trying to think of something for him. 'Well, do you use deodorant?'

Everyone suppressed laughter. The Chinese guy shook his head.

'You *don't?*' Edmund said, feigning surprise and catching everyone's eye. It was clearly a private, long-standing joke. I wanted to pick up my chair and smash it into Edmund's face.

Edmund then asked those of us who were sexually redeemed – who were no longer broken, or never had been – to share a joy of 'living a sexually regular lifestyle'.

'It could be heterosexuality or celibacy,' he said. 'Anyone?'

Silence. It seemed to genuinely surprise Edmund that no one was willing to discuss the intimate detail of their sex lives.

'Okay, for me, I'll start!' Edmund said. 'I'm sexually redeemed. And a joy of being sexually redeemed is I'm able to have my own children; my own flesh and blood. And not in a surrogate style, but by naturally having sex. The first time I saw my Angel in the womb, I cried. The scan! The joy of holding my baby in my arms! When Amanda called me and said "I'm pregnant"' – here Edmund put his hands to his chest and gasped – 'I ran to the jetty and I just praised God. And having a child without any guilt or any condemnation whatsoever, through a proper marriage, through a proper relationship, that's one of the biggest joys of being a sexually regular person today!'

People forced smiles, unable to identify.

'Anyone else? Are you all sexually broken? Are you *all* sexually different?'

The silence was unbearable.

'Well, I'm sexually private!' I offered.

Everyone laughed. Edmund shot me a sharp look but smiled.

'Okay, that is *his* term! Anyone else? All the sexually *nonprivate* people?'

It was clear this wasn't working. Edmund changed tack and asked us to share one major reason why we had moved from being 'sexually different' to becoming 'sexually broken'. This was something I wanted to know too: *Why did these people want to change?*

Edmund threw the question to the Chinese guy. He moved his lips but could barely speak.

'Excuse me?' Edmund said.

'Because it's wrong,' the guy said bleatingly, like a lamb. For a fleeting moment, I swore he was going to cry. Or maybe it was me who wanted to weep.

By the end of the two-hour V-Meet, everyone looked drained. Edmund must have noticed this too, because right before we left, he said something grand and dramatic to leave us on a high note, to give us hope. In case some of us didn't know, he said, his former life didn't stop at being gay. His sexual corruption had become so extreme that he'd even entertained the thought that he was a woman trapped in a man's body.

'Yes, I was a *transgender!*' he said. 'I thought of having a *sex change*. I would have gone for a sex change if a *man* would have wanted to marry me. And yet today, I just *love* my penis so much!'

*

Secret Recipe was a clean family-restaurant chain, which served diabetes-inducing-sized slices of cake. Jerry, Ally and Renik and I met there, listening as the PA hummed with pop classics and power ballads. Ally was the boyish-looking girl I'd met at lunch. She was twenty-four years old and looked thuggishly cool, as though the primary reason for her existence was to not give a fuck. As it turned out, she was just shy. Renik was forty-two, a broad-shouldered guy with dark skin and a ruggedness about him that was softened by a slight belly. With his spectacles,

Renik looked like a handsome young professor.

Ally and Renik shared common ground. They had both been in and out of intensive psychiatric care over the years. Ally had first visited the psych ward after she was caught having an affair with her female cousin, who was married with five children.

'I have ED-ing on her,' Ally said.

'ED-ing?' I asked.

'Emotional dependency,' Jerry explained.

For three years, the women had met secretly, but when the woman's husband found out about it, all hell broke loose. Ally's parents were horrified. Her father demanded to know, 'Why are you in love with this woman? Are you a *lesbian*?'

Ally couldn't quite bring herself to say the words. Instead, she locked herself away and brooded, feeling as though she was going insane. She couldn't stand being wrenched from her cousin. At weird hours, she would find herself walking to her house, as though possessed. The next time Ally was caught by the husband, the police got involved.

Ally was taken to a psych ward, where she was heavily medicated. For about a year after that, Ally was readmitted on and off, taking sedatives and antidepressants. In her spare time, she carefully considered the different ways to kill herself.

Though her parents were devout Catholics, they lived in Malaysia, a melting pot of religions. Desperate, they searched everywhere for a cure for Ally's unnatural attraction to women, turning to gurus at Hindu temples, pastors at the Catholic Church, godless psychologists and obscure organisations they had heard about on the grapevine.

Eventually, they found Edmund and RLM. Jerry and Renik were already members and still remembered the first day Ally joined the group.

Jerry started: 'When I first saw you –'

'I was totally *not* like now,' Ally said. 'I was –'

'Like a zombie,' Renik said, 'that kind of thing.'

'Like a zombie,' Ally said, nodding.

It was at RLM, doped with medication, that Ally decided to hand her life over to God.

'I cried out to him; I screamed to him,' she said now, wide-eyed and beatific. 'And that's when I got the miracle in me.'

Renik had come to RLM in a similar way. Growing up in neighbouring Brunei, he spent his elementary school lunch-breaks with girls jumping rope double-dutch. He didn't really *get* other boys. They were so rough and liked guns; Renik liked teddy bears. The girls, who adored having a boy in their midst, would paint Renik's nails.

As an adult, he'd look back on all the time he'd spent with girls and feel it had rewired his brain. He started seeing other guys the same way his female friends did: they were cute. His same-sex attraction – 'SSA' – gnawed at him. And he was confused. Did he actually want to *be* a girl?

At home, Renik would cry himself to sleep. When he turned sixteen, he moved to the United Kingdom to study. He arrived in England by himself, and, away from family and without anyone looking over his shoulder, he felt the freedom everyone does alone in a foreign country. He could do whatever he wanted and be someone else entirely.

He'd landed in a hive of gay activity. The Midlands' towns and cities were filled with beats, public toilets and parks where men cruised each other at all hours. Phone numbers were scrawled on walls by horny men, and all Renik had to do was call. It was easy. Renik caved.

Still, his belief in God never wavered. He came back from anonymous sexual encounters feeling sick and ashamed. He read his Christian magazines closely, paying particular attention to articles that said homosexuality was something that *could* be changed. 'Such were some of you,' the New Testament proclaimed, 'were' being the operative word. Renik turned to his local pastor in the Midlands for help.

Sensing Renik's worry, his pastor said that on a scale of homosexuality and perversion, it sounded as though Renik was only a 'four' or a 'five', nowhere near a 'ten'.

'Just get back up and try again,' his pastor said.

After Renik returned home to Brunei, something snapped. The low-lying static in his head finally brought on a storm of bad thoughts, and his nervous breakdown was so severe that he was hospitalised for a month. The medication he received gave him hallucinations.

'As a spiritual person, I'd tell you that the Devil was attacking my mind. A doctor would say it's a "chemical imbalance in the brain", but I believe it's a bit of both.'

The beta blockers Renik took reduced his anxiety, but heightened his depression. Concerned at his lack of progress, his doctor said that, from a psychiatric point of view, they didn't believe there *was* anything wrong with same-sex attraction. He also suggested – gently – that perhaps Renik was a little too involved in religion.

'I agreed with him to a certain extent,' Renik said. 'If you're going to focus on something like religion a lot, you have to do it in the right way.'

But he didn't accept his doctor's statement that you couldn't – or shouldn't – get rid of homosexual thoughts. He had read countless stories about ex-homosexuals in America. Some years later, Renik moved to Malaysia's capital. He met a girl at an HSBC call centre, got engaged and started going to RLM, making the ninety-minute journey from Kuala Lumpur to Melaka every month to hear Edmund preach and attend V-Meets.

'Why RLM attracted me was because of Pastor Edmund's own lifestyle,' Renik said. 'He was even worse than I was, but look at him *now*. His life has changed tremendously and I wanted that.'

It wasn't long before Renik and his fiancée fought horribly, calling off the engagement before breaking up entirely. Depressed, Renik started going downhill. Living in Kuala Lumpur meant he was never far from a gay sauna, and he would spend all of his money and time on sex with handsome strangers, which left him light-headed and hollow with regret. On RLM and Pastor Edmund's recommendation, he moved to Melaka to focus on his recovery.

Now, Ally and Renik spoke with the calm and dewy-eyed clarity of converts.

'Do you feel you are cured?'

Ally nodded.

'Do either of you feel attracted to the opposite sex?'

There was a heavy silence.

Ally laughed nervously. 'Uh, yeah ...'

'Oh, it's a personal question ...' I said apologetically.

'Look, to be honest, sometimes I have same-sex attractions,' Renik offered, 'but not where I start fantasising that I want to have sex. A female person now ... I'll find her attractive. I like to see girls in miniskirts and boots.'

'Does it compare to the attraction you felt towards guys? Or is it a different feeling?'

'It's a different feeling ...' Renik started to say. 'And it's a nice feeling. Something different.'

Jerry laughed and said, 'It's like a second puberty.'

'Do you find yourself looking at *guys*, though?' I asked Ally.

'Before, I can't sit with them, I can't talk to them. I was afraid of them! I looked at them as though they were monsters. I was afraid. But now I'm trying to admire them, their looks. Slowly … I'm admiring that.'

For a while, Renik and Ally were even dating *each other*. Physically, it was an unexpected pairing. Renik was nearly twice Ally's age, and although Renik was tall and well-built, Ally – with her slouchy shoulders and razored hair – looked more rough-edged and masculine than him.

'It was a trial, basically,' Renik said happily. 'And it was good. *Very* good. It was good. The first few times we dated, it was … good.'

Good, I wrote in my notebook.

The restaurant's PA system started to play the Céline Dion version of 'All by Myself'. We drained our drinks as Secret Recipe's staff packed up tables around us. I was relieved Renik and Ally weren't detained in psych wards anymore, but I worried about their futures. All Renik knew was that in ten years' time, he wanted to be married with kids. He had always wanted kids; it's just that the option wasn't available when he was with other men.

'Well, without building a uterus,' he said, chuckling softly. 'Then when I was with my fiancée, I was sexually involved with her. So I have "tasted the other side" and I find it more satisfying.'

I nodded, thinking, *Ew*.

On the restaurant's PA, Céline Dion hit a high note – 'Don't wanna be all by myself, any-*mooooooooorrrrrrrre*' – and suddenly everything felt more dramatic and urgent.

'For me,' Ally said, 'it's not five or ten years, but three years. I desire to have kids, because I love kids. I want to have my own kids.'

For weeks after we talked, I was conflicted about what Renik and Ally had told me. Part of me wanted to reach out to them, show photos of me and my boyfriend – of *all* my gay and lesbian friends back home who were in good relationships – and tell them there was nothing wrong with any of us, that long-term relationships were possible. Another part of me felt that was unfair. Here in Malaysia, maybe that couldn't work. Renik and Ally weren't unintelligent or closed-off from the world – Renik had even lived overseas – but they had made a personal decision that homosexuality was wrong. They were happier, they said, and who was I to tell them they weren't?

Out of nowhere, Jerry had asked me: 'So Benjamin, what do *you* think about homosexuality?'

They all stared at me, suddenly interested. I sipped my drink. There wasn't anything left but ice, so I was sipping at air.

'What do you mean?' I asked.

'Why do *you* think people are homosexual?'

I didn't want to lie.

'Can I be honest? I mean, I know a lot of gay and lesbian people. And a lot of them – the guys especially – really feel they were born that way.'

'But do *you* believe they were?' Jerry asked.

'Of course I do,' I said. 'But you're all telling me how you *became* homosexual, and I have to believe that too. It's your story.'

Jerry looked down at his meal, disappointed. I'd spent all this time with them, at the church service and at the V-Meet. I'd heard Ally and Renik's stories. Had I learned *nothing*? Evidence of their work, after all, was all around me. Look at Ally. Look at Renik. Look at Jerry. *Look at Edmund.*

What else did it take?

*

In Malaysia's big cities, you didn't have to look far to find an overwhelmingly beautiful house of worship or religious monument. Every few blocks there were heritage-listed Christian churches or Hindu temples with gods and goddesses spilling from their walls, but it was the mosques that were most impressive. The really outstanding ones were in the north-east oil-rich state of Terengganu, a region that produced most of Malaysia's petroleum. Its capital, Kuala Terengganu, was a sleepy beachside city, lush with green forests and coastlines, and dotted with mansions. It boasted structures like the Crystal Mosque, encased in polished black glass. Another mosque appeared to float on water. Behind my hostel was a mosque so immaculately white, it was blinding in the midday sun. Five times a day, the calls to prayer were broadcast so loudly that the muezzins' mournful acapella suffused every corner of every street.

Hasbullah Wahidul Wahid Mustafar had risen before dawn for prayers every single day of his life. A smooth-faced, broadnosed and serious-looking man in his late twenties, Hasbullah's clothes were a study in monochrome: white collared shirt, black vest and black *mamah*, a stretch of cloth tied neatly around his scalp to signify his advanced level of Islamic study. He was a man of tradition, but he wasn't beyond wearing reflective aviator sunglasses and a chrome watch.

He prayed for his fellow man, for his work and his research, and he prayed for the people he was helping to find a path out of homosexuality. Because that's how Hasbullah regarded homosexuality: a maze through which to navigate, a spiritual conundrum, a puzzle that could be solved.

'Homosexuality is hard to grasp,' he'd tell me later. 'It's a challenge.'

Hasbullah felt he was just the person to unravel it.

Eighteen months earlier, Hasbullah had founded an organisation called the Malaysian Islamic Association of Homosexuality Research and Therapy. The organisation already had hundreds of clients. Most of them weren't homosexual, but siblings, friends or parents who were seeking guidance to help their spiritually corrupted family members. As far as Hasbullah knew, it was the first formal Islamic organisation in Malaysia – and possibly South-East Asia – devoted solely to researching a cure for homosexuality from an Islamic perspective.

Hasbullah hadn't known much about homosexuality himself, but when he was studying counselling at university in Kedah, he regularly encountered clients who spoke of their crippling attraction to the same sex. One of Hasbullah's first clients was a man who wept openly in Hasbullah's office, overcome with grief at his sexual desires for men. Hasbullah had never heard anything like it. The man had cried out to him – weeping and moaning, intensely anxious – 'Mister, help me! Help me, I want to stop this! I tried this and that, but nothing works!'

'They want to stop,' Hasbullah explained, 'but how can they stop?'

In that session, Hasbullah didn't know what to do. What the man was saying shocked him, but, as more and more people came to Hasbullah with the same problem, he began to find it fascinating.

'Did this stuff ever make you feel uncomfortable?' I asked.

'It didn't matter what their problem is,' he said. 'I'm ready to listen.'

Eventually, Hasbullah would ask them what they wanted to do about it. Invariably, the answer was the same: they didn't want to be attracted to the same sex.

Hasbullah had read some books and literature about homosexuality in the context of Islam, but had trouble finding any field research with homosexual people. There was no Islamic organisation dedicated to helping people with same-sex attractions. Hasbullah read online about an American Christian ex-gay organisation called NARTH and contacted them immediately with his plans to start something similar for Muslims. They gave very supportive advice.

Hasbullah and I met at Terengganu State Public Library, an unlikely architectural hybrid of arches, domes, cement and glass slopes. It looked as if a mosque had grown out of a government building. At the entrance was a giant water feature that looked as though a tree had exploded, with liquid gushing out of its mangled remains.

'Homosexuality is not a disease,' Hasbullah explained help-fully as we walked inside the library. 'Homosexuality is a *deviant behaviour*. Everybody is supposed to be on the normal curve, but the homosexuals are outliers. From an Islamic perspective, the Qur'an and the prophet said that homosexuality is wrong, so then it must be wrong. Even if the statistics were that *all* people are homosexual, it will always be wrong from an Islamic perspective.'

His association's members – fellow Muslim academics from psychology, counselling and other disciplines – were starting groundbreaking field work, he said. They needed raw data and anecdotal case studies of how prevalent this problem was among young Muslims. They needed to know what caused it and how to fix it. Fortunately, data was easy to come by. Because most of the association's members worked at universities, they had easy access to students for surveys. And Hasbullah's day job as a counsellor and chaplain at a private Islamic high school gave him regular access to children and teenagers.

When Hasbullah told me this, I must have looked surprised. 'I know,' Hasbullah said, smiling slightly. 'It's a bit evil, right?'

'You're collecting data off the kids?'

Hasbullah nodded, adding he had consent from all parties for his research. 'It's a good way for me to start venturing into how I can help people with this behaviour. Because I need proof.'

'Proof of what?'

Students at Hasbullah's school would come to him with their problems, about home, friends or study. Only some of them would have problems with their sexuality. Hasbullah would ask all students – regardless of their problems – to undertake a questionnaire called the Bem Sexual Role Inventory, a checklist invented by the psychologist Dr Sandra Lipsitz Bem in the early 1970s, fifty questions that would apparently demonstrate whether the person was more male or female. If the child deviated from the normal range, homosexuality was a strong possibility.

'Do the results necessarily mean they're homosexual, though?' I asked.

'No,' he said. 'But depending on the results, I might ask a student to come do another session with me. From that session, he might actually say, "Every night I think of how my friend used to do *this* to me."'

'Like what?' I asked.

'Touching, something like that.' Hasbullah put his hands together and looked solemnly at the floor, as if he was mentally running through evidence to solve a crime. 'If I can stabilise their emotions towards homosexuality, it can help them. It's so that they understand themselves, and understand why homosexuality is wrong.'

'So what sort of questions do you ask?'

'Do you consider yourself as man or woman?'

'Man,' I said.

Hasbullah smiled, embarrassed for me.

'*For example*, I mean,' he said. 'Or: "Do you like flowers more or sports more?"'

Who doesn't like flowers? I thought.

'If you say "flowers", you're more feminine.'

'Ah, okay.'

Hasbullah took me to meet one of his mentors, Dr Abdul Manam bin Mohamed, an academic at one of the leading Islamic universities in the state. He was both a theologist and counsellor, a senior faculty member whose knowledge of the Islamic faith informed all his work. With a stout cylindrical *kopiah* on his head, Dr bin Mohamed was a friendly gorilla-sized man. His hands were gigantic; his fingernails the size of coins. Hasbullah translated for us as we spoke in his office.

'Some students have come to me,' he said, 'and told me they have tendencies in homosexuality. But it's not in a severe level. It's just *mild.*'

He smiled and pinched his fingers together as if to demonstrate. *Only this much.*

Mild homosexuality, I wrote in my notebook, nodding.

'I believe the source of homosexuality is outside *and* inside,' the doctor said. 'Outside, because it's out there in the environment. The urge exists *inside*, of course, but if it's triggered by outside factors, it becomes "emerged". But there are particular cases where the source of homosexuality came from inside – not from outside – and in those cases, it's what in Islamic terms we would call …'

He looked at Hasbullah questioningly and slipped into hesitant English.

'… *satanic?*'

'Satanic!' I said, excited.

'Anyway, it's involved with Satan. There are different spiritual causes. One is satanic, the other is, like … *jin?*'

'Like a genie,' Hasbullah clarified.

'A genie,' I said, imagining a fabulous gay genie.

'Sort of like ghosts!' Dr bin Mohamed said happily. 'There *is* a spiritual element. There are ways in which spiritual entities enter a person.'

He explained that many young Muslim men and women had asked for his help, wanting to be freed from their homosexuality. The first and most important step, he said, was to identify people with these tendencies and separate them from 'the source' – each other. Young homosexuals and lesbians usually came to him in couples asking for help. Dr bin Mohamed explained it was important that all contact between them ceased immediately. They needed to dry out, so to speak. The second step was the 'purification of the heart' – *inabah*, a return to purity, a recovery – using a method Dr bin Mohamed had successfully trialled on people with drug addictions. It was through repetitive prayer and readings of the Qur'an that the spirit could be healed of vices.

When we walked out of Dr bin Mohamed's office, Hasbullah explained the methods in more detail. Hasbullah was really keen to use something called psychoacoustic therapy, where patients listened and recited the Qur'an continuously for marathon sessions, a technique that had yielded many success stories with drug addicts.

'What Dr Manam said was interesting,' I said. 'The idea that homosexuality comes from being overtaken –'

'Possessed.'

'– yeah, by a spirit. So he means, like a demon or something?'

Hasbullah nodded.

'Do you believe that?' I said.

'I believe what he said. Because in Islam, we believe in spiritual entities. There are bad ones and there are good ones. These bad entities cause bad things. They'll make you lose your memories, for example. But some people fight, and then they win. It's like the last prophet says: "Every problem in this world has a solution." This is one of them.'

*

The next morning, Hasbullah picked me up at 5.30 am to take me to morning prayers. As a treat, he took me to the floating mosque that I'd been admiring on our car trips together. It was a voluptuous dome-shaped building, surrounded by seawater that washed over a reef to form a natural lake. During high tide the mosque appeared to float on water. In the lazy dawn light, it looked both blue and orange, as if pulled from science fiction.

Crossing a tiled bridge, I joined the morning worshippers as they took off their shoes and walked inside, the men splitting off from the women. I took a seat on the floor towards the back, watching Hasbullah pray with his fellow men in a line, folding themselves like origami as they bowed, adopting prayer positions in unison. It felt peaceful watching them. I'd decided a while back that while I couldn't commit myself to a religion, I could never be a hardline atheist either. For all the horrors done in the name of religion, something about worship seemed almost fundamental and necessary.

After prayers, we got back into Hasbullah's car and drove for a while. Hasbullah asked me questions about Australia – the city where I lived, what the people were like, how many Malaysians lived there, people's religions – and naturally, homosexuality came up again. What were the Australian attitudes when it came to stuff like this?

'Well, in some parts of Australia,' I said, thinking of my home state Queensland, 'homosexuality was still against the law twenty years ago. Now they're talking about legalising marriage between men and men, and women and women. So I guess the changes have been pretty fast.'

Hasbullah looked ahead, concentrating on the road but listening intently.

'Do you ever think Malaysia might change too?' I asked.

He thought about it for a while. 'You don't know for certain what's going to happen in the future,' Hasbullah said. 'In Malaysia, there is political turmoil. They may change it and make it legal. It depends on the Islamic foundation of this country. Society in Malaysia is changing. Maybe ten years before, we never heard of these types of cases being brought up. But nowadays, it is one of the things discussed openly in forums like television.'

'What's the worst that could happen?' I asked.

'Worst-case scenario?' he said. 'There are countries, for example, where you can marry homosexually. In one house, you might have a son, Christian; a daughter, Muslim; a sister in Buddhism who is gay and unmarried.'

'You see that as too messy.'

Hasbullah nodded. He knew there was a long way to go before the Malaysian Islamic Association of Homosexuality Research and Therapy met his ambitions. But Hasbullah foresaw, in ten years from now, the association becoming the biggest religious organisation dedicated to addressing homosexuality in the Asia-Pacific region, and perhaps the premier Islamic authority on the topic in the world. Within the next few years, he wanted the association to run its own conference where international delegates could share information and develop their own methods for addressing homosexuality. They would create information packs for Malaysian schools and students and provide formal, specialised training for counsellors and psychologists. They would start up camps and retreats to help people of all ages battle their sexual demons. Considering that he'd already built up a national network of hundreds of members in under eighteen months, I didn't doubt his drive.

Even on his days off, Hasbullah kept recruiting new members, including young people from all intellectual disciplines. The broader the skills base, he reasoned, the more professional and robust the organisation would be. The people he approached often didn't know how to respond. They would stare at him silently and would, as Hasbullah put it, ponder.

'And what do you think they're pondering about?'

'I'm not sure. Maybe they are thinking, "Is it okay to research on this topic?" People don't *do* this, right?'

'You are.'

Hasbullah allowed himself to grin.

'It's not common,' he said. '*Yet.*'

'But it will be?'

Hasbullah nodded, determined and serene. 'It will be.'

Hasbullah understood there could be controversy – he had

read about protests against Christian ex-gay groups like NARTH – but he also felt controversy could only be a good thing.

'If there are people supporting me, who think like I do, there also has to be people who hate what I do,' he said. 'It makes the world complete.'

Setting up the association was only the first step. Right now, Hasbullah was applying to study psychology at a leading university in Chicago. He had been accepted once before, but hadn't raised sufficient funds. He felt his work with the association would look good on his latest application. It was pioneering work after all.

We pulled up to a red light. Out of nowhere, Hasbullah said, 'Homosexuality, if not controlled, can destroy the harmony of a family.'

He said it firmly, almost angrily. Confused, I looked up and saw what had triggered that outburst. Above us was a billboard for a whitegoods company, showing a smiling Caucasian family – two parents, a son and a daughter – laughing in the breeze of their portable air-conditioning unit.

'That's why the issue cannot be left out of the mainstream,' Hasbullah said. 'I don't know how it feels – I've never been a homosexual – but being able to understand them a little now, I know it's important. If it's not contained, it will be broken families, leading to more deviant behaviour.'

We sat in silence, waiting for the light to turn green. It seemed to take forever. Finally, we drove past more mosques and lakes, past thatches of forest and a gigantic sign built into a hill that featured the Arabic script for Allah over the words *'Peliharakanlah Terengganu'*: 'May Allah bless Terengganu.'

'It's scary,' he said firmly.

I nodded, now watching him a little warily from the corner

of my eye. 'It's scary,' I said, echoing him.

*

Gay Muslims were easy to find in Malaysia, but that didn't mean they felt comfortable speaking on the public record. To criticise Islam openly was a crime under sharia law, a code that bound Muslims in Malaysia and worked as a parallel system to the country's secular laws. It was easy enough to find out whether someone was Muslim: everyone's religious status was stated on their government-issued identity card. If you wanted the word 'Islam' removed from your ID, you had to go to the National Registration Department and the sharia court and declare officially that you were *murtad* – 'out of Islam' – meaning you had either left the faith or conspired against it. Some interpreted that declaring yourself *murtad* was, paradoxically, a serious crime under sharia – worse, one gay Muslim man told me, than admitting you were gay. It was easier to leave Islam on your ID card and simply shut up about your sexuality.

One gay man I spoke to had studied Islam so thoroughly that he was a qualified imam, but he didn't feel *religiously* Muslim anymore. His problem, he told me, wasn't with Islam itself, but the brand of Islam practised in Malaysia, one that didn't have room for critical thinking when it came to issues like homosexuality. All over the world, there were many Islams, but he felt the type practised in Malaysia proposed one unquestionable version. If he'd been born in the US or UK, things might have been different and he might still identify as a Muslim *and* gay. Over there, he knew there were liberal mosques, but when you lived in a country where the teachings couldn't be contested, there was no room to move. You had to make a choice between your faith and your sexuality.

And if you didn't make a choice, people would make it for you, and that could be dangerous. Azwar Ismail was one gay Muslim man happy for me to use his name, mainly because it had been used so much in the media, especially during that period when people sent him death threats.

An engineer by day and published poet by night, Azwar was a short man with tiny delicate hands, well groomed and urbane in Tom Ford spectacles. The oldest of five children, Azwar was raised in a family devoted to Islam. They prayed five times a day, his sisters wore hijabs, no one wore shorts (they would scandalously rebel against this after high school) and they were banned from going to the cinema.

But when Azwar hit his late twenties, he started coming out as gay to close friends. To his surprise, he didn't get too many hostile reactions. It felt as though his world was decompressing and loosening up. *What the hell*, he thought. He had already come out; he might as well do everything else blacklisted by Islam. For the first time, Azwar went clubbing and drank alcohol, but he still prayed. He also started hanging out with Kuala Lumpur's tight-knit gay community of artists and activists. When Malaysia's most prominent gay organiser, Pang Khee Teik, started a YouTube project inspired by America's 'It Gets Better' campaign, Azwar volunteered to be the one Muslim guy who would talk publicly about what it was like to be gay within Islam.

Azwar's video was always going to attract the most attention, but no one suspected that it would score over 140,000 views on YouTube in a week. Comments poured in, most of them negative and hateful. People told Azwar he was going to hell and others offered to take him there themselves. Many posted verses from the Qur'an condemning sodomy, followed by graphic death threats. After Azwar's video made the news, even Malaysia's cabinet minister for Islamic affairs chimed in, stating he was concerned gay activists were now promoting homosexuality in Malaysia, and hinted at the government taking 'appropriate action' to stop things like Azwar's video polluting the image of Islam. A prominent Islamic cleric said Azwar had 'derided his own dignity and Islam in general'.

Azwar's extended family saw newspaper clippings and called his immediate family to ask whether they knew he was gay. They hadn't known, but they did now. Scared, Azwar sought legal advice to ensure he couldn't be charged for sodomy under sharia or secular criminal law.

In the months this was happening, Azwar's own relationship to Islam was changing fast.

'When I came out, I was still very religious. At that time, I was thinking, *Maybe Islam isn't fixed into one view.* But after some time, I couldn't stand it anymore. Deep inside, I told myself, *If you want to be a Muslim, you don't have to be a Muslim like* those *people. You have your own understanding of Islam.* But whenever I go to the mosque, in the sermon they always talk about negative things. All this hatred. I can't find the authentic Islam that I want, even though I know it exists. In some parts in Indonesia, they have mosques that are very liberal: liberal Muslims.'

He paused, shoulders slumped. 'We just don't have that here.'

*

What about liberal Christians? Was there a counter to RLM? Some gay Christians were trying their best. One Malaysian man told me he had reconciled being gay with Christianity by reading the Bible closely and concluding that being gay was okay, as long as he never had anal sex – 'unholy penetration', he called it – with another man. Another Christian – an ethnic Chinese pastor named Joe Pang – had started Malaysia's first gay-friendly church in Kuala Lumpur. Joe still remembered seeing another man at a Christian gathering tell his story of being both Christian and gay.

'Every night, I kneel down and ask for forgiveness,' the man had told the crowd.

Watching the man tell his story, Joe had wept openly, feeling the man's pain as if it was his own.

'Like him, I would kneel down in my room and cry,' Joe said. 'I'd say, "God, forgive me." Every time I masturbated, I asked for forgiveness. It was a very terrible life.'

Joe was thirty years old now and had the balloon-like face of a kid. His church – the Good Samaritan Metropolitan Community Church – wasn't really a church, but a leased mezzanine of a café with high white walls and blond timber furniture. The lease was about to expire. I arrived for Sunday worship completely drenched from the bruising rain outside. Only a dozen or so gay men and a single lesbian had gathered for worship that day, and Joe looked sheepish. He told me there were weeks the congregation swelled to sixty; other times it went right down to ten. This was a particularly bad turnout.

The service was pleasant enough – a man leading us through songs on acoustic guitar; the entire sermon typed and projected on a screen for a deaf member – but after the service, there was an urgent meeting about the church's future. This was Good Samaritan's last week in the café and they needed to find a new space. On paper slips, church members were told to write down how much they'd be willing to donate to the church each month, before they discussed the pros and cons of the different places they could rent.

On the other side of town, the ex-gay organisation Pursuing Liberty Under Christ – which often taught schoolchildren about the perils of homosexuality – was flush with cash from Christian churches throughout Malaysia. Joe's church was financially anaemic in comparison.

Whenever stories about ex-gay organisations broke around the world, readers often assumed these were fringe groups, freakish, anachronistic relics surely receding in numbers and influence. But there was no stopping the movement. In the Christian world, what started as an American ex-gay movement in the late '70s had given rise to a global network of ex-gay ministries called Exodus International. And although two of its most prominent members – co-founder Michael Bussee and church leader Gary Cooper – eventually renounced the movement altogether, infamously (and spectacularly) leaving their wives for each other, the movement had continued. It remained particularly huge in Asia, and it wasn't just RLM and PLUC in Malaysia. There were Bagong Pag-Asa and the Pathway to Freedom Counselling Center (both in the Philippines), Rainbow 7 (Taiwan) and Choices (Singapore), as well as countless other independent organisations, some that were only just starting up. They were there to help, but you had to want to save yourself or nothing would ever change. They never advertised their services, but if you needed them, there they were. And wasn't that comforting to know?

Who can say 'Amen'?

MYANMAR

In which four in five of the HIV-positive people we interview will probably die from lack of access to lifesaving medication. Key numbers: 65 (the minimum number of US cents you might pay for sex with a man in Yangon); 42 (how many times likelier homosexual men are to contract HIV in this country than their fellow citizens); 2008 (the year Myanmar's biggest distributor of lifesaving HIV medication was forced to stop taking new clients).

*

PEOPLE IN MYANMAR LAUGH at the strangest things. By strange, I mean horrific. Talk to locals long enough, and you'll hear them grimly joke about their poverty, Cyclone Nargis, HIV rates, dying people and even – in hushed tones – the weird, unending nightmare of the Political Situation. In my first week in Yangon, I watched a toddler shit himself by the kerbside, giggling deliriously as liquid poo crawled down his legs and pooled on the cement, the entire time laughing and laughing and laughing and *dear God why wasn't anyone cleaning up after this child?* Later, I passed an elderly woman who was forced to beg because both her hands had been sliced off clean at the wrists. After I gave her some money, almost in tears, she smiled gratefully and held up her stumps as if to say, *Eh, what can you do?*

Death could be funny too. Local hospitals, when pushed beyond capacity, would sometimes dump the dying elsewhere, such as outside the downtown YMCA. I guessed the hospital had hoped the Christian organisation would take one particular man in, but instead he spent his last days by the YMCA entrance, sweating and moaning in the baking heat, shrivelled to bone from dehydration, his *longyi* barely tied around his waist and his balls exposed for the world to see. YMCA residents and strangers watched him die. Some walked around him and pretended not to notice, while others took pity and left a cupcake next to him. Maybe they thought the calories would help. Stories like these were so awful, so beyond the realm of decency, that people who told me them – locals, expatriates and foreign workers who had obviously been in this country too long – couldn't help but laugh while shaking their heads at the hideousness of it all.

If you were a dying person in Myanmar, it was most likely you had contracted one of the big three diseases there: malaria, tuberculosis or HIV. Kyaw Myint had worked in the HIV public health sector for the past decade, often representing Myanmar in high-level talks with UN agencies. At his new NGO's head-quarters, he led me through the basic maths of the situation: roughly 240,000 people in Myanmar were living with HIV right now and 30 to 40 per cent of them needed life-saving antiretrovirals (ARTs) urgently. Only one in five had any chance of getting them, he explained, and –

'Hang on,' I said.

On my notepad, I drew a small circle and filled it in with black.

'So if these are the number of antiretrovirals available in the entire country –' I started.

'Yes,' Kyaw Myint said.

'– but you've got *this* many people with HIV who need them ...'

I drew a much larger white circle around the black circle.

'Yes, yes,' he said, nodding.

'Then what happens to *those* people?' I asked. I pointed to the empty space between the circles, all the HIV-positive people who needed ARTs and weren't going to get them. Looking back now, I see the answer was obvious. Kyaw Myint stifled a laugh and leaned in close, like a dad sharing a conspiratorial joke with his kid.

'They *die*,' he whispered. 'They're going to *die*!'

Kyaw Myint laughed, which I found unsettling. I didn't want to be rude, so I awkwardly laughed with him.

'Ha, ha?' I said nervously.

Between 15,000 and 25,000 people in Myanmar are dying from a lack of ARTs in any given year? In an epidemic described by UN agencies and international NGOs as one of the worst in Asia? In a country that was estimated to have the worst government spending on health *in the entire world*? Hilarious.

Clearly, I had a lot to learn.

*

Myanmar had once been the largest rice supplier and richest country in South-East Asia. You wouldn't know it now. At last count, Myanmar's GDP per capita – a general measure of living standards – stood above Afghanistan's but below North Korea's and the former Sudan's. On average, Burmese people could expect to live to the age of sixty-two.

'Our country is a very *poor* country,' Kyaw Myint said, shaking his head. 'Sometimes the government calls it a "developing country", but it's not "developing". It's the *least developed* country. The lowest.'

When it came to money in people's pockets, Myanmar had become one of the poorest nations in Asia. We were talking about literal money in pockets here: paper notes were the only way to buy and sell things. When I arrived, ATMs and credit card facilities didn't exist. Foreign-owned banks had jumped ship years ago, and state-owned banks were notorious for draining money out of people's accounts without explanation, so most people hoarded money at home. As a result, Myanmar's kyat paper currency had been through so many hands that the notes felt like used tissue paper and were held together with tape. Some notes had mould growing on them.

You were rich if you owned a mobile phone, and most people made phone calls on landlines or improvised public booths – home landlines perched on plastic tables or taped to trees, with someone monitoring the cost of your call. Less than 1 per cent of the population had internet access. There would be no Burmese Spring here anytime soon.

Yangon might have been displaced as the country's official capital, but it was still its most populated city and commercial heart. It was a charming stinker, a grand hymn to bad civic maintenance and disintegrating basic amenities. Yangon's garbage collection system was staffed by crooked-backed adults and crusty-footed kids, who should have been in school but who swept the cement with large brooms and picked up wet, rancid garbage from kerbsides with their bare hands.

The place was full of rotting life: fruit-sellers and hawkers worked on footpaths that looked as smashed as a boxer's mouth, the pavers sitting at odd angles, stained red from spat-out betel nut, Myanmar's drug of choice. It was dangerously easy to fall into an open sewer.

Still, if you could extend your gaze past the cement rubble

and the open drains smelling of horror, there was evidence of Myanmar's former glory everywhere. In Yangon and all over the country, golden pagodas – domes and spires sometimes plated with tonnes of solid gold, some encased with real rubies and emeralds – shone like beacons. They rose up in unexpected places, punching through Yangon's urban mess or Mandalay's stretching fields, like the highest towers of a long-buried city triumphantly pushing its way above ground.

In Yangon, I stayed near a pagoda called the Sule Paya, a golden monument magnificently out of place in the middle of the city's busiest traffic roundabout. On my first morning, I crossed the pedestrian overpass and noticed something interesting: men were cruising each other for sex everywhere around me. It was happening on the overpass itself, the public toilets on either side and the tea house downstairs. Later, I'd discover the cruisers were each drawn to different hotspots for specific types of trade. The cement roadside benches were for older men, while younger men used the pedestrian bridges. The ones after quick sex ventured into the foul-smelling public toilets.

One afternoon, two volunteer staff members of a national organisation supporting men who have sex with men (MSMs) led me and my friend David – a young, ginger Australian academic who spoke Burmese – through the cruising spots. I won't name the organisation for reasons that will become obvious. One of the volunteers, whom I'll call KT, was gangly thin and flamingly camp. He wore white plastic glasses that highlighted his dark face, and a tight white V-neck t-shirt that clung to his ribby chest. His ears were pierced several times – one of the studs was a rainbow triangle – and he sported a rainbow wristband. KT said his family did not know he was gay. How they didn't know would remain an enduring mystery to me. KT was also HIV-positive. His family didn't know that either.

KT's superior was a man I'll call Godfrey. Godfrey was a Burmese man who didn't speak much English but was warm and lovable and physically humungous. Godfrey had a square-ish double chin and the body of a retired steroid-fed quarterback who had gone soft around the edges. With a booming laugh, he told us about a hot man he'd recently been cruising whom he *desperately* wanted to fuck. Godfrey and KT joked with each other in Burmese, before showing photos of an attractive, smooth-faced man on Godfrey's mobile phone.

'He's handsome,' I said. 'This is the man you've been cruising?'

'No, no,' KT explained. 'This is Godfrey's *husband*.'

'Husband?' I asked.

Gay guys in Myanmar, KT explained, called their boyfriends their 'husband'. Godfrey's cruising was making his husband very unhappy, and I said I could understand why. We laughed, before Godfrey asked me bluntly whether I was interested in fucking Burmese men.

'*My* husband wouldn't be very happy about that,' I said.

Godfrey's laugh filled the street. KT linked arms with me as if we were teenagers on a second date. When we crossed the overpass near Sule, guys who recognised KT and Godfrey came squealing up to us, asking me where I was from and what I was doing here, saying I was *asin* (handsome) and 'cute-cute'. Before I could thank them for the compliment, they demanded in no uncertain terms to know the size of my cock. In Myanmar, no one was interested in length, instead asking about my penis width by putting their thumb and forefinger in increasingly bigger circles – *This big? This big?* – while continuing to stroke my arm. Was my cock *ap* (small), *medium* or *cake* (large): as wide as a can of Myanmar Beer? Everyone wanted to know.

'My penis is okay?' I said.

'And are you *queer*?' they asked in patchy English.

'Am I queer?' I said. 'Yes, I'm queer.'

'No!' they said. '*Korean!* Are you *Korean*?'

Several blocks from the Sule overpass was a square pedestrian bridge growing out of the corner of an elevated restaurant whose name, Lion World, was spelled out in green neon. Yangon's male prostitutes hustled for cash outside Lion World every night. One feminine sex worker shyly approached me and raspily said hello. She had the face of a pre-teen and the nicotine-scorched voice of a grandmother. When I said hello back, she smiled with betel-stained teeth.

Another boy looked between twelve and fourteen years old, and that was a generous estimate. He wore a black t-shirt with a Union Jack screenprint and looked as if he'd only just gone through puberty. I refused to believe he was also working on the bridge. It was obscene that someone so young ... Surely he was just loitering ... No one that young could be ...

'He is also a sex worker,' KT said, reading my mind.

'Are you sure?' I said slowly.

'Of course, of course.'

The kid's story was that he was seventeen, but no one seriously believed that. Along with the others, he scanned the passers-by for potential trade, trying to look cool.

Sex work came cheap in these parts. Male sex workers in Yangon charged between 3000 and 7000 kyats (four to nine US dollars) per hour, with the client also paying the hourly rate for the guesthouse. If it was a particularly desperate night, the workers would sometimes go right down to 2000 kyats (2.5 US dollars) or even 500 kyats (sixty-five US cents).

A lot of these boys came from the countryside, which was far poorer than the cities. Their families often had six, eight or even twelve children, with every new arrival making them poorer. Contraception, especially the pill, was a rarity, and basic sex education didn't exist either in homes or schools.

So these boys would take their chances and hitch bus rides to Yangon, some of them without even saying goodbye to their families. They found work in the city's tea houses, hokey snack restaurants that paid their workers criminally low rates but provided food and accommodation. Unused to the 24/7 pressure, a lot of the boys would lose their jobs quickly before realising they couldn't go back home. Some didn't want to return; others just didn't know which bus could take them back to their family. Some would wander onto the pedestrian overpass and encounter the other boys selling themselves for sex. This was a potentially lucrative trade, they would realise. Because when you've lost everything else, you've always got one final asset to sell, especially if you're young.

As KT, Godfrey, David and I gossiped over tall glasses of Myanmar Beer, I watched boys disappear from the bridge. One guy in his twenties wasn't having any luck, despite his teen-model good looks. The painfully young Union Jack–wearing kid had disappeared long ago. New talent was always in demand. Parent-like, I wondered whether they were carrying condoms.

Meanwhile, KT talked animatedly about how he'd recently broken up with his husband and was feeling sad, but, to be honest, 'also kind of horny!' Outside on the overpass, KT had seen a new face he thought was cute: a kid who looked sweet and terrifyingly rough at the same time, like a Rottweiler puppy. The kid sported a mini-mohawk and two huge Gothic-script tattoos of English words on his forearms. One said 'PUNK'; the other said 'FUCK'. These were the kind of tattoos that made you wish his mother had run screaming into the tattoo parlour and pulled him out of there. Red-haired David later told me he'd met Punkfuck previously at the cruising tea house under the Sule overpass. When David asked why he'd chosen those words for his tattoos, Punkfuck said that they summed him up well. He was a punk who liked to fuck.

We finished our beers so KT could get Punkfuck's rates. The other sex workers gravitated towards us too, just in case. I smiled at them and waved, trying to defuse the sexual tension by indicating I was a deranged foreign idiot.

Punkfuck turned out to be expensive by Yangon standards. He charged 7000 kyat (nine US dollars) per hour. KT came back to us, nervous and anxious, asking us whether we thought it was a good price.

'I don't know,' I said. 'By Myanmar's standards, you mean?'

'He's more expensive than others,' KT said. 'He knows he can charge more.'

'You're going to have sex with him *tonight?*'

'Why?' KT asked, panicked. 'Do you think he's too expensive?'

David and I looked at each other.

'Ah, do you have the money?'

KT said he had the money, but still thought it was a lot. Punkfuck leaned against the bridge and surveyed the Yangon skyline as though he didn't care either way. But this deal would be important to him. Getting work was the difference between sleeping with a full stomach or not. KT walked over to Punk-fuck for another quiet conversation, before Punkfuck nodded and disappeared.

'Where did he go?' I asked.

'We're meeting him down the street,' KT said.

KT, David and I left Godfrey behind, who was animatedly

talking to another of the working boys. The three of us walked down the overpass stairs together as KT's nervous chatter bounced around.

'He's so cute!' KT said. 'I like his hair! Didn't you think his hair was *cute?*'

'Um,' I said.

'How thick do you think his cock is?'

'Jesus, I don't know!' I said.

David smiled at the exchange.

'And how big are *you*, Ben?' KT asked. 'Tell me again!'

'I didn't tell you the first time!'

KT laughed. 'Oh, I'm *excited*,' he said. 'I haven't had him before. He's new, I think.' It was only later that I realised KT was implying he'd already had sex with all the others.

Punkfuck met us in the middle of the busy main street. I smiled at him, but his expression was unreadable. *Poor guy*, I thought. I hoped he didn't think all three of us were going to have sex with him at once. Punkfuck crossed the road to a guesthouse's grimy elevator entrance.

'You have a condom, right?' I asked KT.

KT gave me an exasperated look. David and I said we'd wait for him at a nearby noodle stall, waving him off like parents whose child was being bused off to school camp. *Have fun!* We watched them disappear, the elevator doors closing on Punkfuck's sombre face and KT's big gay smile.

David and I stood side by side, not saying much.

'Well,' I said. 'This is weird.'

David, a soulful guy who always seemed deep in thought, nodded.

'Yep,' he said. 'It's pretty weird.'

At the noodle stall, we sat on the kids' plastic stools they had lined up on the roadside. We ordered some noodles that came out swimming in vegetable oil and tasted like metal. Washing the oily noodles down with tea, I thought about what could be happening between KT and Punkfuck at that very moment. KT had told us he liked getting fucked, so Punkfuck probably had him bent over the bed. I was more worried about Punkfuck than KT, to be honest. What kind of life led someone to have PUNK and FUCK tattooed on his forearms and charge nine US dollars to repeatedly place himself inside strangers?

KT wandered out less than half an hour later, even though he'd booked Punkfuck for the full hour. His clothes didn't look any different or ruffled, and his hair didn't look wet from a shower. He just looked blissfully post-coital. Punkfuck wasn't with him. I adopted a faux-concerned parental voice.

'You used that condom, right?'

'Of course!' KT said, grinning with big white teeth.

We hailed a taxi to take us home and we drove in silence. I wondered what David and KT had on their minds. Even though my windowless Yangon guesthouse smelled of mildew and garlic, I just wanted to get to bed. It was only the next day that I even questioned how appropriate it was for HIV community workers to have sex with the people they were supposed to be protecting.

*

Let's take a brief detour through a Beginner's Guide to Homosexual Slang in Myanmar. Repeat after me. *Achauk* (pronounced 'ah-chowk') is a handy, all-encompassing term for any man who has sex with other men. Use it carefully, because it's the Burmese equivalent of 'faggot': derogatory when straight people say it, but used freely between gay guys as a term of bitchy affection.

Then there are three subcategories of *achauk*, each of which comes with a defined sex role. *Apwint* ('ah-pwint', meaning 'open') are Myanmar's queens, who live and dress as women and are always – *always* – on the receiving end of anal sex. The femme sex worker with the bloody smile on the Lion World overpass would have identified as *apwint*. Many are on female hormones for breast development, but few undergo genital sex reassignment. Even if they wanted it, it was unthinkably expensive in this country. *Apwint* were often found dancing in *nat* spirit celebrations or working in hair salons and make-up parlours. If you were an urban Burmese bride-to-be, it'd probably be *apwint* who would design your dress, do your make-up and curl your hair on the day.

Apwint never couple with each other. They team up either with *thange* ('tongue-eh') – macho guys who are relatively open about their sexuality and always on top in sex – or *abone* ('ah-bone', meaning 'hiders'), straight-acting, masculine-presenting men who can be versatile with sexual positions. As their name suggests, *abone* are usually closeted when it comes to their sexual identity.

Some English vernacular has slipped through too. As we've learned already, if you have a steady boyfriend, he is your *husband*. *Gay* is interchangable with *apwint*, while *homo* is the term for *abone* or *thange* guys. If you're a foreigner, don't confuse locals by introducing yourself as 'gay' unless you're wearing make-up or jewellery, and flailing your hands about.

Most of this slang was harmless and funny, but there was also slang for tremendously unfunny things too, such as contracting HIV, which happened often enough in Myanmar to warrant its own suite of euphemisms. If a guy received a positive HIV diagnosis, he might say he'd gotten *thazin*, the name of a native Burmese wildflower that had become synonymous with HIV here, since Médecins Sans Frontières Holland – one of the few organisations in Myanmar that both tested for HIV/AIDS and treated patients with life-saving ARTs – ran clinics named after the flower.

Men might also say they had just won the Myanmar Academy Award for Best Male Actor, gallows-humour code for contracting HIV. When guys explained the slang's origin to me, they laughed uproariously. 'See, the Academy Awards is so hard to get, but HIV is so easy!' they said. 'This is why it's funny. See, you got the Academy!'

'Ha, ha?' I said again.

After the evening with KT, Godfrey and Dave, I returned to the same cruising site during the day with Kyaw Swe, a peer educator with PSI, another NGO focused on preventing HIV. Kyaw Swe distributed condoms, talked to people about their problems and invited them into PSI's drop-in centre for HIV tests. Not all sex workers protected themselves during sex, he told me. I was still troubled by what had happened with KT and Punkfuck. I told Kyaw Swe the story and asked for his opinion.

'This was after hours?' Kyaw Swe asked. 'He was off-duty from his job?'

I nodded. Kyaw Swe thought about it.

'Well, I don't see any problem then,' he said.

Kyaw Swe was handsome: lean and ropey with dark skin, spiked hair and black glasses that framed sad-looking eyes. He was still young – thirty, only a little older than me – but already had two sons aged ten and eight. His eldest was really smart, he said, and had won all sorts of academic awards, especially in maths.

Although Kyaw Swe now had kids and a wife, he had once

been a sex worker, having worked the same streets as Punkfuck for half a decade. He had fallen into sex work by accident. As a teenager, he sold betel nuts in Yangon's local markets for pitiable pay. The markets were a drawcard for tourists, and one night, two American guys took a shine to Kyaw Swe. They offered him money to have sex with them – at least 100 US dollars, maybe more – that converted to a wad of kyats so thick that it supported him for months.

The money Kyaw Swe brought in from sex work was far more reliable than what he made selling betel, so when he got married, his wife let him continue. The idea of him fucking men for cash upset her, but this was Myanmar and their options were limited.

Kyaw Swe was twenty-three when a German client asked him for a tour of things in Yangon that foreigners wouldn't usually see. Kyaw Swe took him to a downtown pagoda festival that attracted huge numbers of locals. There were children everywhere, some of them desperately poor, like the two boys – aged around eight or ten – who caught the German tourist's eye.

'Oh, they are lovely,' the German client said to Kyaw Swe. 'They look very poor, though. Can you bring them to me? I'd like to help them.'

After he introduced the German man to the two boys, Kyaw Swe didn't see them again. But when he was arrested for facilitating child prostitution, he discovered what had happened next: the German tourist raped the boys; he loaded them with money; the boys' parents asked where the money had come from; the police were called in.

'I just thought he wanted to say hello and help the children,' Kyaw Swe said.

Kyaw Swe was sent to Myanmar's notorious Insein Prison for two years. The cells were stinking hot and Kyaw Swe slept shoulder to shoulder on the cement floor with his fellow prisoners, 120 people to a small room. Some Insein inmates were forced to crush rocks, like prisoners in cartoons, making rubble for bitumen and paving. Some, like Kyaw Swe, were assigned to work in lung-corroding mines that were prone to collapsing. Every day, they worked from seven in the morning to six at night with a one-hour break for lunch. When I asked him to describe prison, Kyaw Swe responded in a dead voice.

'It was like hell,' he said.

After his release, Kyaw Swe no longer saw the allure of sex work, but didn't feel he had much choice. He went back to the bridge outside Lion World, but now there was more competition, less pay and new police crackdowns. It wasn't long before HIV peer educators intercepted Kyaw Swe on the bridge. Kyaw Swe educated himself about HIV and sexual health at PSI's Top Centre, meeting other sex workers in a social space for the first time. Soon, PSI offered him a paid job to educate his peers. For the first time, he was thinking about the future for himself, his wife and two boys. He wanted to own a small business, like a tea house, and have one day off a week. He wanted a simpler life with time to hang out with his family and – because he was *thange* – his boyfriend on the side.

To the management at PSI, Kyaw Swe was the perfect candidate for a peer educator: he knew how to talk to working boys. PSI's safe-sex message might have been easy to deliver, but it was a hard sell convincing the boys to use a condom every time. When Kyaw Swe was a sex worker, he often had to pay for the guesthouse and the hotel deposit.

'If you're a customer, you might pay me 10,000. And then you'll say, "And if you *don't* use a condom, I will give you an extra 10,000 kyats." How can I decide? I would take the money, because this short-term problem is more important.'

It was a common attitude in Myanmar. Existence was so hand to mouth that the idea of later getting sick and dying wasn't even worth thinking about. You literally couldn't *afford* to think about it.

If it hadn't been for PSI, Kyaw Swe would still have been out there, often having unprotected sex. Statistically speaking, if he'd kept on working the streets, it was likely that he would have contracted HIV by now.

*

Myths about HIV were prevalent in Myanmar. The most pervasive belief was that if someone had HIV, you would be able to *see* evidence of it. The logic was messy but understandable: if someone was incubating a deadly virus, then surely that person would look as though they were dying. They would look weak and bony, and have lesions that oozed pus. In most people's minds HIV looked like, well, AIDS.

These beliefs were held even by more-educated Burmese. Zin Min Htet was thirty-two years old and an engineer with a PhD. He was smart, had held a government engineering post for years and had even been accepted into international postgraduate courses. When I met him in Yangon, he was dressed like a businessman on casual Friday, wearing an ironed, pink-collared shirt and smelling of cologne.

Zin Min Htet was also HIV-positive. Originally, we'd been scheduled to talk about his work for Myanmar's International HIV/AIDS Alliance, but during a walk to a hotel bar, Zin Min Htet told me the story of how he'd gotten HIV from a long-term boyfriend. The boyfriend had since gone off to work in

Singapore, and Zin Min Htet had no way of contacting him. Zin Min Htet wasn't sure if the boyfriend knew he was HIV-positive.

'I didn't suspect him,' he said, 'because he looked very handsome and strong.'

'Macho, you mean?'

He nodded.

'And you didn't think anyone like that could get HIV?' I said.

He shook his head. 'I wrongly stereotyped that HIV cannot exist in a person who is handsome. This is my misconception.'

Zin Min Htet was *abone* like his boyfriend – versatile and masculine-presenting. They both assumed HIV exclusively affected *apwint,* transgender or feminine men. These were the men usually targeted for HIV tests by NGOs, which came back to sex roles: *apwint* were always on the receiving end of anal sex. Zin Min Htet said he'd learned how HIV was spread only after becoming HIV-positive himself – far too late.

Zin Min Htet grew up in the northernmost part of the Yangon region, in a township called Mingaladon, but moved to the city to attend university. Afterwards, he got a job with Myanmar's Ministry of Science and Technology, regularly transferring from city to city. When he was offered the opportunity to study in Germany and India, he had a mandatory health check, including blood test, standard policy for anyone intending to leave the country. Zin Min Htet was posted in Mandalay at the time and didn't think there would be anything wrong with the results.

But he *had* been getting weird fevers on and off, with increasing frequency. He thought it was just his immune system playing up. When he went back to Yangon's National Health Laboratory to get the test results, they told him he was HIV-

positive. The doctor gave him the results unceremoniously –
without counselling, referrals or words of comfort – then let
him go. His doctor did say one thing, though. Because he knew
Zin Min Htet worked for the ministry, he told him very clearly:
'Don't talk about your blood test results to the government.'

Perhaps it was the shock of the results, or just a coincidence
in timing, but his fever took hold properly soon after his diagnosis. Zin Min Htet's lymph nodes swelled up, his body temperature spiked and constant diarrhoea left him badly dehydrated.
He was away from home and on his own in a Yangon hostel. He
called in sick from work, closed the doors to his dorm room
and stayed in bed for a week.

At the end of that week, one of Zin Min Htet's friends came
to visit, worried about his health. Knowing he looked ravaged,
Zin Min Htet told his friend he was HIV-positive. His friend
didn't flinch, and said his sister worked at Médecins Sans Frontières Holland.

Staff at MSF Holland's *Thazin* clinic diagnosed Zin Min
Htet as also having tuberculosis, a disease that commonly
affects Burmese people with HIV. It's known as an opportunistic infection, because it's easy to infect an HIV-weakened body.
For the first few weeks, Zin Min Htet was on powerful anti-TB
drugs. In the meantime, his CD4 count – the gauge of his
immune system's strength – was plummeting, but he would
have to wait another four months to go on ARTs, since they
couldn't overlap with TB medications.

As Zin Min Htet recovered from TB, he tried sorting out the
logistics of his job. His government post was in Mandalay, an
overnight bus ride from Yangon, but he'd need to stay in Yangon
to commit himself to his forthcoming ART regime. If he slipped
off the strict ART schedule, he would have to start it again.

There were far fewer ART supplies in Mandalay than in Yangon, and no guarantees he would receive his required dosage.

Zin Min Htet's work supervisor was the rector of Yangon University, someone with connections and power, so he took a gamble. He told her he was HIV-positive and asked her whether he could work in Yangon. Troubled, she urged him to disclose his status to the minister responsible for his job. She hoped that the ministry would be able to issue him with an official transfer.

Zin Min Htet sat down and wrote the letter, ignoring his doctor's advice never to tell the government that he was HIV-positive. For the next eight months, he stayed in Yangon on a temporary transfer, started ART treatments and worked as a university lecturer while he completed his PhD. He recovered from the TB, and despite the initial side effects of the ARTs, his health returned.

Then Zin Min Htet's professor received a phone call from the minister himself. Zin Min Htet's file had come to his personal attention, and he demanded that Zin Min Htet take long-term sick leave from his ministry job. Zin Min Htet could be reaccepted into his ministry role, the minister said, but only once his blood tests came back HIV-negative. Everyone knew that was impossible. The message was blunt: *Don't come back.* Knowing this part of his life was over, Zin Min Htet folded and resigned.

Zin Min Htet caught the bus back home to Mingaladon. His parents, two younger brothers and one sister still lived together in relative poverty, and the family relied on Zin Min Htet's income to survive. It was impossible to explain why he'd lost his job without also disclosing his HIV status. He braced himself and told them the news.

'Their reaction was good,' he said. 'They take care of me. But they don't want me to be MSM.'

I laughed. 'So they're okay with you having HIV, but they're not okay with you being an MSM.'

He laughed too. 'Yes,' he said.

Timing was on his side, though. Zin Min Htet looked healthy, and the ART treatment meant his risk of developing AIDS or another opportunistic infection had greatly receded. He was sure he could get another job.

'What would have happened if you hadn't been able to transfer to Yangon in the first place?' I asked.

'I think I was dead!' He laughed, trailed off, then stopped altogether. 'Dead by now,' he said, sombrely.

In his new role working for the International HIV/AIDS Alliance, Zin Min Htet was acutely aware that thousands of people in Myanmar needed ARTs. Some were on waiting lists for the medication – a life-or-death wait – while others didn't even know they needed it. Zin Min Htet would live, but he knew many others would die, especially if they lived outside the city centre.

*

I caught a flight to Mandalay, where I'd been told the availability of ARTs was far worse than in Yangon. It was in Mandalay that I met Than Win. Even though Than Win's birth certificate said she was a 22-year-old man, she was *apwint* and looked more like a fifteen-year-old girl. She was wide-eyed as a calf and kept her wavy, bob-length hair in metal clips like a children's book character.

Than Win lived in a town whose name roughly translated to 'Mandalay New Town', a ninety-minute bus trip from Mandalay, although it could take much longer since 'buses' in this region

were covered utility trucks, which carted produce and sometimes livestock, as well as human passengers. Mandalay New
Town wasn't too different from Mandalay itself: wide streets,
lots of motorcycles and exposed holes in cement drains covered by wooden slats, with poorer people bathing in the public
ablution stations on street corners. The summers were scorching; the rainy seasons muggy and plagued with mosquitoes.

Despite her youth and beauty, Than Win had the gnarled
frame of an elderly woman. Her skin was patchy and dry. The
fingernails of one hand were painted a purply pink, but the
polish was flaking off. She found it difficult to maintain eye
contact, saying she felt ashamed of what she was telling me. She
had big eyes full of trauma, like a Disney-cartoon fawn that had
accidentally wandered into a horror film.

Until recently, Than Win had been a full-time sex worker,
working seven nights a week. She'd left school after fourth
standard, and you needed to finish tenth standard to qualify
for a semi-decent job. During the day, Than Win helped out
her family in the cramped home they shared: Than Win, her
grandmother, two parents, four brothers and Than Win's husband – nine people in one house. Living in such close confines
was difficult on a practical level, and her relationship with her
family was already tense. They knew what Than Win did for
work at night and hated it.

'Don't do that!' her family would say. 'It's not good for your
health!'

Than Win's family hated her construction-worker husband
even more. He would accompany Than Win to score her clients
and ensure she got home safely. When Than Win and her husband returned home after a long night's work, they would often
find her family had locked them out. They got used to sleeping

in the detached room outside.

After a few years, the family's objections quietened down. They realised they couldn't stop Than Win by locking her out. Plus, they were getting money from Than Win, and money was the one thing you couldn't argue with in this country. When business was good, Than Win earned 10,000 kyats in a night (thirteen US dollars), which exceeded the salaries of some professionals in downtown Mandalay.

Her family was right about her health, though. Two years earlier, Than Win had discovered genital warts on her anus, which made her wonder what other horrors were lurking undetected inside her body. Blood tests at Marie Stopes International came back positive for HIV. Than Win was stunned.

She spent days crying her guts out, and her lack of appetite meant she rapidly lost weight. When I asked Than Win whether she knew how she'd caught HIV, she bowed her head.

'I'm pretty sure I got HIV from unprotected anal sex,' she said.

She was one of the many sex workers who knew it was risky not to use a condom, but whose clients often refused to wear one. When your client said no, you weren't in a strong position to convince them otherwise.

'I had to obey,' Than Win said quietly.

When I asked her how often she had unprotected sex with clients, she looked past me.

'Many, many, many times,' she said.

Two of Than Win's uncles had also been HIV-positive, and she had watched one of them die from AIDS-related complications. One uncle had contracted HIV from his wife, who was also a sex worker. The other uncle got HIV from having unprotected sex with men. Shortly after Than Win was diagnosed, she watched that uncle's body crumple, buckle and sag, before completely breaking down. Over months, Than Win saw first-hand how the virus scooped out his immune system and left him completely vulnerable to disease, before a mysterious illness devoured his body.

Than Win kept thinking, *This is going to happen to me. This is going to happen to me. This is going to happen to me. This is going to happen to me.*

It was not a dignified death. In his final days, he lost control of his bowels and had unstoppable diarrhoea, leaking watery shit into the bed. The odour was unbearable and living in such tight confines meant there was no escape from it. It was literally the smell of death.

It was only in the final stages that the family took Than Win's uncle to hospital, because the expense of admission could financially cripple them. By then, it was too late for ARTs: his CD4 count was almost non-existent. He died staining the sheets and smelling of evil. For Than Win, this was HIV's ghastly end point: someone moaning for death and covered in their own filth. It was a glimpse into her future unless she did something soon. After her uncle died and they left the hospital together, Than Win's grandmother scolded her and wailed.

'You've just seen your uncle die like this!' she said. 'Now you see why you *must* take care of your own health!'

The words felt like a curse: Than Win immediately started to feel sick. For years, she had been self-prescribing female hormones to enlarge her breasts and the meds had made her feel lethargic. This was different.

It wasn't long before Than Win was diagnosed with tuberculosis, that common opportunistic infection. Mandalay's NGOs weren't well-equipped to provide ARTs, but they could handle TB at least. But as soon as it had cleared up, Than Win was diagnosed with hepatitis B, and had since developed liver psoriasis as a result. At the age of twenty-two, her body felt like a leaky boat that needed constant maintenance.

Than Win found a community-based organisation that educated her about ARTs. But the clinics that monitored CD4 counts and provided ARTs were all based in the heart of Mandalay and weren't as well-stocked as those in Yangon. To get to Mandalay, Than Win had to take two buses. Not only did the travel take time, but she was also the object of unwanted attention from people on the buses because of her *apwint* appearance.

'Look at me, I'm obviously different,' she said. 'So when I venture into public – on the bus, in the crowds – I don't really feel comfortable.'

She persevered. Getting onto ARTs required attending mandatory counselling sessions intended to provide emotional support, but also to gauge how committed the recipient would be to the medication. No NGO or clinic wanted to waste their limited resources.

Moving to Mandalay's city centre wasn't an option for Than Win. She was annoyed that the government couldn't provide the drugs to keep her alive in her hometown, but she didn't expect the situation to change anytime soon. Talking about this was one of the rare times when she looked angry.

'This kind of convenience is not going to happen,' she said. 'I don't think anyone would be able to expect that for years.'

Than Win knew only a minority of HIV-positive people in Myanmar got ARTs, so she monitored her CD4 levels closely. When I met her, she was within the 500–700 range, which was relatively high for someone with HIV. Her CD4 count would have to be lower – between 250 and 300 – to qualify for ARTs, but some people with CD4 counts that low still didn't get treatment. If stocks were low that season, only people with opportunistic infections would be placed on the ART list. Than Win had even heard of some people *trying* to get tuberculosis so that doctors would give them priority.

While she waited for ARTs, Than Win was taking powerful antibiotics to treat her pneumocystis pneumonia, another opportunistic infection. Her rattling cough kept her up at night, disturbing her sleep patterns and depleting her appetite. She was so weak that she'd sometimes fall asleep in the middle of conversations. She had quit sex work because of her health, so had no income. Her family still disapproved of her. And there was the looming – and very real – threat that she would never get the drugs she needed to stay alive.

'ART is my major necessity,' Than Win said. 'It's the only hope and ultimate goal right now. Nothing else.'

On the buses between her hometown and Mandalay, Than Win had time to daydream. She didn't let her imagination roam far. All she desired was someone in her life to take care of her once she got on ARTs, to remind her to take them and be there when the intense side effects kicked in. Than Win told me that in one Mandalay clinic, she saw an HIV-positive little boy who was starting his course. He must have contracted HIV in the womb, because his mother was nowhere to be seen. His grandmother was taking care of him instead.

'I want someone like that grandmother,' Than Win said.

I didn't want to point out to Than Win that she already had a grandmother. If she thought her grandmother could be that person for her, I figured she would have said so. Than Win didn't mention her husband either, or her parents or her siblings. Despite being surrounded by people, she felt she had no one.

Than Win had an unshakable belief that she'd get ARTs when she needed them. She was travelling so often between her hometown and Mandalay's International Health Care clinic that she had become confident that she'd get to the front of the queue when the time came. She was a familiar face to the staff, and surely that counted for something. Her advantage was the fact that there weren't many people in Myanmar educated enough even to know about the ARTs – people like her uncle. After watching her uncle die, Than Win had made travelling into Mandalay her top priority, no matter how much time it took. Beyond that, all Than Win could do was wait. When I asked her where she saw herself in ten years (I had to keep reminding myself she was only twenty-two), she shrugged.

'Thinking about the future is hard,' she said. 'And to be completely honest, I'm not sure I'll make it to thirty-two.'

*

If you were a man who fucked men and lived in Asia, your risk of getting HIV was 18.7 times higher than the rest of the population. If you were an MSM from Myanmar, that risk became *forty-two* times greater. Some UNAIDS estimates suggested that by 2008, nearly a third of MSM and transgender people in Myanmar had HIV. No other nation in the region even came close to those figures. Something had gone terribly wrong in Myanmar.

If you were HIV-positive in Myanmar, your future was cloudy at best. Most information about HIV was passed by word of mouth, and that information varied from unreliable to downright lies. Hardly anyone had internet access, and NGOs and HIV clinics in Myanmar didn't have a web presence anyway. Many GPs didn't know where or how to refer people to HIV clinics.

One afternoon, I joined the organisation PSI in the middle of a training session for GPs from all over Myanmar to learn the fundamentals of HIV: the causes, the symptoms, the treatment. We were gathered in a tidy, air-conditioned hotel conference room with fifteen doctors, most in their forties or fifties. HIV experts led us through powerpoint slides showing the clinical stages of HIV and symptoms such as mucous, lesions and weight loss. We were treated to searingly unpleasant slides of gingivitis and other possible complications of HIV with horrible names like *recurrent severe pneumonia cryptococcal meningitis, toxoplasmosis, chronic herpes simplex* and something terrible called *HIV wasting.* An information sheet we'd been given showcased graphic photos and details of ulcers, skin conditions and something called 'crust formation'. On the information sheet was the motto, 'None shall be denied.'

Some of these doctors had been practising medicine for years, others for decades. To start with, it was heartening to see them learning this information. Eventually, though, I also felt like screaming at them: *YOU ARE DOCTORS! Shouldn't you know this already?*

Meanwhile, the NGOs struggled. National ART coverage was patchy, and in some places non-existent. MSF Holland's *Thazin* clinics provided the majority of Myanmar's ART treatments, addressing the needs of around 20,000 patients every year, mainly in Yangon. But in 2008, these Yangon clinics were forced to freeze services to all new patients. In a newspaper interview, one executive director of Médecins Sans Frontières described their operations as 'a desperate form of triage'. Every month, doctors were forced to turn away around 240 new HIV-positive people who came to the Yangon clinics seeking help. It didn't matter that these people had CD4 counts that, according to World Health Organization standards, desperately warranted treatment. The clinics had to give priority to the sickest patients, those with a CD4 count of less than 100 – patients who now, technically, had full-blown AIDS. Many died before the treatment could take effect, which amounted to more waste. Although MSF had resumed taking new patients by the time I arrived, it was probable that hundreds – perhaps thousands – of people had died waiting for ARTs.

In the year MSF started turning away patients, the organisation released a public report called *A Preventable Fate: The Failure of ART Scale-up in Myanmar.* In it, MSF was blunt, describing the HIV situation in Myanmar as 'critical' and, more provocatively, blaming the Burmese government for its lack of support. 'The response of both the Government of Myanmar and the international community has remained minimal,' they said. 'MSF should not bear the main responsibility for one of Asia's most serious HIV/AIDS epidemics.'

The report shocked many Burmese with its bluntness. Hardly anyone dared to speak about the government, which people sometimes referred to simply as the 'G'. People danced carefully around the topic, because they never knew who was listening. It was why they referred to Aung San Suu Kyi as 'The Lady', or talked about journalists as 'Js' and politicians as 'Ps'. You spoke in code because people in Myanmar liked to listen in, often out of benign curiosity, but sometimes for more sinister reasons. Markus Buhler, who worked at UNAIDS, said the relationship between the Burmese government and NGO groups had always been complicated and tense.

'It's seen with suspicion by authorities,' Markus said.

'Anything grassroots, huh?' I said.

'Anything grassroots,' he said.

Another NGO worker told me, 'If you're not careful, they'll force you to stop. And if they really have an issue with the work, you'll get arrested.'

Most people agreed that addressing health in general – let alone HIV – was low on the Burmese government's list of priorities. Kyaw Myint said that the only reason the government engaged with HIV was to improve how Myanmar was seen internationally. The government was disseminating some educational information, Markus said, but that was mainly for show.

'They're doing *just enough*.'

Habib Rahman, director of PSI's Top Centre, thought this paranoia was over the top. A bald, no-nonsense Bangladeshi guy, Habib said it really wasn't so bad.

'Look, dealing with the government, dealing with local authorities, you need to be a little bit careful,' he said. 'That is fine. But I can tell you a few things: we are working since 2004 in nineteen cities and have 350 staff. We've *never* faced any major problems from the government. In many ways, they are very supportive. We don't *want* financial support from the government. We are not for that. But what we wish – or what we want – is that they will not *stop* us for anything; they will not *prevent* us for anything. And I think that this enough.'

As long as the government stayed out of their way, PSI was happy. Habib hadn't seen any cases where NGOs working in HIV or with MSMs had run into trouble.

'No, no,' Habib assured me. 'People *think* like that, but it's really not happening.'

Outside Yangon, though, the story was different. Regional

government officials who acted as gatekeepers for HIV community groups could be horrible to deal with, but in unexpected ways. One HIV organisation in Mandalay spoke to me, on condition of anonymity, after being blacklisted by one such official for not complying with his outrageous personal demands.

The organisation, which I'll call Assist, provided education on HIV and home-based care for those already infected. Assist's head, whom I'll call Lo-Lo, was so scared of retribution that he refused to let me visit their headquarters.

'Benjamin, it is impossible for us to bring you to our office due to those sensitivities,' he said on the phone. 'Because to host a foreigner like you, we have to report a full itinerary. We would risk shutting down our CBO [community-based organisation], because of this regional official – that's one reason. The bullshit regulations are another. That's why, instead of visiting us, we will visit *you*. For us to deny you to come to our office is, for us, *quite tragic*.'

We met in the lobby of my Mandalay hostel. They were quite a sight: plump Lo-Lo and his four Assist colleagues, all MSMs, some in loud outfits and one wearing sunglasses indoors. Some of them were HIV-positive, Lo-Lo explained. When I delicately asked who in particular was, Lo-Lo laughed.

'He and he is HIV-positive,' he said, pointing at two of the men. 'But these two,' he added, pointing to the other two, 'are *very* potential.'

Everyone laughed. Maybe I'd been in Myanmar for too long, but I laughed as well.

The regional official in charge of CBO and NGO registration in Mandalay was a man in his fifties, with a wife and children. Lo-Lo said the officer was embezzling funds from Assist, an organisation he was supposed to be supervising. He would arrange meetings with Assist's staff out of work hours at restaurants and bars, demanding things like cameras and mobile phones be bought with Assist's money. He knew Assist received decent funding from international HIV and health organisations and now saw it as a money pit. Sometimes at the meetings, he would even quietly – but firmly – demand to sleep with some of Assist's male staff members, or the male staff members' husbands.

'What?' I said.

'It's actually not so difficult for us!' Lo-Lo said, laughing.

'So you've become a dating agency,' I said. 'Or pimps.'

'No, we have to refuse him,' Lo-Lo said. '"Sir, this time, we cannot arrange for you." But because we said no, we're not close to him now.'

'But he's the gatekeeper to ensure you remain a government-approved CBO.'

'We *are* a government-approved CBO,' Lo-Lo said.

But Lo-Lo added that word had now come from the official that Assist was not to receive funding. When we spoke, Lo-Lo had been forced to go behind his back and speak to the funding bodies directly, explaining the situation. It was a huge risk. If anything went wrong, the operation would be shut down. Assist's ongoing survival was a tightrope act without a safety net.

Later, another NGO worker diplomatically assessed the situation between his NGO and the government. 'Let's just say we're doing okay, *despite* the government,' he said.

Things were getting better. Every NGO worker I spoke to agreed on that. Access to ARTs would get easier and, with the international financing institution Global Fund's support, Myanmar's ART distribution was set to at least double, with targeted projections at 45,000 HIV-positive people on ARTs by 2015.

'It's still not enough,' Markus from UNAIDS said, 'but it's a substantial improvement from now.'

Sex education was getting better too. In the past decade, the number of NGOs that specifically focused on HIV had blossomed. When Markus arrived in Myanmar six years earlier, hardly any of this infrastructure existed.

'NGOs are doing it and they can actually do it quicker and better than government,' Markus said. Still, he added, the Burmese government was far better placed as the country's long-term provider and administrator. For now, though, he saw NGOs working far more intimately with the government's department of health and the national AIDS program.

'New infections are very low,' he said. 'Don't underestimate Myanmar. I'm always surprised. Despite the isolation, I think they're very good at acquiring knowledge with very limited resources.'

It was a relief. Because if nothing about the current situation changed, four out of five HIV-positive people would die waiting for medication.

*

On one of my final mornings in Yangon, I took a taxi to the outskirts of the city, forty minutes from downtown. Accompanying me was Thiha Kyaing, a short, affable, good-looking Burmese guy in his forties who had started a national NGO called Phoenix, which was on the cusp of being formally registered with the government. Thiha Kyaing had offered to act as an interpreter for some *apwint* sex workers who were willing to talk to me. All were HIV-positive and at different stages of treatment.

One of them was Myat Noe, who was twenty years old and wore her hair long, dyed acrylic orange, crimped like a teenage girl at a slumber party and kept together with Mickey Mouse clips. The dress she wore was barely-there short in a tropical flowery print. Despite her tiny frame, she had huge lips, a husky voice and a confident swagger. She had no idea what HIV was until she tested positive.

Myat Noe had grown up in a village called Myeik. Her father was a fisherman and her mother a full-time home-maker. There were six boys and two girls in the family, and she'd been raised as the youngest boy, but always knew she was different from her brothers. Myat Noe insisted on dress-ing as a girl, to the disapproval of her family. No one else she'd met in Myeik was remotely like her – born as a boy but felt like a girl – and she couldn't remember having a single friend in her childhood.

When Myat Noe was ten years old, a 'businesswoman' – otherwise known as a human trafficker – came to Myeik on a scouting mission, looking for a young girl to work as her maid in Yangon. When she found Myat Noe on the street, this woman explained there were other people just like Myat Noe in Yangon, a city of endless opportunity. Myat Noe looked at her rundown village, got on the bus with the woman and never looked back.

In Yangon, Myat Noe lived with the trafficker. She was given a bed, food and clothes, but no money. Roaming around Yangon in her spare time, she began to encounter other *apwint* in the tea houses who danced at *nat* spirit festivals, where *apwint* were revered as spirit mediums in dance ceremonies that predated Buddhism.

Myat Noe left the trafficker and started living with the other *apwint,* and people would come to the *nat* dances just to see Myat Noe's beauty, even though she wasn't dancing. The other *apwint* encouraged Myat Noe to start doing *offer,* a local slang word for prostitution. She was fifteen years old, scared and a virgin, but began working the pedestrian overpass outside Lion World. It didn't take long before the customers came to her. For the first few times, getting fucked from behind – often roughly – meant pain and bleeding, but she soon got the hang of it and was charging 3000 kyats an hour. Selling herself was worth more back then. She never used condoms. She'd never even heard of them.

Two years later, she was diagnosed as HIV-positive. She got her diagnosis at PSI's Top Centre after some peer educators referred her onwards.

'They explained very well,' Myat Noe said. 'They even explained that it wasn't something to be scared about and how I could live with treatment, so then I became very relaxed.'

They showed Myat Noe how to use condoms and it was the first time she'd ever seen the rubbery things.

'When you went back to work with condoms,' I said, 'what happened with the clients?'

'Some refused,' she said. 'They don't want to use them.'

'Did you have sex with them anyway?'

'I told them I'm HIV-positive. See, there are two kinds of clients. One: before I start working, they'll ask for condom. Two: they don't know what a condom is. They've never seen it before. So sometimes they say, "I'll give you more money to fuck you without the condom."'

'And what do you say?'

Myat Noe raised an eyebrow, then fluttered her lashes at me.

'They give me more, I let it be.'

Even though Myat Noe had been diagnosed at PSI, she hadn't gone back. She knew she should regularly monitor her CD4 levels, but something was stopping her from returning.

'Why haven't you been monitoring your CD4 count?' I asked.

'I don't want to monitor it,' she said simply.

'What are you scared of?'

She looked away. 'I'm scared to take drugs.'

'Why are you scared of taking drugs?' I asked.

'Because of the side effects! Some of my friends had a changed appearance because of the drugs!'

It was true: before I spoke to Myat Noe, I'd spoken to several other sex workers who had been on ARTs for years. They were grateful that their lives had been saved by the drugs, but hated how the medication aged them, making their cheekbones more prominent. I could barely conceal my surprise when one *apwint* sex worker told me she was thirty years old. Work and medication had aged her terribly and she looked far older than my own mother, who was in her late fifties.

'What are you more scared of?' I asked Myat Noe. 'Getting sick from HIV or the side effects of drugs?'

'I don't want to change my appearance,' she said firmly.

'What will you do if you get sick?'

She blew air softly with her mouth, pouting the way kids do when they're bored.

'Then I will go onto ARTs,' she said.

I asked how confident she was that she'd be able to access ARTs if she needed them. She looked at me searchingly, a trace of worry on her face, as though wondering whether I knew something she didn't. The horrible thing was, maybe I did.

'I'm not ready for ARTs just yet,' she said.

'Do you know where to get them when you need them?'

'Some people talk about some place, but I've never been there,' Myat Noe said. 'To be honest, I don't know. My only worry about when I'm on ARTs is that I need caregivers. Because there is no one around me.'

Eventually, we changed the subject and talked about other stuff that didn't matter. She asked me about Australia – what it was like, where it was in the world – and how it was that I was travelling by myself. Casually, she asked me where I was staying in Yangon, and as I began to reply, Thiha Kyaing – who had been acting as our translator – started chuckling. Myat Noe only asked me this because she was wondering whether I'd like to have sex with her. When I started laughing too, Myat Noe posed faux-seductively for me on her chair.

I ended our conversation the way I end all my interviews: I asked Myat Noe whether there was anything she wanted to add, or if she had any questions herself. She thought about it, then spoke slowly and carefully in Burmese to Thiha Kyaing, who relayed her question back to me with a curious, dry look.

'She would like to know,' Thiha Kyaing said, 'how *you* can help *her.*'

I hadn't expected that.

I started reeling off the names of some NGOs, but had trouble explaining where to find them. There were some places, I said, that might be able to help, like MSF's *Thazin* clinics, and another one called *Médecins du Monde,* and there was also PSI … but you know of them already, and there's Phoenix, of course, and others, but I don't know their addresses off the top of my head –

I was rambling.

I didn't know how to answer her question. I didn't know what response she was looking for. In Myanmar, no one knew what the future would bring. 'What can you do to help me?' she had asked. And, to my shame, I couldn't quite bring myself to look her in the eye.

INDIA

In which we visit the latest country in the world to have decriminalised homosexuality, travel thirty hours in a train and march in a pride parade involving a lesbian group with a staggering acronym. Key quote that was not used in this story, but is pivotal nonetheless: 'Look at how we've been treated, the most harmless of minorities' – Ashok Row Kavi. Intensity of food poisoning while researching this story (on a scale of one to ten): eight.

*

IN THE MIDDLE OF a six-hour taxi ride from Delhi, I paused at an outdoor cement urinal that smelled – weirdly – of human shit, wondering whether I'd made a terrible mistake. According to my estimates, we were in the middle of nowhere and it made me anxious. 'Middle of nowhere' wasn't an exact coordinate, but when you're in India on your own, relying on a driver who doesn't speak English and becoming paranoid that neither of you knows where you are, it's difficult to be precise. Plus the cold was fuddling my brain. The chill had an almost liquid quality, the way it seeped through my beanie, gloves, multi-layered thermals, down my jeans and into my shoes. No one had told me the subcontinent could feel so Arctic.

Our destination was near Haridwar, one of India's holy cities and a well-known site of pilgrimage. On the map, though, our target was a tiny cluster on the side of the road, a cameo appearance from humanity: it would be all too easy to miss.

I zipped up and scurried into the cab's backseat. The driver shook his head and reclined the passenger seat to show me I could lie completely flat.

'Sleep,' he said, pointing. 'You sleep.'

It was 1.30 am. I liked the way he thought.

As I slipped into unconsciousness, the driver turned up the heat to block out the cold that was entering through every crack. Outside, the temperature continued to plummet, breaking Indian meteorological records. Across the country, thick wafts of movie-set fog were causing epic train delays, forcing stranded passengers to sleep on station floors with blankets pulled over their faces, and giving platforms the look of giant makeshift morgues after a natural disaster. That night, people died from exposure to the cold in neighbouring Uttar Pradesh, India's most populous state.

The driver woke me up three hours later. We had arrived at Patanjali Yogpeeth, also known as Patanjali University. It wasn't really a university, but rather a strange hybrid of health research institute, conference centre and massive yoga retreat. I shouldn't have worried about missing it: the entrance for the guests' quarters was huge, a white concrete frame recalling the entrance to a Hollywood studio, set off by warm glowing lights. Juvenile palm trees sprouted alongside manicured pathways, bordering tidy flowerbeds of gerberas and chrysanthemums.

Staff dressed in military gear asked me for my papers, then walked me to my room, protecting themselves from the cold by pulling heavy blankets over their shoulders and scarves around their faces like improvised balaclavas.

My bathroom was a slab of cement with a basin and faucets.

The showerhead didn't work, so I bathed the way most people in India did: by filling a large bucket with as much hot water as possible and then scrubbing myself raw while crouching on the freezing concrete. In bed, I cocooned myself in blankets. I couldn't doze for long: my glow-in-the-dark watch told me I'd have to be awake soon. In less than two hours, I'd have my first chance to see the guru I'd come to meet. One of the most powerful and influential men in India, he had gathered millions of disciples and devotees worldwide, attracted by his claims about the curative power of yoga and ayurvedic medicine. It was believed that his practices could cure cancer and reverse diabetes, but his most controversial claim was that he could cure people of homosexuality. Of course, I had heard this before, but Ramdev was different. In India, he was a household name.

Swamiji Baba Ramdev was known by many names: Baba Ramdev, Swami Ramdev, Yogarishi Swami Ramdevji or, simply, Babaji. If you showed his photo to any Indian on the street, they would recognise him immediately. His picture was plastered outside traditional ayurvedic pharmacies throughout the country: long, slick black hair, bushy beard and squeezable, always-smiling face. In his youth, he had resembled an Indian version of the apple-cheeked American actor Mark Ruffalo. No one knew Ramdev's real age, but most people believed he was in his late forties or early fifties.

Ramdev led the simple life of an ascetic – steamed vegetables; strict sexual abstinence; same old orange robes day in, day out – and reportedly didn't even have a bank account in his own name, but he was ridiculously rich. His empire of yoga camps, ayurvedic drugs, fruit juices and natural toiletries was estimated to be worth 25 million US dollars. *India Today* declared him to be the twenty-ninth most powerful person in the country. To his 80 million followers worldwide, and 20 million regular television viewers who followed his morning exercises, Ramdev was not a mere yoga instructor but a holy leader and cult hero. No matter whether they were Hindu, Muslim, Sikh or Christian, Ramdev said everyone could benefit from his teachings.

In mid 2009, there had been a huge nationwide campaign to repeal Section 377, a colonial hangover that effectively outlawed homosexual sex in India. Ramdev used this moment to become a prominent anti-gay campaigner, insisting that homosexuality was a sexual abnormality, which he could cure.

'The verdict will encourage criminality and a sick mentality,' he said in a press statement. 'This kind of thing is shameful and insulting. We are blindly following the West in everything. This is breaking the family system in India. Homosexuals are sick people. They should be sent to hospitals for treatment.'

∗

At Patanjali, my alarm went off. I hadn't really slept. It was still dark outside. I could hear my fellow yogis opening their doors, switching on lights and shuffling their feet. Outside, loudspeakers stirred us from our rooms.

'The yoga session will start at 5.45 precisely,' they announced in English. 'The yoga session will start at 5.45 precisely.'

We slowly filed outside, crossing our arms close against our bodies and watching the steam of our breath as we joined the human river headed for the amphitheatre. Most of the people were Indian, but a number of the delegates had flown here. Some had East Asian backgrounds, but a decent number were white people from America, Europe and Australia, hippies who had hit retirement and were looking for enlightenment. Everyone was dressed bizarrely. The freezing weather demanded multiple layers of clothing, but we were also heading to a yoga class that required breezy, flexible apparel. People wore loose tracksuit pants *and* fur stoles; polyester jackets *and* Thai fisherman pants, over thermal leggings and *with* a suit blazer.

When we reached the yoga hall, I couldn't stop staring. It was a majestic space, a beautifully lit amphitheatre with 250,000 square feet of cement floors and padded cotton mats. The story went that Baba Ramdev had started teaching yoga in a modest 250-square-foot room. This amphitheatre was 1000 times bigger.

As musicians played drums on-stage, we cracked out our morning stiffness. I sat on my mat with my legs in front of me, reaching over to stretch my hamstrings. There was movement on the stage, a smudge of orange I immediately knew was Baba Ramdev. Later, I would see crowds of people walk up to touch his feet before backing away quickly, as if making contact with holy fire. We all stood to acknowledge his presence. Following everyone else's lead, I raised both arms in salute, humming a general *ohm* in his direction. Despite the Hitler Youth connotations, the gesture was a genuinely beautiful thing: a collective of people harmonising our voices. It was as if we had connected on a metaphysical level.

Baba Ramdev signalled for us to sit down.

'Welcome everyone,' he said into the microphone, his voice echoing through the space.

He was wrapped in his usual robes: day-glo orange, the same colour you'd find at a rave. Two giant screens on either side of the stage projected Ramdev's image as if he were Bono at a U2 concert. Zoomed in close, you could see all his features in high definition. He looked older than in the program's photos and his right eye was visibly damaged, blinking out of sync with the left. However, his beard was as healthy and as thick as ever: an upside-down beehive with afro-level density. It was the kind of beard you could lose cutlery in.

In a few quick moves, Ramdev refolded his robes from a flowing neck-to-toe number into the skimpiest pair of running shorts imaginable. Now displaying his famously luxurious mat of chest hair, he led us through the moves slowly and methodically: slow-motion star jumps, long-limbed cat stretches, knee-to-nipple leg pumps, bridge-like spine arches. In the middle of that last stretch, a middle-aged Indian woman in front of me released a fart, a floppy honking arse-trumpet that resonated throughout the chamber. The man next to me completely lost his shit, giving up on the stretch to collapse with his head on his mat, spasming with laughter.

'These are traditional Indian exercises,' Ramdev said in English, ignoring the echoing fart.

The moves became more complicated: Russian Cossack leg thrusts, thalidomide-baby elbow claps. We briefly retreated to familiar territory with salute-the-sun routines, but soon Ramdev was performing them as fast as a breakdance, complicated manoeuvres that looked as if they'd cause permanent spinal injuries in most people. Ramdev pinned his hands on the floor in a push-up pose, flinging his entire body and legs through his arms – back and forth, back and forth – before sitting with his legs crossed to show us something cool we could do with *pranayam* breathing. Closing his eyes, he sucked in his gut to make a concave shape between his ribs, a hollow big enough to fit your entire face. He jiggled his gut around rapidly, like a lava lamp in time lapse. We applauded. It was as impressive as it was gross.

If these were the moves that were supposed to straighten out gay people, I would be gay for the rest of my natural life.

As the conference went on, I warmed to Ramdev. A lot of what he said made sense. He told people to reduce their meat consumption, not just because it was a good Hindu thing to do but also because of environmental concerns. He believed in chewing your food properly, eating raw vegetables and limiting the use of air-conditioning and heaters, because global warming and energy consumption concerned him. Ramdev was also a beautiful orator. In Hindi, he described the other delegates who had gathered there as 'saints and seers'.

In the afternoon, Ramdev held a two-hour Q&A session in a cavernous auditorium. Shirley, the conference organiser, sat beside Ramdev on-stage and sorted through a Santa-sized pile of letters, selecting the questions she considered the best or most interesting. Those of us who couldn't understand Hindi wore headsets that broadcast a live English translation. Some of the questions were general; others were bizarre: *How do we reduce obesity in woman after HRT? How does one eat right, and when should one eat? Which yoga practices should and shouldn't be done during the menstrual cycle? Can yoga address autism? What about yoga for muscular dystrophy? How can we use yoga to help enlarge our prostates? Can yoga help with multiple sclerosis?*

Ramdev nodded and answered each question in the affirmative: yoga could help with all these things. All of them. He insisted you would never need anti-wrinkle cream if you did yoga, citing his sisters as living evidence. Yoga could also cure osteoporosis and cancer. If you had glaucoma, eye drops and laser surgery weren't necessary. Natural ayurvedic medicines could easily reverse the condition. In fact, he'd recently cured a woman of glaucoma with a simple natural remedy, combining white onion, ginger and lemon juice, which the woman administered directly to her eyes. My eyes involuntarily watered thinking about it.

'I can't tell you to recommend this to your patients in the West,' he told us, clapping his hands together and laughing with a donkey wheeze. 'Over there, they'd *sue* you! So perhaps you can "recommend" it to them, but don't "tell" them to do it! And don't tell them *I* told you!'

He laughed again. I imagined it was the kind of laugh that came after convincing someone to squeeze onion, ginger and lemon juice into their eyes.

Then came a question about sex.

'When we do more yoga,' Shirley read out in English to Ramdev, 'should we also feel like wanting more sex?'

Ramdev smiled again, greatly amused for someone who'd apparently never had sex himself. It was the first time sex had been mentioned during the conference and he approached the answer boldly. 'Through yoga, wives and husbands will have balance restored,' he said. 'They will be loyal to one another from the core of their hearts. When you do yoga, sexual disorders will be removed.' He nodded, certain in his convictions. 'Through yoga, your sexual desires will be balanced.'

The following day, when I got to meet Ramdev one-on-one, I could see he was wrong about the wrinkles. Crows feet had gathered around his eyes, though his skin was still smooth like a polished apple. There was also a single crease on his forehead, as though someone had run a blunt fingernail through it.

Ramdev had agreed to grant 'private' interviews, albeit ones in which we would be surrounded by his all-male entourage, one of whom was a man in a business suit who would translate Ramdev's Hindi for me. Ramdev understood English well enough, but needed help communicating his responses. After we sat down together, surrounded by his team, I asked him about some of his health claims, like the one that yoga had the power to cure people of HIV. Ramdev laughed – everything seemed to amuse him – and said he stood by those claims.

'I never claimed to have personally cured HIV,' he said. 'But as far as HIV is concerned, there are three things that I've witnessed and claimed, and will say even now. One is the viral load. The CD4 counts responsible for your immune system, in some people with HIV, have decreased from 700 to 800 to as low as twenty-five.'

I nodded, understanding. By this stage a person would technically have AIDS.

'But through *pranayam* breathing, the CD4 count becomes normal,' Ramdev said. 'The decrease in viral load is significant. The infection normalises. Even now, there are patients who experience these benefits.' He looked me in the eye, as if to challenge me. 'It can still be achieved with any patient you wish to refer or to send.'

On one level, I was impressed: Ramdev was familiar with the language of HIV and knew about CD4 levels and how viral loads worked. But the idea of AIDS patients doing breathing exercises to boost their immune system?

'Then in 2009, with the repeal of Section 377 –' I started.

Ramdev nodded, putting up his hands and interrupting, knowing what I was about to ask.

'When I visit the US or the UK, people – the gay community, gay individuals – they look at me and think, "Oh, this could be a dangerous person."'

He laughed again, raising his eyebrows at his entourage as if to say, *Am I right?* They nodded their agreement and laughed back at him.

'But I think *positively* of their conditions! It's a *habit*. It's a wrong habit, and also, it's a mental disorder.' He switched to English, as if to make his statement more official. 'Homosexuality,' he said, 'is a *bad mental habit.*'

His interpreter looked at me sternly to make sure I'd understood. I nodded.

'The perversion can extend up to a level,' Ramdev continued, 'where people wish to have *sex with animals.*'

'Right,' I said, taking notes. 'So it's a sliding scale, then. A spectrum.'

Ramdev turned out his palms and nodded. 'It's a spectrum of perversion, from normal sexual desire to perverted sexual desire. Most male homosexuals? They are actually *heterosexual,* you know. They have their usual sexual relationships with women, but they also wish to have homosexual behaviour sometimes. So it's normally an extension, a perversion of normal behaviour.'

'And what about female homosexuals?' I asked.

Silence.

'Lesbians,' the translator said ominously in English.

Ramdev shot me a little smile, as if he'd heard a dirty joke. 'Oh, it's also the same thing! If they were *purely* lesbian, you could argue that it was biological. But behaviourally, *they* are heterosexual also. Only the minority – 1 per cent – of these people are purely not heterosexual, purely gay or lesbian. Most are not attracted to each other sexually, but to each other as individuals. And then it becomes ...'

'Something else?' I offered.

'Something else,' he said. 'These relationships can have a normal spectrum, but also a perverted spectrum. The practice of *pranayam* and meditation can give us a mastery over it, so we'll be able to get out of the bad habit. People want to come out, but they don't feel confident enough because they don't have *tools* to come out.'

I looked at Ramdev confused, before I realised he didn't mean 'coming out' in the usual sense, but 'coming out' of a life bound by homosexuality. Looking at his beaming face, I felt conflicted: what he was saying made me squirm, but I also wanted to reach over and squeeze his adorable cheeks. For someone so insane and hateful, he was almost lovable in a cartoonish way. How horrible could he possibly be?

'You say you can cure all this,' I said.

Ramdev sighed. '*Pranayam* and meditation can help.'

So Baba Ramdev's infamous de-gayification program was all about *breathing* correctly? *Pranayam* was the basis of breathing techniques taughed in yoga classes all over the world. I thought of my yoga classes back in Australia. Often these classes were packed full of gay men who wouldn't be straightened out even if you surgically inserted metal rods into their spines.

'Do you see homosexuality as a Western import?'

Ramdev shrugged. 'This is not a Western or Eastern thing. Only a bad habit. It's unproductive sex! It's like throwing the seed into the fire.'

'Like masturbation, then.'

Upon hearing that word, everyone nodded and murmured disapprovingly.

'Have people come to you for advice?' I asked. 'I mean, say if I was to come to you and say, "Baba Ramdev, I am a homosexual, help me," what would you say to me? What step-by-step advice would you give?'

'Of course I would help,' he said. 'We'd start with the *pranayam* practice, and that will lead the way forward –'

'It's as simple as that?'

Ramdev gave me an exasperated look, like a teacher working with a dim child.

'It's those four breathing practices that you're aware of now,' he said.

'The internal change comes from practice,' a member of his entourage whispered urgently.

'Uh-huh ...'

Ramdev snapped. 'Next question!' he said, shaking his head, decidedly offended. 'Stop this! Stop!'

His entourage bit their lips and looked away awkwardly.

'Stop this!'

So we stopped.

*

In New Delhi, I sat in a plush hotel room, sipping tea and listening as someone gossiped to me about Ramdev.

'Oh, I'm *convinced* he's gay,' Dr Anjali Gopalan said. 'You see him with those young boys on his TV shows ...'

'You mean his disciples?'

'Whatever they are,' she said. 'The way he touches them and looks at them ...'

I laughed. Anjali raise her eyebrows, mock-serious.

'There's something there!' she said.

Anjali Gopalan was in her fifties and had thick salt-and-pepper hair, an intimidatingly intelligent brain and the constant suggestion of mischief in her eyes, as if she was plotting something diabolical. She also had a lot of history with Baba Ramdev. Before, during and after the repeal of Section 377 – the so-called ban on homosexuality – Ramdev and Gopalan often appeared on nightly current affairs programs to spar about the issue. In that time, Anjali's face became synonymous with the fight against Section 377. After all, it was her organisation that was the petitioner in the case of *Naz Foundation v. Government of NCT of Delhi.*

One of Anjali's most memorable confrontations with Ramdev had taken place when they were miked up in TV studios in separate cities, waiting for the host to introduce them. Because the connection was already live, guests were able to talk among themselves. Baba Ramdev had gestured to Anjali on the monitor and snidely asked the TV producer a question.

'So, she is also like *this*?' he said, implying she was a lesbian.

'You know, Babaji,' Anjali said, 'I am *exactly* like you are. There is no difference between you and me. Meanwhile, it looks like you've found one *great* way to sell more of your medicines.'

Furious, Ramdev was about to fire back when the cameras started rolling.

'Oh, he was so fucking angry with me,' Anjali said. 'He's a vicious queen.'

Whenever they had these televised debates, Ramdev was hostile but also appeared confused by Anjali. Unlike the flamboyant gay male activists Ramdev was happy to dismiss and mock, here was a woman whose title was 'doctor' and who dressed traditionally and conservatively. It was hard for Ramdev to attack Anjali for being stupid or an outsider to Indian culture. And she was also straight.

'He didn't know where to place me,' Anjali said.

Anjali was famous throughout India for establishing the Naz Foundation in 1994, an HIV organisation that now occupied a five-storey building, including three levels where twenty-seven

HIV-positive kids lived. Some were orphans, others had been given up by HIV-positive parents who could no longer take care of them. On the walls were brightly coloured murals of butter-flies and birds. It looked like a well-funded day-care centre you'd find anywhere in the world, except for its panoramic views of New Delhi.

When it started in 1994, the Naz Foundation had focused exclusively on men who had sex with men. Anjali had worked in New York City at the height of the AIDS crisis and saw close male friends die hideous deaths: slow, painful and shrouded by stigma. She saw how quickly the virus spread and knew India would be hit soon. When she got back to Delhi, Anjali teamed up with a doctor named Rajiv – who was also straight – and together the pair would go to Delhi's gay cruising parks with sample medications and supplies for sexual health tests.

'Poor man,' Anjali said, chuckling, thinking about Rajiv now. 'Rajiv didn't know what hit him. These boys would fall in love with him, but he was so good.'

They met with a lot of resistance. Older queens in the park would tell the younger boys not to listen to Anjali. She had come from the West, they said, and was spreading false rumours about a disease that didn't exist. Some of them specu-lated that the real reason Anjali was there was that she, like Baba Ramdev, wanted to make them all straight. Anjali laughed thinking about it now but, looking back, realised she had been on a steep learning curve too.

'You're very clear in the States when you go through your training,' she said. 'People are either straight, bi or gay. Here, in India, there's like this whole other world. One had to relearn everything.'

For a start, most of these Indian men didn't identify as

'gay'. They had no sense of community or even sexual identity. The Naz Foundation set up phone lines, which they advertised in public spaces where men were known to have sex. Besides the men themselves, parents called in constantly, bemoaning the fact that they'd discovered their son sleeping with other men. When Anjali and other Naz counsellors told parents homosexual behaviour wasn't a disease, the parents weren't convinced.

'Every time we counselled parents, we'd beat our heads against the wall,' Anjali said. 'It always came to this: "If you think we should accept our son as he is, and it's really normal and natural for our son to be like this, then why is it *criminal?*"' Anjali looked at me with both her palms facing upwards, exasperated. 'How do you argue with that?' she said.

Anjali and the other counsellors tried persuading the parents that Section 377, a law that dated back to 1860, was an unfair legislative relic and that they were doing everything they could to fight it. The parents were never convinced. Deep down, Anjali, too, felt that nothing was ever going to change. The Indian legal system was infamously slow and inefficient, and sexual minorities would never be attended to with any urgency. Every other day, Anjali would end up at the local police station, negotiating with the cops to release Naz Foundation outreach workers from detention. They would be caught in the parks trying to engage with men about safe sex, and the cops would haul them off. The police gruffly explained to Anjali that her staff were technically promoting an illegal behaviour. For Anjali, the breaking point came when the Naz Foundation discovered a young Indian man who had been forcibly given shock treatment for being gay. When Anjali and Naz took the case to the National Human Rights Commission, they were

told it wouldn't be investigated – once again, because homosexual sex was illegal.

Out of exhaustion and anger, Naz teamed up with the
Delhi-based non-profit Lawyers Collective in 1995. The timing
was canny: Lawyers Collective had just been funded to work
specifically on HIV issues and shared the belief that Section
377 could be repealed on both civil rights and public health
grounds. If Section 377 was repealed, they felt, it would
decrease HIV rates dramatically. Once the ban on homosexual
sex was lifted, you could speak openly about it and educate
people about safe sex. Lawyers Collective had already drafted
the petition for repeal and just needed a responsible party to
file it. In 2001, Anjali filed the petition with the Delhi High
Court in the Naz Foundation's name.

*

Lawyers Collective was headed by a human-rights lawyer
named Anand Grover. But Anand was not India's Harvey Milk.
Like Anjali, he wasn't even gay. Nowadays, Anand worked
upstairs in a narrow building that relied on a gated elevator
with a human operator. His office reminded me of the *Being
John Malkovich* film set: the walls leaned inwards and the dimen-
sions felt impossible. Volumes of legal tomes lined up in glass
cabinets. Receptionists worked hidden behind towering stacks
of manila folders.

Anand seemed ageless and had the kind of face that made
white hair look so terrific that you looked forward to turning
grey. He wore a crisp white cotton shirt, thick-framed designer
spectacles and coloured rubber wristbands for different chari-
ties over his expensive wristwatch. His heart was grassroots; the

rest of him was fabulously tailored. Although Anjali said she'd always been skeptical that their joint efforts to dismantle Section 377 would fail, Anand said he'd been sure of success.

'I was always 100 per cent confident,' he told me. 'There is a mountain to be climbed. You can see it; you *have* to climb it. It may take time. You may fall. But then you will go ahead, because it *will* be climbed. There's no doubt about it, because it's patent injustice.'

Anand had worked extensively in cases relating to homosexuality and HIV since the late 1980s, when he represented Dominic D'Souza, a gay man who was fired after being diagnosed as HIV-positive. Doctors refused to treat D'Souza and he was detained in a sanitarium for two months by state officials who insisted they were serving the public interest. D'Souza's mother approached Anand and his team to initiate a lawsuit to have Section 53 – the law that allowed D'Souza to be fired and detained – declared unconstitutional and a denial of due process. They lost the case and everyone was shattered. In 1992, as D'Souza was dying, Anand promised him that he'd keep on with the work they had started together.

After D'Souza died, Anand became obsessed. Gay men approached him for representation if they were being blackmailed. Anand would take on four new pro bono HIV-related cases per month. His wife – herself a lawyer and co-founder of Lawyers Collective – said he'd gone mad, and Anand knew she was only half-joking. After years of working on these cases, he felt the root cause of each one was the same: Section 377. If India got rid of that law, most of these cases would disappear. And, technically, it wasn't just gay men who infringed Section 377.

'The act was only against gay men on the face of it,' he said.

'But if I'm heterosexual and have anal sex or oral sex with my female partner, I'd go to jail too. You have to understand this section.' Anand looked at the ceiling and recited directly from Section 377. '"Whoever voluntarily has carnal intercourse with a man, woman or animal – against the order of nature – shall be punished." What is the meaning of "against the order of nature"? A practice which does not beget children! Penis is the culprit –'

'As it always is,' I said.

Anand laughed, agreeing.

'As it always is. And the explanation says, "penetration that is sufficient to constitute this offence". So penile penetration is a *must.*'

This provided an interesting loophole if you were a woman. Lesbians were completely ignored by Section 377. If you were a queer woman in India, this was one of those rare cases in which discrimination actually swung in your favour. When Anjali, Anand and Lawyers Collective started mobilising for the fight against Section 377, some lesbians in India became nervous. They remembered a 1995 case in Sri Lanka, in which petitioners lobbied against a similar colonial law called Article 365. Not only did the repeal fail, the campaign made things worse. The previous law, the government decided, wasn't discriminatory *enough*, so they created an amendment called Article 365A, which criminalised same-sex relationships between anyone – men *and* women – as an act of 'gross indecency'. Female-on-female sex was now punishable by up to twelve years' imprisonment in Sri Lanka, solely because activists had spoken up. It was the court's perverse way of redefining equality.

Anand and Lawyers Collective, aware of these concerns, arranged open meetings and forums for anyone who felt they had a stake in the repeal. Queer people from gay to *hijra,* transgender to bisexual, poor to middle class, arrived to debate the campaign. In the meantime, the case tediously bounced from the Delhi High Court to the Indian Supreme Court and back to the Delhi High Court. For most people, the wait would have been frustrating. But in the years it took for the case to pass between the courts, Anand noticed something else developing.

'By 2006 and 2007, there were talk shows and chat shows. Everybody was saying, "My daughter is gay," "My son is this," "My brother is that, and I support them."'

Journalists and commentators started talking about the petition too. The issue occupied increasing inches of column space in newspapers and divided the Indian parliament. The Health Ministry declared its support for repealing Section 377 for public health reasons, while the Home Ministry denounced the petition. Having two government ministries publicly contradict each other gave the repeal an advantage, forcing the court to push its final arguments through. Suddenly, it was announced that the two-judge bench overseeing the case would deliver a swift verdict.

Indians and expatriates sent emails and text messages to each other with the news: *They're deciding tomorrow.* Anand got the word in Geneva where he was working for the UN. In India, and around the world, people stayed up in anticipation.

The next morning, the Delhi High Court was packed with activists, lawyers, reporters and spectators. Judgements in other cases had to be read out first, but the crowd was there for *Naz Foundation v. Government of NCT of Delhi.* As the two-man bench entered the room, everyone stood up, bowed to both Chief Justice A.P. Shah and Justice S. Muralidhar, and then sat down. A silence descended.

'I will read out the conclusion,' Shah said. 'We declare that

Section 377 IPC, insofar it criminalises consensual sexual acts of adults in private, is violative of Articles –'

A gasp went around the room. Some people squealed. Anjali couldn't tell whether they were expressing horror or joy. She wished her legal vocabulary was stronger. Had they won or not?

'What's he saying, what's he saying?' she asked the man next to her, a lawyer she didn't know. 'What does it mean?' Smiling, he leaned over and explained.

In homes across India, the rolling ticker-tape display on the bottom of television sets explained the verdict in capital letters: 'BREAKING NEWS: HOMOSEXUALITY IS LEGAL. HC: CONSENSUAL SEX BETWEEN SAME SEX ADULTS IS LEGAL.'

Later, Anjali would recall the moment over and over.

'My god,' she said. 'It was such *fun*.'

In Delhi, *hijras* led dances among repeal supporters who held up banners for photojournalists. In Mumbai, 1500 kilometres away, it was monsoon season and the city was being pissed on by rain. It didn't matter: people ran or caught rickshaws or taxis to each other's homes to see the news, remaining glued to the TV sets for hours. People skipped work. Many wept. Religious groups fumed. The Bharatiya Janata Party (BJP), India's conservative opposition, had always been against the repeal. And while few things were capable of uniting India's diverse Muslim, Christian and Hindu groups, they were all united in denouncing this. Furious, Baba Ramdev declared he would immediately file a petition with the Supreme Court against the decision.

On that day, though, it was clear which side the news producers were on. As they reported the news of Ramdev's petition, every TV station managed to find the most bizarre footage of

Ramdev possible, including shots of him doing Russian Cossack leg thrusts and that weird thing he did with his gut. It made it hard to take him seriously.

Several days after the court verdict in Delhi, a still-buzzing but exhausted Anjali Gopalan was in bed when her phone rang. On the other line was a man's voice she didn't recognise, telling her that he represented Baba Ramdev and that his people were going to have her kidnapped and killed. Normally, this would have been chilling, but after the previous few days, Anjali was exhausted.

'Look,' she said down the phone line. 'I don't think you've seen me. It's not so easy to kidnap me.'

'Women like you,' continued the caller, 'have singlehandly ruined the moral fibre of this country.'

'Well, thank you very much,' she said, sighing. 'I'll take that as a compliment.'

Then she hung up.

The next day, she told her colleagues at the Naz Foundation what had happened. They were appalled.

'You must file a police report and ask for protection,' they said.

'Are you mad?' Anjali said. 'Ridiculous! *This* is what you're going to get killed for? Fuck this shit.'

So far, nothing had happened. After a decade's worth of drama in campaigning for queer rights, Anjali had recently started as a volunteer at a Delhi shelter dedicated to caring for abandoned, neglected and abused animals. Considering the number of stray dogs, cats and cattle I'd seen on Delhi's streets, it sounded like a job without any end in sight. It was as though she was always looking out for the next disenfranchised group to take care of.

'You can't help yourself, can you?' I said.

Anjali shrugged mock-innocently.

Maybe Baba Ramdev was right. It always started with homo-sexuals before progressing on to animals.

*

My hotel in Delhi – if you could call it a hotel – was a hole in the wall with the vaguely brothel-ish name of Hotel Express 66. It was bang in the heart of the city's busiest road, an artery for trade that connected Delhi to its main railway and metro station. Outside the hotel, stray dogs with long snouts and droopy nipples wove through human legs, as those human legs wove through a bitumen chaos of cattle-drawn carts, motorcycles and three-wheeled auto rickshaws. Teenage boys sat on the ledges of the main bridge of Desh Bandhu Gupta Road eating snacks, feet dangling over the edge, seemingly oblivious to the fatal drop. Men pissed into open-air urinals on the kerbside only to have their piss run back onto the footpath and road. Everything stank. It was an ever-evolving smell, usually consisting of petrol fumes, faeces, human urine and an exciting hint of fire. At night, even with the windows closed, the smell seeped inside. As I slept, I collected it in my lungs.

In the morning, barely conscious and heavy-lidded, I caught the metro into the suburbs to meet the man known as the god-father of India's modern gay movement, who'd supported the Section 377 repeal movement from the start. Ashok Row Kavi had even discussed with Lawyers Collective the possibility of filing the petition himself, but the problem was that he lived in Mumbai at the time.

When I got off the train and walked the back streets towards

Ashok's apartment, I sighed with relief: this was as close to quiet as you could get in Delhi. Instead of the screaming of car horns and the smell of burning, there was birdsong and the sound of lone hammers doing construction work. It wouldn't be this quiet for long. This area was in demand. Older houses were being dismantled all over the neighbourhood in favour of new, full-floor apartments. When I mentioned the development in his street, Ashok nodded happily.

'Oh, India's just exploding,' he said. 'It's like gay culture here too.'

Although he was indoors, Ashok wore a full winter jacket and beanie. He lived in a fifty-year-old building with bad wiring, which meant that an electric heater could blow the fuse. But there was a serene quality to his apartment too. He kept two aquariums full of bright fish, bookshelves packed with litera-ture and warm fairy lights strung throughout the place.

Ashok was in his mid sixties, but had a constant expression of wry amusement that made him look far younger. He had an infectious, puckish personality, called everyone 'darling' and always referred to his male friends by female pronouns. When someone phoned in the middle of our chat, Ashok greeted him by airily asking, 'And who are you fucking at the moment, you filthy pig?'

Ashok was the first gay man to talk about his sexuality in the Indian press. After he came out as gay in the 1980s, he became notorious and the press endlessly interviewed him about homo-sexuality. For years, Ashok remained the sole openly gay public figure in India. He founded two major institutions: India's first gay magazine, *Bombay Dost*, and the Humsafar Trust, which remained one of India's peak organisations for sexual health in gay men, MSMs and transgender people. People called him the godfather of India's gay rights movement.

'Oh, I'm not the *godfather*,' Ashok said now. He put his hand to his chest, feigning humility. 'I'm called *amma*, which means mum. And as a mother, I *earned* that title.'

Like Dr Anjali Gopalan, Ashok had also had his fair share of encounters with Baba Ramdev. Ashok asked to see my photos with him. He adjusted his glasses to examine them, made a face, then handed back my camera.

'I'm glad you spoke to him,' he said. 'I think he's *weird*. In fact, I'm very sure that he's in the closet.'

'People do keep saying that,' I said.

'He only has men around him,' Ashok said. 'He only nurtures guys. Closet queens. What did he have to say to you about homo-sexuality?'

I told Ashok that Ramdev has described homosexuality as a 'bad habit'.

'*Eeee!*' Ashok squealed. 'I could slap him! He's a *yoga teacher*. What he speaks on is yoga, and yoga is a physical science sup-posed to harness spiritual energies. It's got nothing to do with pure spiritualism. I once said to him on television, "You're not even properly Hindu. Most of the stuff you teach is rubbish." But it is frightening. He's got 80 million followers, most of them total weirdos.'

Queer sexualities were not new to India, Ashok explained. Everyone knew about the *hijras*, similar to transgender men – who dressed and lived as women – also known as the so-called third gender of India. But there were other precedents, like the ancient practice of holy prostitution in some Hindu temples. *Jogappas*, male devotees of the Hindu goddess Yellamma, had dressed in the saris and jewellery of married women and sexu-ally serviced men as a display of their religious devotion. There was also the obscure Hindu concept of *Vanaprastha*, a stage in the Vedic ashram system where men, in old age, would renounce everything, including their property, wife and family. They'd go to a forest or ashram, get fully nude and stay nude until they died. Ashok quipped that this had been a handy option if you were old, married and closeted. It was British colonialism that introduced new rules and moral structures into Indian society, and laws such as Section 377 made sex largely taboo, even though this was the birthplace of the *Kama Sutra.*

Now the gay scene was expanding quickly, with social groups, fundraisers and parties sprouting up, especially in the wake of the Section 377 repeal. Still, Ashok had reservations about how the scene had evolved. Recently, someone had held a gay party at a Hindu religious hostel about 250 kilometres from Delhi, which had been raided by the police. Partygoers were outraged at the authorities, but Ashok was more appalled at the party's organisers.

'Gay men take such horrendous risks!' he said. 'That's my gripe. "Stay out of trouble, guys. There's enough shit on our plate already!" A hundred of them were there! Can you believe it?'

'Still, it's quite bold of them,' I said.

'It *is* bold,' Ashok conceded. Then he shook his head as if to add: *but also stupid.*

A lot of the Delhi parties were for the young urban elites, gays with a tertiary education, a full-time job and money to burn, who were looking for a quick fuck. Meanwhile, Ashok pointed out, lesbians were still getting bashed and gay men were still contracting HIV through bareback sex and lack of education. It felt vulgar to him that these parties didn't give anything back to their community.

'To the guys holding these expensive parties, I ask: "Why don't you collect fifty rupees extra? When each ticket is 400 or 500, surely you can pay fifty rupees extra for one of your own who's been bashed up somewhere? Where is your sense of charity?"'

Tuesdays and Saturdays were gay nights in New Delhi. Since the repeal, the nights had become far more open and, ironically, *less* gay. Gay parties now attracted a more mixed crowd, with many straight women – mainly models and wannabe actresses – rubbing shoulders with fashion designers and magazine editors. To get into one particular club, you needed a special SMS forwarded by a friend. Ashok didn't want to go, but knew the organisers and sent me the exclusive SMS to show at the door. It seemed a little incestuous – a club night where everyone would know someone else – but maybe that was the appeal.

Later that night, I showed my phone to security guards and paid a 500-rupee (eleven US dollars) entry fee, which was steep for this country. The place was packed with young men and as dark as blindness. As my eyes adjusted, I saw these men were uniformly young, twinkish, educated professionals, including IT specialists and film-makers, engineers and media types. Beers started at 250 rupees and went right up to 500, a colossal price in India, where you could pay a rickshaw driver a mere twenty rupees for a fifteen-minute drive home.

It wasn't long before I was monumentally drunk. Older men shouted me drinks and demanded in unsubtle terms that we go back to a hotel and fuck immediately. Strangers kept plying me with liquor, lighting my cigarettes and dragging me to the carpark because they had something very important they wanted to tell me in private, which was always a fervid plan of fucking in a hotel room. One guy – an aeroplane engineer in his thirties, who wore a black jacket and blue paisley satin shirt – became smitten with me and asked, over and over, to see my bare feet. The attention was flattering, but soon the place was nightmarishly packed, and I felt I was either going to pass out or vomit. After pushing my way out into the night, I hailed an auto rickshaw and headed back to Hotel Express 66 alone, my face going numb with the cold. After I paid the driver, I looked in my wallet and realised I'd spent hundreds – possibly thousands – of rupees on alcohol. Ashok was right: Delhi's gay parties had become freer since Section 377, but the gay nightlife existed only for the people who could afford it. And in a country like India, that wasn't many people at all.

*

From Delhi, I took a south-bound train to Bangalore to move closer to the equator. I needed to defrost my bones. The train route cut India down the middle like a scalpel, and the entire ride would take over thirty hours.

I had already experienced some of what India's vast rail network had to offer. When travelling from Baba Ramdev's Patanjali headquarters to New Delhi, I had mixed up my tickets and ended up booking a last-minute journey in standard passenger class. The experience was so searingly uncomfortable that it became comical. Children hid and slept in the overhead luggage compartments while women spat peanut shells directly onto the floor. In the toilets – which were somehow worse than I could ever have imagined – there was a brown smear of *something* on the mirror. At each stop, men threw themselves violently into the carriage and smashed their bodies into impossibly small spaces, as if playing a human game of Tetris. Strangers asked to sit on my lap, got angry when I said no, then sat on my lap anyway.

For the thirty-hour ride to Bangalore, I decided it was important to book an air-conditioned sleeper carriage. Once on board, I found the toilets were relatively clean and unexpectedly fun. You could choose from either an Indian squat-style or a Western toilet, but both had the same wonderful capacity of emptying directly onto the railroad tracks. You sat down, let the wind caress your naked butt and then happily watched as everything flew out into the open air. *Whee!* I squealed. Perhaps I'd incurred brain damage from Delhi's cold, but I felt like a kid again.

My carriage companion was a young guy in his early twenties with a sunny face and a chubby body, his hair and beard clippered like peach fuzz. After I forcefully shoved my backpack under the seat facing his, we smiled at each other and I extended my hand.

'I'm Benjamin.'

'Hello,' he said. 'I'm Harsh.'

Harsh actually introduced himself by his real name, but later asked me to change it to the moniker he used in online chatrooms. Harsh was an only child, had never left India and was desperate to get out. He was studying French so he could visit Paris. He knew everything about the Netherlands because he wanted to live in Holland. When he asked to see my passport, the look on his face as he scanned the stamps was a mixture of awe and grief. He passed it around to our neighbouring passengers and people whistled.

Harsh was too enthusiastic and talkative not to be gay. During the train ride, he also displayed a catty streak that could momentarily stun me into silence.

'You don't take very good pictures,' he said, flicking through my digital photos. 'You don't plan ahead very well,' he said, after I explained my itinerary. 'Your wallet is ugly,' he said, looking at my leather billfold.

Struggling to find some common ground, I looked at his stack of magazines, including the Indian edition of *GQ*. Harsh was studying to be an engineer, but he had zero interest in the field. His dream was to work in fashion.

'Would your father have preferred you be an average engineer or an incredibly successful fashion designer?'

Harsh didn't blink. 'Average engineer,' he said, still smiling.

The names that obsessed Harsh were those of the blockbuster designers showcased in *Vogue* and by labels such as Versace and Burberry.

'Tom Ford,' he said, almost sighing. 'He is a very good designer.' Harsh cut eye contact and spoke very softly. 'He is gay, you know.'

'Yes,' I said slowly. 'A lot of male fashion designers tend to be.'

'Marc Jacobs,' he said, lowering his voice again. 'He is gay too.'

I nodded, choosing my words carefully. 'Do you have any gay friends, Harsh?'

That was all it took. Harsh leaped out of his seat like he'd been burned, his eyes wild and bulging. He shook his hands wildly around his mouth, a clear gesture for me to *shut the fuck up*. He turned around to see if the passengers across from us had heard.

'You!' he said, whispering violently, leaning back in his seat so he couldn't be seen. 'You are also …' He mouthed the word: *gay?*

I nodded.

Harsh snapped the curtains to our alcove shut. He looked as if he were about to explode. At first, I thought he was angry, but when I examined his face properly, he had an odd expression: as if he'd just won a lottery but couldn't tell anyone in the room in case they stole the money from him. What were the chances? Of all the people on the train, we had found each other.

'You,' he said again, whispering, 'are gay.'

'Yes,' I said, grinning. 'You too?'

Harsh remained silent. Instead of speaking, he balled his hand into a fist and bit it, looking outside the window, as if he'd found himself, finally, in another country.

*

Over the next thirty hours, Harsh and I spoke in hushed tones, taking our meals behind closed curtains. He asked me when I came out, whether my family knew about me and what my boyfriend was like. He then found a modest stash of porn on my laptop and asked if he could copy it onto his hard drive. He told me about his robust sex life and how he would go cruising online all the time – every gay man in India had a Planet-Romeo profile – or engage in mutual groping with strangers up the back of buses. Barely anyone in his life knew he was gay, though. I'd known guys like Harsh and they always made me sad. They had heaps of sex with many different men but not one platonic gay friend.

His parents, he said, had always impressed on him the importance of good grades at university. But his college grades slipped dangerously when he started cruising for more and more gay sex. Harsh was obsessed; his sexual appetite was huge. He found it hard to concentrate on his studies and kept flunking a subject called Network Analysis. In his view, gay sex was destroying his life. He sought out a psychiatrist.

'What were you looking for the psychiatrist to do?' I asked.

'Some kind of magic,' Harsh said, smiling sadly.

Harsh would travel twelve hours on a bus from his engineering college to Bangalore. After the psychiatric appointments, he would sleep in cheap hotels by himself before catching a bus back to college the next day. His first psychiatrist prescribed him a fifteen-day trial course of pills, the name of which Harsh didn't remember. When he didn't notice any change, he went to a younger doctor. That doctor suggested nothing was actually wrong with Harsh, that he was perfectly normal, adding that he believed most people were bisexual, to some extent.

Emboldened by the idea, Harsh came out to a select group of friends, who were straight but promised to be discreet with Harsh's secret. But there was no way Harsh could come out to his parents, and he suspected he never would.

'I'm telling you the truth,' he said. 'If society changes, particularly towards gay men, I'll be the first one to come out. I'll come out immediately.'

'Section 377 was all over the news,' I said. 'Did that trigger any conversations with your parents?'

'No!' he said. 'You can't talk about that sort of stuff. Everyone saw it on the news, everyone knows about it, but no one *talks* about it. You can't. I tried talking to my *masi*, my mother's sister, who's like my next mother. But I know even she would never support me on this.'

Harsh put down his cutlery and started talking passionately.

'People should start talking about this,' he said. 'People should have this in their mind. It should not be a new thing for them.'

'But don't things like the repeal of Section 377 *make* people talk about it?'

'You tell me,' Harsh said, leaning in. 'In the train, have *you* ever said the "G" word?'

'No,' I said, taken aback. 'You told me not to.'

'Because *I* know the reaction of other people!' he said, turning around. 'You don't know the culture of India. Like pride parades. Who goes for pride parades? No one! Pride organisers go. Who else goes there? You tell me one.'

'You wouldn't go, then.'

'Hell, no,' he said. 'If my parents see me on the TV, what am I going to do? You have to be very rational in this.'

'So what else needs to change?'

'The thinking. The mentality. People need to be educated!'

Harsh spoke with the fervour of someone who had a lot of ideas but had never been able to share them with anyone. But he was confusing me too: if he wanted Indian people to be educated about gay and lesbian rights, didn't the fight against Section 377 do just that?

'For a time. For a *time*,' he said. 'But it was just a moment. It just fluctuated. The news came, and then ...' He flicked out his fingers into the air: *Then nothing.* 'Those organisers organising these gay parties? They should organise it on a larger scale. And all these parties, they charge you, like, 350 rupees per person, right?'

'Right,' I agreed. 'More, actually.'

'So this money should be given to newspaper societies and magazines to publish articles.'

I couldn't help but laugh. 'Wait: you want to *pay* magazines to publish articles about gay people?'

'Yes! Who would publish a gay article otherwise? These rainbow flags, it won't do any good. You have to be revolutionary.'

'Paying people to write stories about you isn't revolutionary,'

I said.

'Yes!' he said.

Harsh and I disagreed a lot, but he had the big mouth of someone who would make a good activist. When I told him this, he laughed darkly.

'No way. Because to be an activist, you have to have guts and can't have anyone you can disappoint. You need to be very brave. And I have many people that I cannot let down. My parents come first. Not all this bullshit.'

Later, in the north-west city of Pune, I had dinner with a friend and talked about what Harsh had said. I partly understood his frustration, but mostly I felt he was being a dismissive prick, especially when it came to gay organisations and pride marches. Then I remembered that I had never been to a pride march myself.

'You've never been to a gay pride parade?' my friend Mario said across the table, laughing. 'Ever?'

I realised how this looked. Here I was, an openly gay guy who came from Australia – home to one of the most celebrated gay events in the world – and I'd never attended a pride march. I wanted to tell Mario that I wasn't one of those self-hating gays who avoided all public demonstrations of gayness, but maybe that wasn't entirely true.

'I guess it's just not my thing,' I said weakly.

Mario nodded non-judgementally, which made me feel worse.

I remembered watching footage of the Sydney Gay and Lesbian Mardi Gras on TV as a teenager. This was before I'd come out as gay myself. Part of me was fascinated, but mainly I was cringing inside. These parades were all about flaunting muscles, leather, speedos, glitter and waxed arses in chaps, shoulders draped in feather boas; whereas my thing was more about staying indoors, reading quietly in bed and *not marching in public*. I clearly remembered thinking at the time, *If this is what it means to be gay, kill me now*. It probably wasn't the healthiest mindset, I now realised.

Mario told me about the pride march in Mumbai he'd attended back in August 2008. The atmosphere had been electric. It was the first such march ever held in Mumbai, and – a year before the repeal of Section 377 – gay sex was still technically illegal. Mario looked skywards, grinning as he thought about it now.

'You get to a point in the march where you're standing on this bridge, looking out over the water, across the ocean and over all the marchers,' Mario said, 'and it's just about the most beautiful thing you've ever seen.'

That was enough for me. A few days later, I boarded a train headed for Mumbai.

*

Suketu Mehta's *Maximum City* – his sprawling memoir and portrait of Mumbai – starts off with this: 'There will soon be more people living in the city of Bombay than on the continent of Australia.' Take those 21 million people, my country's entire population, and cram them into a city geographically smaller than Hobart and you have the population density of Mumbai. As I hauled my gear from the train in the syrupy heat, I could feel it immediately. Bunches of smiling, dirty-footed kids almost ran into me, flying makeshift kites of plastic bags attached to thread. Families of homeless women, aunts and kids huddled on traffic islands, all of them wearing brightly coloured clothes dusted with what appeared to be cocoa, but was actually grime

and soot. Endless traffic pushed past, oblivious to their existence, while the giant shadows of shopping malls they'd never
enter loomed over them.

This was a city of hustle and dogged enterprise. Tied-up
barn animals watched blankly as their four-legged comrades
were slaughtered and sold in hut-like stalls. *Hijras* tapped the
windows of taxis and the sides of rickshaws, asking for money
from passengers with dry expressions on their faces that said,
Give a lady a break. Shoeless teenagers sold helium balloons to
passing pedestrians, as men crossed the road holding hands –
a sign of platonic friendship and respect. At Goregaon train
station, I gave money to an old lady who'd had the fingers on
both hands sliced clean off. Her paddle-like palms were stained
with muck. In some ways, Mumbai was a grim city, but there
was also a jolt of energy to the place, an underlying optimism.
Things could only get better, after all.

I'd already been in touch with the organisers of the upcoming Queer Azaadi Mumbai Pride Parade (QAM). This year, it
was going to be big. In 2008 – the march Mario had attended –
they'd had 500 marchers. The next year there'd been 2000.
This year, QAM expected roughly 3500 people, and there
would be a new week-long festival leading up to it. QAM was
going to be the biggest queer event ever held in the world's
most populous democracy.

To organise an event like that, you had to field a vast volume
of emails every day without losing your cool. Messages were constant and came at all hours: questions, responses, confirmations,
costings, budgets, schedules, agendas, minutes, congratulations,
encouragement, thinly veiled passive-aggressive remarks, squab-
bles, reprimands about the number of thinly veiled passive-
aggressive remarks being distributed.

On a Saturday night, exactly a week before the march, QAM called one of its final meetings at Mumbai's Humsafar Trust headquarters. Humsafar was the organisation Ashok Row Kavi had started. In fact, Ashok had lived at the headquarters years earlier. It was modest, even cosy: a storage space, a pantry-sized bathroom, a tiny kitchenette, an office with two desks and a living room for gatherings. I tagged along to the meeting with Srini Satya, a smart guy in his late twenties who worked full-time and volunteered the rest of his waking hours to QAM. He was one of those gung-ho volunteers who made himself heard at meetings, winning people over by virtue of an easy confidence that came from being slightly too handsome for his own good.

The organisers were a diverse lot. There was a young male journalist from the *Times of India*, a beautiful and alarmingly thin transgender woman named Urmi from a dance troupe, and a shaggy-haired twenty-something entrepreneur who'd just opened a gay men's clothing shop nearby. Over thirty people crammed into the living room with its red-carpeted floor, sitting around in a circle as a leonine man named Pallav drove the meeting forward.

One of the major points agreed on was that everyone should feel welcome, including families and kids. One guy raised the issue of face-painting, and whether marchers should come to the parade already decorated.

'It *is* handy if someone wants to hide their face,' someone said cynically.

'It can be beautiful as well,' Srini offered.

As QAM's week-long program unfolded, I went to film screenings in restaurants and an indoor fete where you could buy books and have your tarot read. Groups of us went to dinner afterwards and introduced ourselves by offering both our name (someone else's idea) and a graphic description of our penis (my idea), which set off an evening of drunken laughter and foul jokes. One evening, everyone walked to the beach and settled into tiered seats to watch transgender women and *hijras* lip-sync, dance and rumble to classic Bollywood songs as the sun went down. In stark contrast to the throbbing, sexually suggestive songs I'd heard at Japanese drag queen shows, these were the most heartbreakingly mournful melodies I'd ever heard, based on epic Urdu poetry. Throngs of big-toothed kids – some of them homeless – drifted in, bunched up alongside me and wriggled in their seats, dancing. They knew all the words and sang along, even to the sad ones. Especially to the sad ones.

*

When you've been in India for a month without contracting food poisoning, you become cocky and complacent. You break the rules. You drink water from carafes, order garden salads and start going to the toilet like everyone else: no toilet paper, just water and your left hand. Staying at Srini's place, I would leave my toothbrush on his windowsill and gargle with water from his shower. I did pretty much everything travellers are told not to do. And so it transpired that the night before the QAM pride march, I spent the evening rushing to the toilet every hour, close to tears, leaking what felt like hot soup. It was as if my guts had become a faucet of horror, passionately rejecting something evil inside me.

I didn't sleep. The next morning, the bags under my eyes made me look as if I'd been assaulted. I felt frail and dehydrated, as though I'd been out in the unblinking sun for an entire day without water. Srini was already awake and dressing for the parade in a grey polo top and bright orange wrap with a rainbow trim.

'Are you getting into costume?' he asked.

I wondered if a diaper constituted a costume. Already, the day's heat was seeping through the walls and the thought of taking a bumpy rickshaw to the parade made me nauseous. My guts clenched horribly. Avoiding eye contact with Srini like a shame-ridden dog, I rushed to the toilet again and closed the door behind me.

'Ben?' Srini said through the toilet door. 'I'm going to order a taxi so we don't have to take a rick.'

'That's a good idea,' I said through gritted teeth. 'I'll pay.'

We arrived early, landing at a large public sports oval of red dirt. Teenagers played cricket while bleary-eyed shift workers slept on benches around the gates. Sleep-deprived, I followed the workers' lead, finding a space on a park bench and falling asleep. When I woke an hour later, throngs of people had arrived for the march. Most were local Indians, but there were also men from the United States and England, and women from Australia and Germany. I made friends with a bunch of teenage American exchange students, rude with good looks and youth.

Just past midday, the crowd grew and stretched across the oval until there was barely room to move. Thousands of people had gathered around a stage on the far side of the oval. Middle-aged, middle-class women carried placards that said, 'I'm Proud of My Gay Son,' while *hijras* arrived in hordes, holding hands and wearing elaborate pots on their heads, decked out in saris of every imaginable colour. People led call-and-response chants in Hindi, carrying banners and flags, and I didn't see one painted face in the crowd. These people didn't care if they were recognised. On the oval, the *hijras* danced the *Karakattam*, a Tamil

Nadu folk dance, shrieking and whooping as an American exchange student joined in and the drumming grew more frenetic. Newspaper photographers, sensing an opportunity to convey the international flavour of this event, pounced on the *hijras* and the American girl as they squealed and laughed.

A car pulled up behind the stage and the Bollywood actress Celina Jaitley got out wearing rainbow fairy wings. Everyone adored Celina, who had fiercely debated on TV for the repeal of Section 377 in the lead-up to the court ruling. I was standing there, awestruck, when I noticed an Indian prince standing to my left.

Prince Manvendra Singh Gohil was a little jetlagged, having just flown back from Chicago after his second appearance on *Oprah* to update her on the progress of gay rights in India. He might've been tired, but he still knew how to make a joke.

'Hello, Your Highness,' I said, quietly introducing myself.

'Pleased to meet you, Benjamin,' he said. 'I am Prince Manvendra Singh Gohil of Rajpipla and I breed hermaphrodites.'

It was his standard introduction. Manvendra might have been provincial royalty, but he also had a degree in farming and bred earthworms professionally. The self-proclaimed only openly gay royal in the world, Manvendra was in his mid forties, had a thin moustache and long manicured fingers. His laugh was adorably muppet-like.

Manvendra's story was as famous in India as it was tragic. When he publicly came out as gay in 2006, people in his home state of Gujarat burned effigies of him in protest. To them, he was an abomination. Gujarat was ruled by the BJP, the Hindu fundamentalist party that in 1996 had burned down cinemas screening *Fire*, a film which matter-of-factly depicted lesbian love. Unsurprisingly, Manvendra's father publicly disowned him in a statement to the local newspaper.

Still, Manvendra continued living at the palace. By that stage, he didn't talk much to his parents outside formal settings and he was already running his HIV organisation, the Lakshya Trust, and involved in the case against Section 377. He wrote supporting documents for the Naz Foundation's original petition, stating that he was both royal and openly gay, and reciting the history of ingrained homosexuality in traditional Indian culture over centuries. Homosexuality had been rampant in the royal families forever, he told me, and was especially so these days. He'd said so in the court documents.

'You really used the word "rampant"?' I asked.

'I can prove it!' he said.

I laughed. 'Do you know that, or are you just speculating?'

'We know that for sure. Our gay network is very strong in India! We know who is gay and who is not. There are a *lot* of royals who are gays or lesbians, but they don't talk about it. They're all closeted, we know that for a fact.'

Someone in the crowd bumped into me hard and we were cut off mid-sentence. Turning around, I faced a particularly foul-looking drag queen, pouting at me from underneath her sunglasses as if I'd hurt her feelings. She was shorter than me, a little chubby and her ill-fitting outfit – plush novelty top hat, ridiculously tight red dress – was an assault on the eyes.

'Excuse me,' I said coolly.

'Don't you recognise me with my beautiful hair, bitch?' she said.

I peered closer and gasped. 'Ashok?'

Ashok Row Kavi laughed as he lowered his sunglasses, then gave Manvendra and me each a kiss. A luxurious brunette wig came right down past his shoulders, and he was holding an

A3-sized banner printed by the new gay magazine *Fun*, which was Manvendra's latest enterprise. The banner had the slogan: 'Better to Be Gay than Grumpy.'

For once, engines were stopped on the main roads leading to Mumbai's coastline, and the honking of ricks and cars ceased as they watched the entertainment. Every queer group from Mumbai and beyond seemed to be there, including the group Lesbians and Bisexuals in Action, who had either the most appalling or inspired acronym of all the groups – I couldn't decide. Trumpets blew in the park as the parade set off, and a giant rainbow flag was passed over the heads of the marchers at the front. The crowd gave a gentle roar as dozens of drummers kicked and punched out a rhythm to accompany us.

A long-haired, wild-eyed lesbian, Sonia, led the parade. During the past week's QAM events, Sonia had displayed a superhuman ability to holler with animalistic enthusiasm from the base of her gut. She had recently broken her legs in a drunken accident, though, so Sonia was wheelchair-bound for the parade. Despite not being able to use her legs, Sonia's face was wild with happiness.

'ARRRRRRRRRRRRRGH!' she screamed.

The drums were deafening. The American college students gyrated and sweated alongside the *hijras* under the giant flag. *Hijras* grabbed each other's forearms in a crossed monkey grip, spinning wildly until they were a blur, daring each other to go faster. Parents carried small kids on their shoulders. And on his own, multi-tasking with his mobile phone as he marched, was the lawyer Anand Grover.

As we marched with Manvendra, Ashok explained the significance of the parade's route. The red patch of dirt from which we'd started was the place where Gandhi had issued his clarion call to the Indian people to fight for independence from the British in 1942.

In the middle of the march, I moved to the edge of things – partly to take photos, but also because I needed a break. On any other day, I would have been enjoying myself. But after the food poisoning, I was dehydrated, sweating and dizzy. Then I heard someone call out.

'Ben!' he bellowed.

Hovering over me was Srini, the gung-ho QAM volunteer, standing on a cement pedestrian bridge that stretched over the road. Waving back, I climbed the stairs to where he was. Monkey-like, I used my remaining energy to boost myself up onto the railing, dangle my legs over and look down. The drop was possibly fatal, but I felt safe. In the distance, I could see thousands of marchers – not quite the 3500 expected, but close – from all over the world, dancing and stomping to the beat of the drums. Bringing up the back of the parade were the girls from LABIA. The giant rainbow flag was passing right beneath us.

I had never liked the rainbow flag before this. I'd always thought it was a little over the top, retina-searing and too, well, *gay*. It took going to India – where even the poorest and most disenfranchised people dressed in vivid greens and reds, and saris of pinks and golds – for it finally to feel right to me. Watching the flag trail under the bridge, I thought of Harvey Milk's San Francisco of the '60s and '70s, when the jeans were tight and the homosexuals were furious. No one could re-create the Castro Street of that period, but as I watched the men and women dance in Mumbai, I felt what seemed to be a similar energy, the same spirit, the unbeatable optimism that came only after an arduous, bleak stretch of digging upwards, followed by the daylight of major victory.

My stomach was still cramped from the food poisoning, but sitting on the bridge I felt the illness begin to subside. Behind me was the ocean, the natural port that had always connected Mumbai to the rest of the world. What Mario had told me was right: this was one of the most beautiful things I'd ever seen. It was my first ever march and I had a lot of mixed feelings. Gastro was one of them, sure, but there was something else. We might have been in Mumbai – in India, in Asia – but it felt bigger that that. It was possibly the heat or my illness talking, but in that moment, watching everyone march for a single cause, what I felt was something closely resembling pride.

ACKNOWLEDGEMENTS

MY UTMOST GRATITUDE TO everyone at Black Inc., especially my publisher and prince of an editor Chris Feik, for his unwavering support, faith and guidance. Thank you also to Nikola Lusk, for her killer editorial chops. Without them, this book would be a mess, worse than any Asian squat toilet you could imagine, and I've seen some doozies. Special thanks to my co-conspirator and literary agent Benython Oldfield, not just for being there during my nervous breakdown in a forty-degree Beijing heatwave, but for all the future breakdowns he will inevitably witness.

Researching and writing *Gaysia* was generously supported by the Asialink Writing Residency at Peking University (Beijing, China), the Youkobo Art Space (Tokyo, Japan) and the Varuna Writers' House fellowship (Katoomba, Australia). A hat-tip to my Varuna comrades Anna Goldsworthy (who read early chapter drafts and offered invaluable notes), Linda Jaivin, Shalini Ahkil and, of course, my dear friend Krissy Kneen.

I made heaps of friends writing this book, and I'm especially grateful to Pear Bunsupa and Kristian Dowling (Pattaya, Thailand), Aya Hamashima (Tokyo, Japan), Rachel Ryan (Yangon, Myanmar), Martin Cosier, Jen Clark, Sally Brand, Carl Flanagan, Silvano Zheng, Dinah Gardner and Yusu 'William' Wang (Beijing, China) and Srini Satya (Mumbai, India) for the stellar company. Back home, I'd like to *apologise* to my friends for my neglect (especially to Meg and Ross, Kate and Roger, Rebecca and Jeremy, Julia and Kalem, and Kirana and Tyrone, whose weddings I missed while writing this book).

Seriously, though, thank you to all my friends, especially my writing buddies. Lorelei Vashti and Michaela McGuire have both been very helpful with advice, because that's the kind of people they are. Fiona Stager and the staff at Avid Reader in Brisbane have been there from the start. And of course, thank you to my honorary wife and best friend Anna Krien, for having my back, keeping my sanity in check and somehow always making the horror seem bearable, even funny.

Thank you to my family – Mum, Dad, Gar-Jer, Gor-Gor, Tammy and Michelle – for, well, basically everything. And to my criminally handsome boyfriend Scott, not just for his patience, support and superb brain, but for not dumping my sorry arse while I was gallivanting around Asia writing this goddamned book, acquiring various repulsive illnesses before returning to him an absolute mess. Researching these stories reminded me I'm one lucky son of a bitch to have him in my life.

Over the course of writing this book, I employed dozens of translators and interpreters whose work fills these pages. I also interviewed hundreds of people on-record, and dozens more off-record or as background. To everyone who shared their stories, perspectives and insights with me, I am deeply indebted and humbled. My final thanks are reserved for them.